Lecture Notes in Computer Science 3432

Commenced Publication in 1973
Founding and Former Series Editors:
Gerhard Goos, Juris Hartmanis, and Jan ·

T0216376

Michael Beigl   Paul Lukowicz (Eds.)

Systems Aspects in Organic and Pervasive Computing – ARCS 2005

18th International Conference on
Architecture of Computing Systems
Innsbruck, Austria, March 14-17, 2005
Proceedings

Volume Editors

Michael Beigl
University of Karlsruhe
Telecooperation Office (TecO)
Vincenz-Priessnitz-Strasse 1
76131 Karlsruhe, Germany
E-mail: michael@teco.edu

Paul Lukowicz
University for Health Science, Medical Informatics and Technology
Innsbruck, Austria
E-mail: paul.lukowicz@umit.at

Library of Congress Control Number: 2005921801

CR Subject Classification (1998): C.2, C.5.3, D.4, D.2.11, H.3.5, H.4, H.5.2

ISSN 0302-9743
ISBN 3-540-25273-8 Springer Berlin Heidelberg New York

Springer is a part of Springer Science+Business Media

springeronline.com

© Springer-Verlag Berlin Heidelberg 2005
Printed in Germany

Typesetting: Camera-ready by author, data conversion by Olgun Computergrafik
Printed on acid-free paper   SPIN: 11398196   06/3142   5 4 3 2 1 0

Preface

The key challenge for future computer system is dealing with complexity. On one hand this involves internal system complexity which has increased exponentially over recent years. Here the main objectives are to maintain system reliability and to keep the design and maintenance effort manageable, while at the same time continuing to provide new functionality and increasing system performance. This has been the focus of so-called autonomous computing, which aims to bring self-configuration and repair to a wide range of computing systems.

On the other hand future computer systems are more and more becoming integrated into the fabric of everyday life and thus have to deal with the complexities of the real world. They will become smaller, more appropriate for their use, integrated into everyday objects, and often virtually or physically invisible to the users. They will also be deployed in a much higher quantity and penetrate many more application areas than traditional notions of computer systems. This requires computer systems to be adaptable within a much wider range of possible tasks, subjected to much harsher conditions.

To provide such features and functionality, computer devices will become tinier yet still increase in system complexity; they must consume less power, while still supporting advanced computation and communications, such that they are highly connected yet still operate as autonomous units. Pervasive and ubiquitous computing research addresses such issues by developing concepts and technology for interweaving computers into our everyday life. The principal approach is to enhance system functionality and adaptability by recognizing context and situations in the environment.

Organic computing deals with high system complexity by drawing analogies from complex biological systems, with the human-centered goal of self-organization. It addresses both internal system complexity of conventional systems and the complexity involved in pervasive environments dealing with the real world. Thus organic computing investigates the design and implementation of self-managing systems that are self-configuring, self-optimizing, self-healing, self-protecting, context aware, and anticipatory. It touches upon a number of exciting research topics including ultra-low power consumption, scalability and complexity of devices and systems, self-awareness, adaptive networking, and smart behavior of systems.

Many papers submitted to the Architecture of Computing Systems Conference (ARCS) address these aspects of adaptable, self-organizing systems. For computer system hardware, reconfigurable hardware allows us to optimize the system performance based on the application context, relieving software developers from detailed consideration of the inherently inflexible hardware constraints. Adaptive methods for managing resources and tasks enable (embedded) microprocessor systems to be both real-time aware but also very low in their power consumption. In software, middleware agents are able to cope with changes in application and environment, thus still providing a minimum of functionality even under difficult and changing conditions.

Adaptive ad hoc communication networks and context-aware pervasive systems and applications provide the functionality mostly visible to the end user of such systems. To achieve this extent of adaptivity a large variety of methods were used – many of them borrowed from nature. The papers in this book present a good profile of such novel methods and their application in the area of computing systems.

This year the ARCS conference selected 18 papers from a competitive field of 52 submissions from 12 countries. All papers accepted for presentation were peer reviewed and discussed in the first step in an online discussion among members of the international Program Committee. In the PC Meeting then the final decisions were made based on these reviews and the online discussions. Care was taken to avoid any conflict of interest by handing out papers and discussion papers only to PC members not involved in or related to the work.

We would like to take the opportunity to thank the numerous people who supported us in organizing the paper program and the conference: the Program Committee members for their efforts in reviewing many papers; Uwe Brinkschulte for supporting us by serving as the Workshops and Tutorials Chair; and the General and Program Chairs, Christian Müller-Schloer and Theo Ungerer, for sharing their experience with us and helping us to organize the paper program and the conference.

We extend our gratitude to several organizations that provided financial and organizational support for the ARCS conference. Volker Schanz from the ITG provided the legal framework and the ARCS Fachausschuss, the organizational body of the conference. Financial and organizational support came from the APS+PC group, which organized and funded a special session with several interesting invited talks. Donations also came from our benefactor, Siemens AG. We would also like to thank Christian Decker and Michael Biebl for their help during the electronic submission process, and the University for Health Sciences, Medical Information and Technology in Innsbruck, Austria for hosting the conference.

January 2005   Michael Beigl
                                                          Program Chair ARCS 2005

                                                                  Paul Lukowicz
                                                          General Chair ARCS 2005

Executive Committee

Conference Chair: Paul Lukowicz   University for Health Sciences, Medical
Informatics and Technology, Austria

Program Chair: Michael Beigl   University of Karlsruhe, Germany

Workshops and
Tutorials Chair: Uwe Brinkschulte   University of Karlsruhe, Germany

Program Committee

Shigeru Ando	University of Tokyo, Japan
Nader Bagherzadeh	University of California, Irvine, USA
Frank Bellosa	University of Erlangen, Germany
Uwe Brinkschulte	University of Karlsruhe, Germany
Roy Campbell	University of Illinois at Urbana-Champaign, USA
Alois Ferscha	University of Linz, Austria
Paul Havinga	University of Twente, Netherlands
Wolfgang Karl	University of Karlsruhe, Germany
Jürgen Kleinöder	Universität Erlangen-Nürnberg, Germany
Rudolf Kober	Siemens AG, München, Germany
Spyros Lalis	University of Thessaly, Greece
Erik Maehle	Universität zu Lübeck, Germany
Christian Müller-Schloer	University of Hannover, Germany
Joe Paradiso	MIT Media Laboratory, USA
Burghardt Schallenberger	Siemens AG, Germany
Hartmut Schmeck	University of Karlsruhe, Germany
Albrecht Schmidt	LMU Munich, Germany
Karsten Schwan	Georgia Institute of Technology, USA
Rainer G. Spallek	Technische Universität Dresden, Germany
Peter Steenkiste	Carnegie Mellon University, USA
Yoshito Tobe	Tokyo Denki University, Japan
Hide Tokuda	Keio University, Japan
Theo Ungerer	University of Augsburg, Germany
Klaus Waldschmidt	University of Frankfurt, Germany
Lars Wolf	University of Braunschweig, Germany
Martina Zitterbart	University of Karlsruhe, Germany

Organization

The Architecture of Computing Systems (ARCS) Conference was organized by
the ITG (Informationstechnische Gesellschaft – Information Technology Society) and the Special Interest Group on Computer and Systems Architecture of
the GI (Gesellschaft für Informatik – German Informatics Society), supported
by OCG (Austrian Computer Society), OVE/GIT (Austrian Electrotechnical
Association) and electrosuisse (ITG), and held in cooperation with ACM.

Sponsor

Siemens AG, Munich, Germany

Table of Contents

Application Adaptable Systems

Pervasive Computing and Communication

Energy Management for Embedded Multithreaded Processors with Integrated EDF Scheduling

Sascha Uhrig and Theo Ungerer

Institute of Computer Science, University of Augsburg,
86159 Augsburg, Germany
Tel.: +498215982353, Fax.: +498215982359
{uhrig,ungerer}@informatik.uni-augsburg.de

Abstract. This paper proposes a new hardware-based energy management technique for future embedded multithreaded processors with integrated Earliest Deadline First (EDF) real-time scheduling. Our energy management technique controls frequency reduction and dynamic voltage scaling depending on the deadlines, the Worst Case Execution Times (WCET), and the real execution times. Hard real-time capability can be guaranteed for aperiodic threads and for threads with deadlines shorter than their period. Our evaluations show that energy consumption can be reduced up to about $\frac{2}{3}$ of a comparable software-based algorithm.

Keywords: energy management, energy-aware program execution, real-time scheduling, multithreading, EDF scheduling

1 Introduction

The reduction of energy consumption is an important research field because of the rapidly growing number of battery-powered mobile and embedded devices. Hard real-time is often an essential requirement for such systems. This paper focuses on energy management in embedded processor cores in combination with real-time applications. The aim is to reduce the total energy consumption by optimizing power consumption without delaying the completion of the real-time threads.

In CMOS devices, the power consumption is proportional to the square of the supply voltage and linear to the frequency:

$$P_{cmos} = aC_L V_{DD}^2 f,$$

where a is the activity of the circuit, C_L is the output load capacity, V_{DD} the supply voltage, and f the frequency. Obviously, power consumption can be reduced dynamically by decrementing supply voltage and clock frequency. Unfortunately, supply voltage depends on clock frequency and, using lower frequency, the processor's performance is reduced too. Hence, in real-time systems, we have to control frequency in a way which does not harm the real-time behavior of the system.

M. Beigl and P. Lukowicz (Eds.): ARCS 2005, LNCS 3432, pp. 1–17, 2005.

We developed a multithreaded Java microcontroller – called Komodo microcontroller – with hardware-integrated real-time scheduling schemes [1, 2] for application in embedded real-time systems and ubiquitous devices. The Komodo microcontroller is able to perform a thread switch without any overhead. Thus, instructions of active threads are executed in an overlapped fashion inside the core pipeline; the EDF scheduler hardware ensures that the thread with the earliest deadline is the thread with the highest priority. Due to hardware multithreading, instructions of other threads are executed within latency cycles of the thread with the highest priority without interfering with its execution (latency bridging).

We investigate mechanisms to minimize energy consumption using hardware-based energy management techniques that are made possible by a multithreaded processor core with integrated EDF scheduling. In particular, we show that energy saving techniques like frequency reduction and voltage scaling can be controlled more efficient by the integrated EDF energy management than using conventional operating system methods. Our hardware-integrated energy management algorithm chooses automatically in each processor cycle the frequency and voltage level that is currently required to perform a real-time application without any miss of deadline.

The next two sections show state-of-the-art energy saving mechanisms and related work. Section 4 presents the extensions for hardware-based energy management within the processor-integrated EDF scheduler and in section 5 we evaluate our approach. Section 6 concludes the paper.

2   State-of-the-Art Energy Saving Mechanisms

Commercial processors use a number of techniques for saving energy like pipeline gating, several suspend or sleep modes, and reduction of frequency and supply voltage. Intel's XScale [3], Transmeta's Crusoe [4] and the MSP430 [5] from Texas Instruments work with software-controlled techniques of frequency reduction and voltage scaling.

We describe shortly the energy saving features of the XScale and the Crusoe processors, because we use their electrical properties (voltages and frequency rates) for simulating our hardware-based energy management. Both processors are able to run at several frequencies using different supply voltages. A change of frequency requires among other tasks to complete all outstanding memory accesses, to set the external SDRAM to self-refresh mode, and to disable the interrupt controller. Most tasks are done automatically, but, nevertheless, they need time for execution. The whole process of changing frequency requires up to $500\mu s$ in the case of the XScale. Using the Crusoe processor, the time required for a supply voltage change depends on the distance of the two voltage levels. The maximum value is about $896\mu s$ in the default configuration.

Pipeline Gating [6] is a technique for selectively disconnecting parts of the processor, especially pipeline stages. So the energy consumption can be reduced by uncoupling unnecessary parts of the pipeline without concerning any other component. In contrast, frequency and voltage scaling affect the whole circuit.

3   Related Work on Real-Time Energy Management

Different directions of research targeting real-time applications are present: energy management controlled by the application, the operating system, or by the hardware itself. Application-based power management requires special power control sequences within the application's program code. Shin et al. [7] present a technique for automatic insertion of power controlling code based on a WCET analysis before runtime. The suggested mechanism is feasible for hard real-time systems.

In contrast to application-based techniques, other approaches focus on frequency and voltage reduction controlled by the operating system, especially by its thread scheduler. Pillai et al. [8] present several energy-aware scheduling schemes similar to the EDF scheduling scheme for low-power embedded real-time operating systems. Jejurikar et al. [9] focus on the problem of task synchronization in combination with energy-aware task scheduling. Pouwelse et al. [10, 11] describe a hybrid approach, which is based on an extended Linux OS with a so-called *energy priority scheduling*. The parameters for the scheduler are given by the application.

A theoretical approach for an energy saving technique using EDF scheduling is presented by Krishna et al. [12, 13]. Their energy management is based on an offline thread schedule, the online schedule, an offline and an online function, which describe the amount of work to do. Aydin et al. [14] additionally use a speculative speed adjustment for periodic real-time tasks.

All presented techniques are based on a single-threaded processor core and a software-based energy management. Energy management investigations concerning multithreaded processors pertain simultaneous multithreading and are made by [15, 16]. Energy management of a multithreaded single-issue processor with integrated Guaranteed Percentage (GP) hardware real-time scheduling was evaluated by ourselves [17, 18].

All existing processors and research approaches (except our GP energy management) suffer from the inefficiency of software control: Calculating the optimal frequency and the supply voltage by software requires a software overhead. Additionally, most control techniques assume a continuous frequency control which is not realistic. In real processors, frequency is selected by binary clock multipliers and dividers, i.e. only discrete frequency levels are possible. A more efficient solution is a hardware-based energy management, i.e. the processor core decides to run at the optimal frequency and voltage level by itself and is able to readjust frequency and voltage during thread execution.

Another drawback of existing energy management techniques in combination with real-time scheduling is the often used assumption, that the deadline of each thread has to be equal to its period. Krishna et al. and Aydin et al. additionally require an offline thread "execution" for determining the *amount of work* function and the offline schedule itself for the energy management.

4   Hardware-Based Energy Management Mechanism

4.1   Thread Model

For our energy management technique we permit arbitrary activation of threads with the constraints that all threads are independent and that a thread will only be restarted after its completion, i.e. at most one instance of each thread is active at a time. In the case of periodic threads, we do not make the assumption that their deadlines are equal to their periods.

For the realization of our proposed energy management technique, several characteristics of the execution of a thread are necessary. Fig. 1 illustrates the required values which are measured in execution cycles. The figure is divided into two scheduling areas: the upper area describes the *regular thread scheduling* which is similar to Krishna's offline scheduling, with the difference that it is generated online by the knowledge of the WCETs and the deadlines of the already completed and all actually active threads. The lower area mirrors the scheduling depending on the real runtime behavior of the threads, i.e. the *runtime scheduling*. In addition to these two schedulers a third scheduler, not shown in the figure, called *execution scheduler* is present. It is responsible for the selection of the thread executed within the multithreaded processor pipeline in the current clock cycle. Because of the latency bridging, the scheduling decision temporarily alternates between different threads.

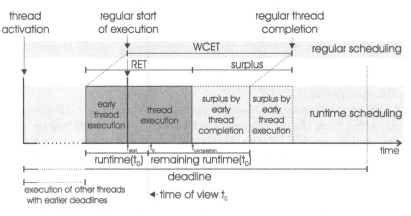

Fig. 1. Characteristics during the execution of a thread.

The *deadline* and the *WCET* are given by the application and stored as constants within the energy management unit. The *surplus* are the remaining cycles from thread completion to the regular (planned) completion of the thread assuming that all previous threads have exhausted their *WCET* too. The *runtime(t_0)* represents the amount of execution cycles the current thread has executed up to time t_0. In general, due to the multithreaded execution and the *surplus* of the previous thread, an *early thread execution* takes place and thus, the *runtime(t_{start})* is greater than zero at the *regular start of execution*. At thread completion, the *runtime($t_{completion}$)* is equal to the real execution time (*RET*). The *remaining runtime(t_0)* is the number of cycles the thread will run from time t_0 (assuming its WCET), i.e., the difference between the *WCET* and the *runtime(t_0)*. The surplus is the sum of the surplus by early thread completion and the surplus by early thread execution (surplus of the previous thread).

4.2   Methodology

The idea behind the hardware-based energy management mechanism is that the active threads rarely need the time calculated as WCET for the actual execution as it is reported in [19]. Thus frequency can be reduced such that all threads terminate as late as possible but not later than the time predicted by the schedulability analysis (depending on the WCETs). As a consequence, the supply voltage can be adapted to a level corresponding to the throttled frequency, which may lead to a tremendous energy saving. Because of the direct relationship between the selected clock frequency and the required supply voltage, determining the optimal clock frequency is the real challenge.

Using a software-based solution, frequency and voltage selection is only possible at the time of a thread suspend or activation (intertask DVS) or at dedicated points during thread execution (intratask DVS). In contrast to a software-based version, our hardware-based energy management is able to observe the progression (in execution cycles) of all active threads continuously. Thus, clock frequency and supply voltage can be adapted dynamically during the thread's execution to approximate the optimal execution speed.

At the time of a thread suspend the presented energy saving mechanism registers the number of execution cycles remaining to the regular thread suspend, i.e. the surplus. Due to the surplus of the just suspended thread the execution of the thread directly following can be slowed down. The optimal frequency $f_{reduced}$ can be calculated by the formula

$$f_{reduced} = \frac{WCET}{surplus + WCET} * f_{max},$$

where f_{max} is the maximum frequency of the processor, $WCET$ is the WCET of the new thread, and *surplus* is the surplus of the just suspended thread. If the processor is working at the calculated optimal frequency $f_{reduced}$ and the new thread requires its complete WCET, its execution completes exactly at the time planned by the schedulability analysis. If the new thread does not need its WCET for execution it offers a surplus to the following thread. Usually only fixed frequency levels are provided by the processor. So the optimal frequency cannot be selected and a frequency higher than the optimal one has to be chosen. As result, the really required energy is higher than the theoretical necessary energy.

4.3   Implementation

To realize the EDF energy management the following set of five hardware registers are required for each hardware thread slot:

$WCET_{reload}$: This register is addressable by the software. It contains the reload value of the WCET.

$WCET_{surplus}$: The $WCET_{surplus}$ register is an internal register within the energy management unit. At every thread activation it will be automatically reloaded with the value stored in the $WCET_{reload}$ register. During runtime it will be decreased according to the algorithm described below.

$WCET_{remain}$: This register is very similar to the $WCET_{surplus}$ register. The difference between these two registers is the way of decrease also described below.

DL_{reload} : The DL_{reload} register holds the deadline of the corresponding thread. It is software addressable.

DL_{count} : At the time of a thread activation, this register will be initialized with the value of the DL_{reload} register. It is decremented in every clock cycle and is responsible for the thread scheduling. Both deadline registers are required for the thread scheduling and are already available within the priority manager.

Depending on the thread scheduling, selective registers are updated in every execution cycle by hardware. Both *reload* registers have to be set by the application with the help of special instructions.

Register Actualization: The $WCET_{surplus}$ and the $WCET_{remain}$ registers have to be updated corresponding to the actual thread execution. That means, the $WCET_{remain}$ register of a thread is decremented iff an instruction of this thread is executed in the actual execution cycle, i.e. it reflects the execution cycles remaining until the maximum thread execution cycles. Whereas the $WCET_{surplus}$ register has to be reduced iff the corresponding thread is currently the regular thread, i.e. assuming the WCET of all previously executed threads. At the time of thread suspend, the $WCET_{surplus}$ register mirrors the surplus which is available for the execution of other threads.

The scheduling decision of the regular scheduler depends only on the deadlines and the WCETs of all active threads. The execution scheduling evaluates additionally the fill level of the instruction windows, possible latencies, and the real completion of the threads.

Fig. 2 demonstrates the correlation of the scheduling parameters, the scheduling decisions, and the decrease of the WCET registers. The scheduling parameters *deadline, latencies, IW (instruction window) fill level*, and the *active* flags are required for the *execution scheduling*. The WCET register sets are only required for the energy management. The $WCET_{surplus}$ and the $WCET_{remain}$ registers are updated depending on the *regular* respectively the *execution scheduling*. A set of all registers is available for each hardware thread slot.

Frequency and Voltage Control: For frequency and voltage control an additional third scheduler, the *runtime scheduler* is required, which is not shown in figure 2. Its task is to determine the thread with the highest priority in execution. In contrast to the *execution scheduler*, the *runtime scheduler* ignores the fill levels

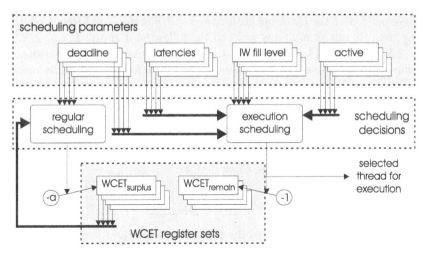

Fig. 2. Decrease of the WCET registers in correlation with the scheduling. The decrease value a depends on the selected execution frequency.

of the instruction windows and occurring latencies. Thus, the *runtime scheduler* designates the current active thread with the highest priority disregarding its feasibility.

For the selection of the execution frequency, the energy management unit has to distinguish between three cases:

1. The decision of the *runtime scheduler* is invalid. In this case, no active thread is available. Frequency and supply voltage can be reduced to the minimum level.

2. The decisions of the *runtime scheduler* and the regular scheduler are identical. The maximum number of cycles the thread will be executed is known within the register $WCET_{remain}$ and the number of cycles available till the regular completion of the thread is stored in register $WCET_{surplus}$. The execution frequency can be reduced or has to be increased to

$$f_{reduced} = \frac{WCET_{remain}}{WCET_{surplus}} \times f_{max}.$$

3. As last case, the regular thread is not the same as the thread determined by the *runtime scheduler*. This means, a previous thread completes before its WCET and its surplus is available for the execution of the thread selected by the *runtime scheduler*. The execution frequency has to be set to:

$$f_{reduced} = \frac{WCET_{remain\_runtime}}{WCET_{surplus\_regular} + WCET_{surplus\_runtime}} \times f_{max},$$

where $WCET_{remain\_runtime}$ and $WCET_{remain\_runtime}$ are the corresponding registers of the thread determined by the *runtime scheduler* and $WCET_{surplus\_regular}$ is the $WCET_{surplus}$ register of the regular thread.

We assume that the clock generator works with a clock divider without any settling time. In our simulations we used the following divisors: 1, 1.5, 2, 2.5, 3, 3.5, 4, 4.5, 5, 10, and 14. How we determine the optimal execution frequency is now shown at the example of case 3 (see above). The following formula must be fulfilled by the minimal possible frequency:

$$f_{reduced} \geq \frac{WCET_{remain\_runtime}}{WCET_{surplus\_regular} + WCET_{surplus\_runtime}} \times f_{max}.$$

$f_{reduced}$ is derived from f_{max} by a clock divider. Div_{num} is the numerator and Div_{denom} the denominator of the clock divider:

$$f_{reduced} = f_{max} / \frac{Div_{num}}{Div_{denom}}.$$

Combining both formulas leads to the following inequation:

$$f_{max} / \frac{Div_{num}}{Div_{denom}} \geq \frac{WCET_{remain\_runtime}}{WCET_{surplus\_regular} + WCET_{surplus\_runtime}} \times f_{max}$$

$$\Leftrightarrow$$

$$Div_{denom} \times (WCET_{surplus\_regular} + WCET_{surplus\_runtime})$$
$$\geq Div_{num} \times WCET_{remain_{runtime}}$$

Using the mentioned clock divider, all multiplications can be mapped to shift operations and at maximum one addition. In parallel to the frequency selection, supply voltage is chosen using a lookup table and the calculated frequency divider as index. In contrast to the voltage which is set immediately, frequency is set after a delay iff an increased voltage is required (see 4.5). In between, the processor continues working at the lower frequency.

4.4   Readjusting Frequency

In most cases, the selection of the optimal frequency is not possible. Therefore, the energy management technique has to choose a frequency higher than the optimal one because otherwise the actual executed thread could terminate after the regular termination. While the thread is executed at the higher frequency than the optimal one, the progression is also higher than required.

At the time the thread's progress reaches a level such that frequency can be decreased below the optimal one, the energy management slows down the processor to this frequency. Additionally, supply voltage could be decreased. The dynamic readjustment of frequency and voltage at any time during thread execution can only be afforded by a hardware-based solution which monitors the thread's progression consistently.

4.5   Impact on WCET

Using the policy described in section 4.4, an increase of the execution frequency may be necessary. In this case, the supply voltage has to be adapted first (because of the capacity of the circuit) before the execution frequency can be increased. We called this delay the *frequency increase delay* which is the only impact of the energy management to the timing behavior of the system. The WCET of each thread has to be increased by the *frequency increase delay*. The necessity of this delay can be demonstrated by the following situation: The processor is running at a low frequency and a low supply voltage. Now, a new thread with the highest priority is activated. Because of the unknown runtime behavior of the new thread, the processor has to run at the highest frequency and voltage. Thus, first voltage has to be increased and just after voltage reached the required level, i.e. after the *frequency increased delay*, frequency can be increase too.

Another case, in which the *frequency increase delay* is important is the simultaneous change of the regular thread and the thread with the highest priority. Hence, due to the unknown runtime behavior of the second thread, the processor has to run at highest frequency. To allow running at high frequency immediately, supply voltage has to be set to the highest level before the first thread completes regularly, i.e. when the $WCET_{surplus}$ register of the first thread is less than the *frequency increase delay*.

4.6 Drawback During Switching

Within all software energy-management techniques known to us, voltage and frequency switching is done in one iteration. Hence, this step takes at least as long as the voltage needs to reach the required level (assuming a voltage increase) and no useful work can be done in the meanwhile. Our hardware-based energy-management controls frequency and voltage in two steps without halting the processor. It still runs at the lower frequency until the voltage reaches the upper level. The time, the processor runs at the lower level is taken into account at the selection of the target frequency and voltage. Therefore, a high number of voltage and frequency changes is rather an advantage than a disadvantage.

5 Evaluation

5.1 Processor Models

As proof of our concept we built the described energy management technique into the VHDL model of the multithreaded, single-issue Komodo processor core with integrated EDF scheduling [2, 20]. Besides the energy management itself, we integrated a clock divider with 11 different output frequencies. To avoid the assumption of $f \sim U$, we used the more realistic voltage levels derived from the Crusoe respectively the XScale processor and the appropriate clock dividers shown in table 1.

All benchmarks are performed by simulating the VHDL model. The frequency divider supports the clock dividers shown in table 1. Each benchmark is simulated twice: first using the voltage levels similar to the Crusoe technology (Crusoe-style), second using the voltage levels corresponding to the XScale technology (XScale-style). In addition to these two technologies we used three different energy management techniques per benchmark:

Table 1. Voltage levels assumed for the simulation derived from the XScale and the Crusoe processor's supply voltage levels.

Clock divider	XScale's voltage [V]	Crusoe's voltage [V]	Clock divider	XScale's voltage [V]	Crusoe's voltage [V]
1	1.1	1.3	4	0.85	0.8
1.5	1.0	1.05	4.5	0.85	0.8
2	1.0	0.95	5	0.85	0.8
2.5	1.0	0.875	10	0.85	0.8
3	0.85	0.85	15	0.85	0.8
3.5	0.85	0.8			

1. Assuming a single threaded microcontroller with pipeline gating requiring in gated mode 40% of the total energy consumption.
2. Assuming a single threaded microcontroller and a software-based EDF energy management similar to that presented by Pillai et al. [8].
3. The multithreaded microcontroller with integrated energy management. We assumed an overhead of 8% energy consumption for the additional hardware effort. This value is derived from the additional hardware cost for energy management.

Energy consumption is estimated by tracking the core frequency in combination with the selected voltage level and the formula of section 1. Because energy is proportional to the clock frequency we just calculate the relative energy consumption.

5.2   Benchmarks

We performed two synthetic benchmarks and a realistic benchmark for evaluating the behavior of the hardware-based EDF energy management.

Synthetic Benchmarks: Each synthetic benchmark consists of four threads with a growing processor utilization. The WCETs and the periods of all threads are chosen in the way that the theoretical processor load of a whole benchmark is 100%. During the execution of both benchmarks, the real processor utilization is growing from nearly 0% at the beginning to finally 100% of computing power.

Within the first benchmark ($EQUAL$) all four threads were activated simultaneously with identical periods. Figure 3 illustrates the activation and the growing real computing time of the threads. In contrast, the threads within the second benchmark ($DIFF$) were activated at different times using different periods (see table 2).

The relative energy consumptions of the three different processor models using the energy management techniques pipeline gating (PG), Pillai software energy management (Pillai) and hardware-based EDF energy management (EDF) are compared as function of the real processor utilization using the processor models similar to the Crusoe respectively the XScale technology. Figure 4 and 5 show the results of the $EQUAL$ benchmark and figure 6 and 7 mirror the relative

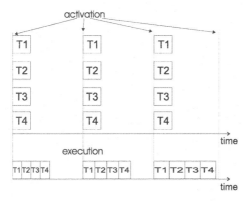

Fig. 3. Thread activation and execution during the *EQUAL* benchmark.

Table 2. Periods and WCETs of the *DIFF* benchmark.

	Period	WCET	Utilization
Thread 1	100000	11655	11.6
Thread 2	20000	7900	39.5
Thread 3	55000	6160	11.2
Thread 4	25000	9425	37.7

energy consumption of the *DIFF* benchmark. The figures do not show the total energy consumption of the whole benchmark but rather snap-shots of energy consumption at the appropriate utilization level.

Three curves are shown in all four figures. The one starting slightly above 40% and reaching 73% represents the energy consumption of a processor core supporting only pipeline gating. Because of the assumed energy consumption of 40% in gated mode the minimum energy consumption is likewise 40%. Due to latency bridging, the maximum energy consumption is less than 100% of the energy consumption, i.e. in the case of 100% processor utilization, there are still unused clock cycles left for pipeline gating. This phenomenon can be observed in all measurements.

The second curve, mostly in the middle describes the energy consumption of the benchmarks using a software-based energy management similar to the Pillai technique. The relative energy consumption using the *EQUAL* benchmark behaves as expected. In the case of the *DIFF* benchmark the energy consumption using the Pillai energy management exceeds the energy consumption of pipeline gating. This behavior can be explained by the software overhead of the energy management and the readjustment of frequency and voltage only at each thread activation and suspend. Because of the disadvantageous distribution of the threads in the *DIFF* benchmark, this phenomenon appears only here.

The lowest curve in each figure shows the relative energy consumption resulting from the hardware-based EDF energy management. The *EQUAL* benchmark is a very uniform benchmark which leads to the approximately proportional energy consumption in figure 4. In contrast to *EQUAL*, *DIFF* is a very inhomo-

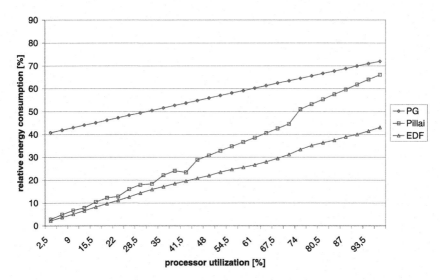

Fig. 4. Relative energy consumption of the *EQUAL* benchmark (Crusoe-style).

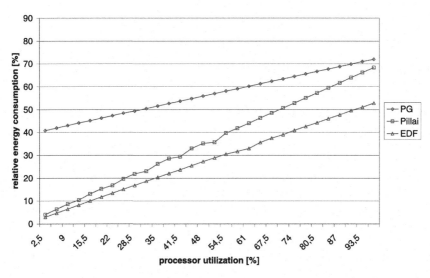

Fig. 5. Relative energy consumption of the *EQUAL* benchmark (XScale-style).

geneous benchmark, which leads to a more or less advantageous arrangement of active threads. The low point at about 90% processor utilization using the Crusoe-style model is a result of an advantageous thread arrangement. The flattening of the energy curve at growing processor utilization can be explained by the increasing overlapped thread execution, i.e. with the growing number of usable latency cycles.

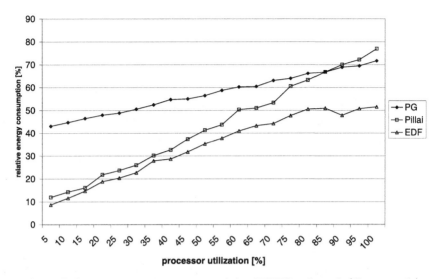

Fig. 6. Relative energy consumption of the *DIFF* benchmark (Crusoe-style).

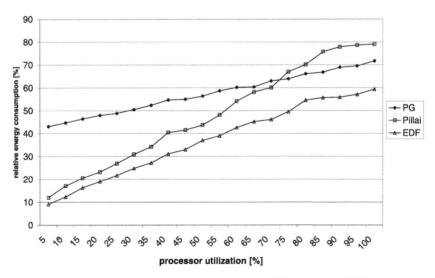

Fig. 7. Relative energy consumption of the *DIFF* benchmark (XScale-style).

Realistic Benchmark: For the realistic benchmark, the Komodo microcontroller prototype was built into an autonomous guided vehicle (AGV). Four hard real-time threads control the movements of the vehicle and are used for evaluation. The microcontroller's inputs are the data sent by a line camera, its outputs are pulse width modulated signals (PWM) for two driving engines. The task of the vehicle is to track a steering line on the floor. The four threads perform the following tasks:

1. Receiving Camera Data: This thread is responsible for receiving the digital pixel values sent by the line camera. The data is stored in a Java array. The camera thread is activated each time a pixel is received and deactivates itself after writing the received data into the array. After receiving a whole picture, the array is transmitted to the second thread.

2. Recognizing the Line: The task of this thread is to recognize the line that guides the vehicle based on the data within the array. This thread is only active during the line detection, otherwise it is deactivated.

3. Calculating Steering Data: Together with the data of previous line pictures and the information about the actual positioning of the line, this thread calculates the new driving direction and speed. These two values are forwarded to the next thread.

4. Generating PWM Signals: This thread's job is to use the values of direction and speed for calculating PWM signals.

Methodology: Because real current measurements cannot be made using a FPGA prototype and an ASIC is much too expensive, the measurement methodology combines real input data from the AGV prototype with a VHDL simulation of the Komodo microcontroller including the different energy management techniques (pipeline gating, software-based energy management, and hardware-based energy management).

First, the vehicle's control program was executed on the FPGA prototype inside the vehicle. During the first 3.2 million clock cycles a logic analyzer records the signals sent from the line camera. The second step is to use the logged data as input to the simulation running the same vehicle program yielding the frequency and voltage changes and the number of cycles with gated pipeline.

Results: Figures 8-9 present the results of our simulations. The x-axes mirror the time in base clock cycles and the y-axes show the energy consumption relative to a processor without any energy management. The peaks above 1 in figure 9 stem from the assumed overhead of 8% of energy consumption of the base processor because of the added energy management hardware.

Figure 10 summarizes the simulation results by showing the fractions of energy consumption during the simulated time interval. Each column represents the required energy in the specified technology in comparison to a Komodo microcontroller running at full speed all the time. These values are calculated using the formula in section 1, where C (the capacity of the whole circuit) and f are normalized to 1.

The leftmost bars show the energy consumption using pipeline gating and the highest voltage of the corresponding technology. The reason for the large energy saving of about 51.5% is the low overall processor utilization with an average of 22.6% over the whole time interval. Because we assumed that the energy needed in gated mode is still 40% of the energy in running mode, the required fraction of energy (48.5%) is higher than the overall utilization.

The bars in the middle of figure 10 mirror the results using a software-based energy management similar to the one presented by Pillai et al. within a single threaded processor core. It reaches energy savings of up to 82%.

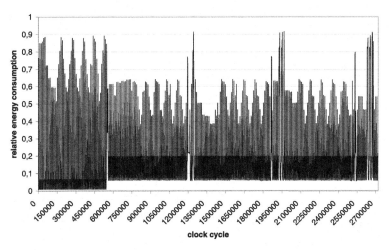

Fig. 8. Energy consumption using pipeline gating and software based energy management (Crusoe-style model).

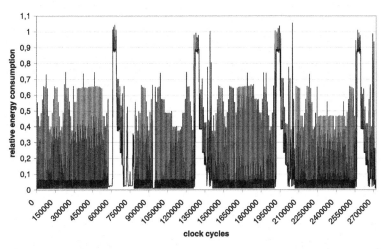

Fig. 9. Energy consumption using hardware based EDF energy management (Crusoe-style model).

The remaining bars show the results using the hardware-based frequency/voltage adjustment and pipeline gating. This combination reaches the best results with the least energy consumption due to the fast frequency and voltage switches, the usage of latencies and the fact, that the processor is not idle during voltage/frequency switching. Because of more available voltage levels and a lower voltage at the slow clock rates, the Crusoe-derived version outperforms the XS-cale version.

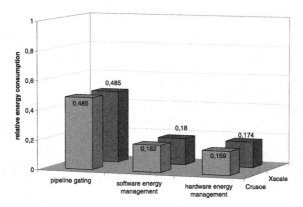

Fig. 10. Total energy consumption of the AGV benchmark normalized to a Komodo microcontroller running at full speed.

6   Conclusions

This paper presents a new management technique for reducing energy consumption within multithreaded real-time systems. Frequency adjustment and dynamic voltage scaling are managed exclusively by hardware. The management technique is based on the Earliest Deadline First (EDF) scheduling scheme implemented in the multithreaded Komodo microcontroller which is used for benchmarking.

One advantage of hardware-controlled energy management over software-based solutions is the ability of using extremely short periods of underutilization for reducing energy consumption, where software-based solutions are not able to react fast enough. The second advantage is the ability to slow down real-time thread execution at any time during thread execution. Thus, our technique is able to compensate the disadvantage of discrete frequency levels. As third advantage, it should be mentioned that our hardware-based energy management is suitable for both, periodic and sporadic real-time threads. Especially in ubiquitous systems, energy management for aperiodic real-time threads is important.

Our evaluations show that energy consumption could be reduceded to $\frac{2}{3}$ of an comparable software-based solution. The consumed energy never exceeds the amount consumed by the software-based algorithm. Additionally, the software-based algorithm supports only periodic threads.

References

1. Kreuzinger, J., Schulz, A., Pfeffer, M., Ungerer, T., Brinkschulte, U., Krakowski, C.: Real-time Scheduling on Multithreaded Processors. In: 7th International Conference on Real-Time Computing Systems and Applications (RTCSA 2000), Cheju Island, South Korea. (2000) 155–159
2. Kreuzinger, J., Brinkschulte, U., Pfeffer, M., Uhrig, S., Ungerer, T.: Real-time Event-handling and Scheduling on a Multithreaded Java Microcontroller. Microprocessors and Microsystems **27** (2003) 19–31

3. Intel Corporation: Intel PXA26x Processor Family Developer's Manual. (2002)
4. Transmeta Corporation: Crusoe TM5500/TM5800 System Design Guide. (2002)
5. Texas Instruments: MSP430x43x, MSP430x44x Mixed Signal Microcontroller. (2004)
6. Li, H., Bhunia, S., Chen, Y., Vijaykumar, T.N., Roy, K.: Deterministic clock gating to reduce microprocessor power. In: International Symposium on High-Performance Computer Architecture (HPCA). (2003) 113–122
7. Shin, D., Kim, J., Lee, S.: Intra-task voltage scheduling for low-energy hard real-time applications. IEEE Design and Test of Computers **18** (2001)
8. Pillai, P., Shin, K.G.: Real-time dynamic voltage scaling for low-power embedded operating systems. In: ACM Symposium on Operating Systems Principles. (2001) 89–102
9. Jejurikar, R., Gupta, R.: Energy aware task scheduling with task synchronization for embedded real time systems. In: International Conference on Compilers, Architectures and Synthesis for Embedded Systems, Grenoble, France. (2002) 164–169
10. Pouwelse, J., Langendoen, K., Sips, H.: Energy priority scheduling for variable voltage processors. In: Int. Symposium on Low Power Electronics and Design (ISLPED), Huntington Beach, CA, USA. (2001)
11. Pouwelse, J., Langendoen, K., Sips, H.: Dynamic voltage scaling on a low-power microprocessor. In: 7th ACM International Conference on Mobile Computing and Networking (Mobicom), Rome, Italy. (2001) 251–259
12. Krishna, C., Lee, Y.H.: Voltage-Clock-Scaling Adaptive Scheduling Techniques for Low Power in Hard Real-Time Systems. In: Proceedings of Real-Time Applications Symposium. (2000)
13. Krishna, C., Lee, Y.H.: Voltage-Clock-Scaling Adaptive Scheduling Techniques for Low Power in Hard Real-Time Systems. IEEE Transactions on Computers **52** (2003)
14. Aydin, H., Melhem, R., Mosse, D., Mejia-Alvarez, P.: Power-Aware Scheduling for Periodic Real-Time Tasks. IEEE Transactions on Computers **53** (2004) 584–600
15. Brooks, D., Bose, P., Schuster, S., Jacobson, H., Kudva, P., Buyuktosunoglu, A., Wellman, J.D., Zyuban, V., Gupta, M., Cook, P.: Power-aware Microarchitecture: Designing and Modeling Challenges for Next-generation Microprocessors. **20** (2000) 26–44
16. Seng, J., Tullsen, D., Cai, G.: Power-sensitive multithreaded architecture. In: 2000 IEEE International Conference on Computer Design: VLSI in Computers and Processors, Austin, TX, USA. (2000) 199–206
17. Uhrig, S., Ungerer, T.: Fine-grained power management for multithreaded processor cores. In: ACM Symposium on Applied Computing (SAC 2004), Nicosia, Cypres. (2004)
18. Uhrig, S., Ungerer, T.: Fine-grained power management for real-time embedded processors. In: RTS Embedded Systems, Paris, France. (2004) 129–146
19. Ernst, R., Ye, W.: Embedded Program Timing Analysis Based on Path Clustering and Architecture Classification. (In: International Conference on Computer-Aided Design (ICCAD '97)) 598–604
20. Uhrig, S., Liemke, C., Pfeffer, M., Becker, J., Brinkschulte, U., Ungerer, T.: Implementing Real-time Scheduling Within a Multithreaded Java Microcontroller. In: 6th Workshop on Multithreaded Execution, Architecture and Compilation (MTEAC-6) in conjunction with 35th International Symposium on Microarchitecture (MICRO-35), Istanbul, Turkey. (2002) 57–64

Reducing System Level Power Consumption
for Mobile and Embedded Platforms

Ripal Nathuji and Karsten Schwan

College of Computing,
Georgia Institute of Technology,
Atlanta, GA 30332
{rnathuji,schwan}@cc.gatech.edu

Abstract. The power consumption of peripheral devices is a significant portion of the overall energy usage of a mobile platform. To take advantage of idle times, most devices offer the ability to transition into low power states. However, the amount of energy saved by utilizing these sleep states depends on the lengths and number of idle periods experienced by the device. This paper describes a new process scheduling algorithm which accumulates device usage information in the form of device windows to make power a first class resource: it attempts to increase the burstiness of both device accesses and idle periods, and it provides enhanced behavior for timeout-based sleep mechanisms. An initial implementation based on the default Linux scheduler demonstrates the algorithm's and approach's ability to reduce the average power consumption of devices by increasing device sleep times and reducing transition overheads.

1 Introduction

Mobile devices have become a popular platform for both personal and commercial applications. The increased use of these devices has in turn emphasized the demand for maximizing their battery lifetimes, making power efficiency a critical design goal. Indeed, in order to enable these devices for end users, it is often necessary to employ software techniques in addition to hardware optimizations to achieve the battery lifetimes required by end users. As a result, commercial systems now routinely employ power reduction techniques, ranging from dimming displays, to spinning down disk drives, to turning off (or placing into sleep modes) devices during idle times [1, 2].

An issue faced by most current dynamic techniques for reducing energy usage is that they should not lead to reduced productivity in mobile device usage. Stated more precisely, system metrics like job throughput should not be unduly affected by devices operating in sleep or idle modes. In other words, while reductions in energy usage indicate the need for increasing the burstiness of device usage and thereby improving the extents of device idle times, the consequent changes in the ways in which jobs are executed must not substantially reduce user-centric measures of job scheduling like throughput or response time.

M. Beigl and P. Lukowicz (Eds.): ARCS 2005, LNCS 3432, pp. 18–32, 2005.

This paper explores a new system-level technique for process scheduling which uses information about a process's device usage to make scheduling decisions. In particular, device usage information is correlated to a process using device windows. The goal of the resulting *window-based* process scheduler is to utilize this information to schedule processes in a manner which (1) increases the burstiness of device accesses, and (2) increases the durations of idle periods.

As with related work [3, 4], we assume that the determination of when and how long to put devices to sleep is made at the operating system level, in part because the OS has ready access to the internals of device drivers and performance counters needed to implement effective power measures for power reduction. Consequently, our initial implementation of device window-based scheduling extends the Linux process scheduler on a hardware platform representative of portable devices, using an experimental version of a handheld device that uses Intel's XScale processor. Experimental evaluations of window-based scheduling rely on application scenarios that emulate reasonable device usage patterns. Power measurements use a wireless network device based on the standard 802.11 sleep protocol. These measurements illustrate the ability to save power with this scheduling approach. An analysis of time spent in low power modes and device accesses is also provided. Results indicate improvements of up to 18% in time spent in a low power state and 25% in average power consumption with our wireless 802.11 device.

2   Related Work

There are multiple approaches to the problem of energy reduction in portable devices. Recent processor architectures like Intel's XScale permit dynamic frequency and voltage scaling (DFS/DVS), which can be used to reduce power consumption during program execution [5]. Process schedules can be adjusted to take advantage of these techniques while also meeting application-level requirements like task deadlines [6, 7]. In order to build power-aware hard real-time systems, a design framework that allows for the exploration of power/performance tradeoffs is proposed in [8]. By combining system-level techniques with application-level adaptations, further savings in energy usage can be attained, as shown for multi-media applications [9]. Other methods use compiler-based information to create a compiler/OS collaborative system for frequency scaling [10].

In [11], the authors present an operating system approach that extends the lifetime of a system to some user-specified length by making power a first class resource, and by allocating power strictly to processes. This approach is extended to modified scheduling algorithms in [12]. While increasing device lifetimes, these approaches, however, do not provide any user-level guarantees like throughput or deadlines. In [13], the author utilizes hardware performance counters to perform energy accounting, and proposes energy-aware scheduling techniques based on this accounting.

There has been substantial research on utilizing device idle periods, much of it concerned with communication devices. In [14], the authors propose the use of a separate low power channel to better determine when to turn off the device. In [1], a modification of the 802.11 protocol at the client and base station is used to collaboratively determine when to put a wireless device to sleep. An adaptive protocol for making device-level sleep decisions is introduced in [15]. The approach is based on the secondary effects of powering down wireless devices on higher layer protocols such as TCP. For greater flexibility, in [16] the authors propose a new application interface for system I/O to provide energy-aware resource usage.

For multiple devices, given a predetermined task schedule and device usage list, [17] describes an algorithm to determine a schedule for device sleep/working states. Given perfect knowledge of tasks' device usage, [18] presents an algorithm that schedules tasks so as to maximize device idle periods. In [19], the authors combine this approach with decisions about when to turn devices on or off using runtime information about per-process device utilization.

Our approach is inspired by the multi-processor scheduling algorithm presented in [20], where the authors utilize processor-cache affinity information to schedule tasks to minimize cache overheads. We develop a power analogue of that approach, the goal being to reduce power consumption by bursting device accesses. The idea is to develop a lightweight dynamic process scheduling algorithm that manipulates inter-device usage characteristics in order to reduce system-level energy consumption. Unlike previous work, we attempt to provide power-enhanced scheduling without any specific information from applications or compilers.

3   Motivation and Approach

3.1   Background

It is well-known that the sizes and distribution of device idle periods can dramatically affect the amount of power that is saved by putting them to sleep. We focus on two particular interactions between idle periods and power saving mechanisms, which are the interactions of idle time distributions with (1) state transition overheads and (2) sleep timeout overheads. Figure 1 illustrates how the distribution of idle periods can affect these attributes. The example depicts a scenario with four periods of device usage. Power state transitions are represented with dotted arrows, and timeout periods with dashed areas. Note that timeout periods overlap with idle periods of the device.

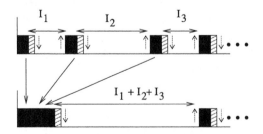

Fig. 1. Bursting Device Accesses.

When the three periods of device usage are coalesced into one larger one, total idle time remains the same, but the device avoids two timeout periods and four state transitions. This results in an increased time spent in sleep state with the same idle time (due to both timeout and state transition overheads). As an example, a wakeup state transition for the 802.11 wireless device can take about $250\mu s$ during which time the card consumes the amount of power required for the idle state [21], resulting in an energy consumption of approximately .2mJ per wakeup when the card consumes 755mW more power in idle mode than in sleep mode [22]. The energy cost of a timeout period is given by Equation 1, where P_{idle} is the average power consumed when idle, P_{sleep} is the sleep power of the device, and t_{to} is the timeout period. Each timeout that is avoided saves E_{to}. Using our wireless example again, with a typical timeout value of 10ms, E_{to} is approximately 7.55mJ. Therefore, by reducing the number of timeouts, and by amortizing the cost of both timeouts and state transitions with longer sleep periods, 'bursting' device accesses can benefit power consumption. For the specific case of wireless network devices, this behavior is also exploited in [22].

$$E_{to} = (P_{idle} - P_{sleep}) * t_{to} \tag{1}$$

The principal goal of our scheduling approach is to manipulate process schedules in order to provide power-efficient inter-device usage times. Given perfect knowledge of device usage requirements for processes, it is possible to determine an optimal schedule for both process execution and the associated schedule for toggling the sleep modes of devices. This paper's approach addresses the more common scenario in which the operating system must schedule processes and manage device states without apriori information about device usage. As a result, we do not require applications to adhere to a specific API to take advantage of device window scheduling, nor do we assume hints or program information provided by compilers. Instead, the idea of process scheduling based on device windows is to dynamically develop information about a process's pattern of device usage based on its past behavior. Past behavior is collected using device windows, which are then used to help schedule processes in order to create suitable inter-device usage times. Stated concisely, (1) device usage information collected at runtime is used to estimate the lengths of device usage patterns, based on which (2) process schedules are changed to better distribute device idle periods (*i.e.*, increased burstiness).

An interesting issue with device idle periods is to make them large enough to enable low power modes but also sufficiently small to avoid device timeouts. This is because systems use timeouts to determine when or whether a device should enter sleep mode. That is, a device enters sleep mode after some pre-determined timeout period and is woken up as soon as it is used by some process. The aggressive approach of using very small timeout values can lead to overall increases in energy usage due to the overheads of frequently toggling device states, and it may also cause additional, wakeup-caused delays for the applications using the device. Conversely, using a conservative timeout value can result in achieving only a fraction of the total possible energy savings. In this context, then, one task of device window scheduling is to create 'good' inter-device usage times.

In order to illustrate the approach, assume that only one device is under consideration and that the scheduler is aware of whether or not a process will use the device the next time it runs. Given this information, the scheduler can 'burst' device access by first scheduling all of the tasks that will use the device and only then running the tasks that will not (or vice versa). Unfortunately, schedulers do not have perfect information about future device usage by processes and must, therefore, use some predictive mechanism. The mechanism advanced in our work assumes that processes begin executing with 'empty' device windows. Whenever a process executes on the CPU, its device window is updated to reflect whether or not the device is used. We next define device windows and their usage in more detail.

3.2 Device Windows

The role of device windows is to provide information to the scheduler in order for it to determine the next process to be scheduled. There are two kinds of device windows: (1) process device windows and (2) system device windows. *Process device windows* are used to estimate the likelihood of a process utilizing a device during its next execution period on the CPU. For each device in the system, a unique device window is included in the state of each process. These device windows are updated whenever a process stops executing on the CPU. Specifically, device windows are implemented as statically sized sliding windows. Each time a process is removed from the processor, the window entries are shifted to the right, and the 'last' (leftmost) bit is set if the device was used during the past execution period.

In addition to the device windows allocated to each process, our scheduling algorithm requires some system-wide state. This is realized with *system device windows* that capture system state rather than per-process information. Similar to process device windows, there is a unique system device window for each device. These windows are updated simultaneously with process device windows whenever a process is removed from the processor. Figure 2 illustrates the design of our system with respect to device window state.

Given process and system device windows, the scheduling algorithm determines the most appropriate process to schedule next. When doing so, the scheduler must compare the significance of multiple device windows. This comparison is performed by determining device window "values". The *value* of a device window is a function of its bits. One possible function is to count the number of

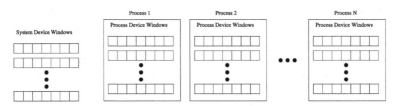

Fig. 2. System Device Window Design.

'set' bits in the device window. With larger device windows, however, it may be necessary to not just consider the number of set bits, but also their distribution. For example, consider a device window of [00101] and [11000]. Both have two set bits, but the latter window represents a process that has used the device during its two most recent execution periods. To quantize this difference, device windows can also be compared by the binary values of their bits. In the example, this would result in comparing device window values of 5 and 24. Note that this approach exponentially reduces the significance of a device window bit whenever the window is shifted. Therefore, we define device windows that calculate their values in this manner as 'exponential' device windows. The decision of which type of device window to use is left as a design parameter. In our experiments we utilize exponential device windows for process state, and normal device windows for system state.

An issue is the size of both system and process device windows. With larger windows, the scheduler can accumulate usage data over longer periods of time. The tradeoff, however, is that the information in a longer device window may not accurately represent the current execution characteristics of the process (*i.e.* the data may become stale) for low latency devices. Similarly, small device windows may be too dynamic for higher latency devices. Therefore, device windows should be sized in proportion with the latency of the respective devices to which they are assigned. For system device windows, we utilize a static size of 'one' to allow the scheduler to quickly adapt to changes in device usage patterns of the system.

A final attribute of device windows is the use of window value thresholds. Thresholds are used for both process and system device windows. For process device windows, if the value of the window is greater than the threshold, then the scheduler will predict that the process is likely to use the device the next time it runs on the CPU. We define the *Active Device Set* (*ADS*) of a process as the set of devices for which the device window value is greater than the threshold. For system device windows, if the window value is greater than the threshold, the scheduler will consider that device as being active in the system. Similar to processes, we define the system *Active Device Set* as the set of devices which are determined to be active in the system. Table 1 lists the various device window parameters discussed in this section.

3.3   Device Window Scheduling

The goal of energy-efficient scheduling is to obtain burstiness in device usage. That is, if a device is not currently being used, then preference should be given

Table 1. Device Window Parameter Definitions.

Parameter	Definition
size	number of bits allocated for a device window
value	set bit count (normal) or binary value (exponential) of device window
threshold	comparison value for a device window
ADS	set of device windows for which value > threshold

Table 2. Scheduler Parameter Definitions.

Parameter	Definition
$S_{0,i}$	1 if System device window value less than threshold for device i, 0 otherwise
$S_{1,i}$	1 if System device window value greater than threshold for device i, 0 otherwise
$P_{0,i,p}$	1 if Process device window value less than threshold for process p and device i, 0 otherwise
$P_{1,i,p}$	1 if Process device window value greater than threshold for process p and device i, 0 otherwise
$W_{i,p}$	Process window device value for process p device i
$W_{i,max}$	Maximum window device value for device i
λ_i	Weight value for device i

to processes that are not likely to use it. If a device is in use, then processes with high device window values should be preferentially scheduled. We term the previous action as 'idle bursting' (IB) and the latter as 'device bursting' (DB).

As described in Section 3.2, the scheduler utilizes threshold values along with system device windows to determine what devices are active in the system. If a device is active, the scheduler will try to perform device bursting for it, otherwise it will attempt to perform idle bursting. In particular, as described in Table 2, the parameters $S_{0,i}$ and $S_{1,i}$ denote whether the scheduler should perform idle or device bursting, respectively, for device i. Given the parameters in the table, we define the maximizing function in Equation 2, where K is the number of devices considered by our scheduler.

$$M(p) = \sum_{i=1}^{K} \lambda_i (S_{1,i} P_{1,i,p} W_{i,p} + S_{0,i} P_{0,i,p} (W_{i,max} - W_{i,p})) \qquad (2)$$

The value returned by Equation 2 depends upon the bursting mode currently occupied by the process system. The $W_{i,p}$ value for a process is only included in the returned value if the scheduler should perform device bursting for device i. Similarly, the value $(W_{i,max} - W_{i,p})$ is factored in the value of the maximizing function if the scheduler should perform idle bursting. Given the scheduling parameters and our maximizing function, our simple scheduling algorithm is Algorithm 1. The precise behavior of this process scheduling algorithm depends upon the number of devices under consideration.

Algorithm 1 Device Window Scheduling Algorithm.

$\forall$ *Processes* $i, j \in$ *Runnable*
    Choose *Process* i s.t. $M(i) \geq M(j)$ $(\forall j \neq i)$

Scheduling with a Single Device. Given a single device, the behavior of device window-based scheduling is straightforward. If the scheduler determines that it should perform idle bursting, it will choose the process in the run queue that has the smallest window value, thereby attempting to elongate an existing idle period. Similarly, if device bursting should be performed, the scheduler searches for the process with the largest window value, since a higher window value signifies an increased likelihood that the process will use the device when it is scheduled on the CPU.

Scheduling with Multiple Devices. When the scheduler must consider multiple devices, its behavior is best described using the idea of Active Device Sets (*ADS*). In particular, the algorithm will give highest preference to processes whose Active Device Sets match the system *ADS*. If no such processes exist, preference is given to processes whose device sets intersect as much as possible with the system *ADS*. Note that the scheduler gives least preference to processes that have device sets disjoint from the system *ADS*.

Device Weight Values. The notion of device weights is included in the maximizing function in order to allow the scheduler to give preference to scheduling for particular devices. Specifically, these weights can be used to give preference to creating idle periods for high latency devices with larger timeout values and larger state transition overheads. The motivation is that it is often beneficial, in terms of system power, to increase the number of state transitions for a low latency device in order to allow a device with higher overheads to remain idle.

4   Scheduler Implementation

4.1   Linux Scheduler Modification

Our initial implementation of device window scheduling is based upon the epoch-based Linux scheduler. The default Linux scheduler picks a runnable process which has the maximum value returned from the *goodness*() function. This function will return zero if the process has zero time quantum remaining. If all processes are out of time quanta, the scheduler reassigns quanta to initiate another epoch.

We utilize the *goodness*() function to implement device window-based scheduling. In particular, if a process is both runnable and has a non-zero quantum value in the current epoch, we add the value returned by our maximizing function in Equation 2 to the goodness value. Therefore, we do not modify the usual behavior of the Linux scheduler in terms of epochs and assigned quantum values. Instead, we attempt to provide improved device access behavior by reordering process execution in a given epoch.

4.2   Performance Considerations

Given the scheduling algorithm described in Section 3.3, the scheduler can starve certain user tasks by continually scheduling processes that are either I/O- or

CPU-bound. This can result in poor performance with respect to application-level requirements like response time or other soft real-time guarantees. Our implementation of device window process scheduling prevents such behavior by taking advantage of time epochs in the Linux scheduler. Specifically, tasks cannot experience starvation because our scheduling algorithm will not extend a process's time quantum to increase the length of an idle or busy period for a device. Instead, we attempt to make device usage/idle periods as bursty as possible within the constraint of the epochs. This ensures that applications do not experience any less service than they would with the normal Linux scheduler.

5   Experimental Evaluation

5.1   Sitsang Evaluation Platform

Device window scheduling is experimentally evaluated on XScale-based platforms using Intel's Sitsang evaluation board. This evaluation board is based upon the Intel PXA255 processor. The PXA255 processor integrates the Intel XScale microarchitecture with various controllers and peripherals including a memory controller, universal serial bus support and DMA controller. The evaluation board offers additional features, including a CompactFlash slot, infrared receiver, and a slot for Secure Digital memory cards. The operating system used with the evaluation platform is a patched version of the Linux 2.4.19 kernel.

We have chosen to use this evaluation platform for two reasons. First, it is somewhat representative of the future 'high end' cellular phone platforms now being developed. Such platforms are intended to replace what are now multiple devices carried by end users, like PDAs, cell phones, or calculators, into single, multi-function devices able to carry out a wide variety of tasks. XScale processors are used because of their high level of energy efficiency, their support of both frequency and voltage scaling, and similar capabilities. The Sitsang platform represents a simple model of such future devices in a PDA-like form factor, but with limited device connectivity. To evaluate the scheduler, we attach a Linksys WCF11 wireless network card to the Sitsang board, as well as a USB hard disk.

5.2   Operating System Modifications

We modify the Linux 2.4.19 source with the scheduler implementation described in Section 4. This modification consists of modifying the existing *goodness*() function to utilize our maximizing function when applicable, and the addition of device window state in both process and global state. We modify the scheduler to update device windows whenever a process is removed from the CPU.

In order to support the experimentation described in this section, we also modify the Linux operating system to include some monitoring functionality. The modification implements monitoring functionality in order to detect when processes uses the devices under consideration (802.11 and disk). This information is then used to update the process and system device windows in the scheduler. In particular, we update monitoring state whenever a process either reads or writes to these devices.

Table 3. Experimental Applications.

Application	Description	Devices Used
A	Background tasks	None
B	Data computation and transmission	802.11
C	Periodic data update	802.11
D	Audio Streaming	802.11
E	Image Streaming	802.11
F	Audio Streaming w/Save	802.11 & Disk
G	Image Player	Disk

5.3 Application Scenarios

The ability to save energy through process scheduling strongly depends on the mix of application processes running on the mobile device. The experiments conducted in this paper envision scenarios with applications that would reasonably be executed on a mobile device. Table 3 lists the applications being used.

Our experimental evaluation attempts to reflect reasonable platform usage by creating different scenarios, each comprised of multiple applications. All of these scenarios include sporadic background computational tasks (application A). Application B is a simple application that performs computations and then transmits data over the network. This application mimics the behavior of many programs executed on mobile platforms, including those that manipulate data obtained from sensors or context, and then send it back to a data sink. Application C imitates the type of updates a cellular phone or PDA may send over the network to a back end server. The remaining applications are used to capture multimedia program behavior.

Table 4. Experimental Scenarios.

Scenario	Applications Used
1	A,B,C
2	A,B,C,D
3	A,B,C,E
4	A,B,C,F
5	A,F,G

Given the list of applications, Table 4 depicts the experimental scenarios executed in the evaluation of device window-based scheduling. We next describe the metrics that are used to quantify the benefits of device window scheduling.

5.4 Evaluation Metrics

As described in Section 3.1, the intent of device window-based scheduling is to improve energy efficiency by increasing the lengths of device usage periods and idle periods. By increasing the lengths of idle periods, the approach (1) creates sleep periods that previously would not exist due to timeouts (*i.e.*, the original idle periods are shorter than the timeout value) and (2) amortizes the costs of state transitions and timeout periods with longer sleep periods. Given these two characteristics, device window scheduling should directly impact the average energy consumption of a device.

For our first four experimental scenarios, we utilize power measurements of our wireless device to evaluate performance. The fifth and final experimental scenario focuses on the disk device. In particular, we investigate how this process scheduling approach influences the access behavior experienced by the device. We do this by collecting and analyzing traces obtained during the execution of the experimental scenario. In particular, we analyze the traces using the formula given in Equation 3. Both of these evaluation methods are discussed in more detail below.

$$M_{perf} = \frac{t_{sleep}(t_{to})}{\#S_{trans}} \tag{3}$$

Power Measurements. Power measurements with and without device window scheduling are conducted for the wireless device scenarios. The goal is to experimentally illustrate the benefits derived from the increased burstiness of inter-device usage distributions for creating periods of low current draw in devices. For the device sleep algorithm, the standard 802.11 sleep mode is invoked with the *iwconfig* system utility. Since our wireless card is a compact flash device, it uses a power supply voltage of 3.3 volts. To prevent reducing this supply voltage during measurements, we use a 'current sensor IC' (integrated circuit) to measure the current flowing to the CF socket, without disturbing the voltage source. The output from the current sensor is then amplified via an analog circuit to obtain measurements. We simultaneously measure the source voltage, as well, in order to obtain accurate average power numbers. An oscilloscope samples both channels at a 4kHz sampling rate, and is capable of buffering 4 seconds of data at a time. Therefore, we obtain repeated measurements during a scenario execution to get the average power consumption over a two minute window. We present the mean and standard deviation of these final values as our result.

In addition to these values, we analyze the distribution of current values to determine how much time the device spends in a low power state with and without our process scheduler. The reasoning behind this metric is that the overall power benefit of our scheduler is dependent upon the energy characteristics of the device. Therefore, we compare the percentage of time that the wireless device spends in low power state in our scenarios to illustrate the capability of the device window scheduler to increase the sleep time a device experiences.

Disk Access Analysis. As described earlier, we utilize the metric given as Equation 3 to evaluate the performance of our scheduler in our final experimental scenario. The amount of sleep time the device experiences is the numerator of our formula (t_{sleep}), and is a function of the timeout value (t_{to}) that is considered. In particular, we utilize our execution trace to calculate the time between accesses.

If such a period is longer than the considered timeout value, we calculate the difference as sleep time, and add two state transitions (one to power down device, and one to power it up for the subsequent request). Note that this metric is directly proportional to sleep time, and inversely proportional to the number of state transitions (S_{trans}). We present the result of this metric as a function of possible timeout values. In this particular case, the disk device does not support the types of timeout values we consider, but we feel that it is reasonable to perform this general analysis of the traces as an evaluation of the behavior of our scheduler.

5.5   Evaluation Results

We present the results of power measurements in the first four experimental scenarios in Table 5. First, it is apparent that device window-based scheduling significantly impacts the average power consumption of the wireless device. Savings from 50mW to 100mW, or about 10%–25%, can be observed. We also see substantial improvements in the time spent in low power mode. These improvements vary from 6%–18%.

Table 5. Power Results of Wireless 802.11 Device.

Scheduler	Scenario	Average Power	% of time in Low Power Mode
Default Scheduler	1	417±4 mW	33%
Device Window Scheduler	1	313±8 mW	51%
Default Scheduler	2	389±5 mW	39%
Device Window Scheduler	2	336 ±8 mW	48%
Default Scheduler	3	547 ±12 mW	16%
Device Window Scheduler	3	496 ±11 mW	24%
Default Scheduler	4	411 ±7 mW	40%
Device Window Scheduler	4	363 ±3 mW	46%

In addition to improving average power consumption by increasing the percentage of time spent in low power mode, the device window scheduler also (1) reduces power by saving energy when it avoids timeout periods and (2) reduces state transition overheads by amortizing their costs over longer sleep periods. We illustrate these benefits with our fifth and final experimental scenario.

Figure 3 presents the analysis of our disk access trace with the evaluation metric given in Equation 3. The figure shows that device window scheduling creates extended sleep periods, and for longer timeout values, creates sleep periods that would otherwise not exist. In the particular case of a disk device, this behavior is the result of allowing better write back behavior due to bursting and elongated idle times. This type of disk write behavior is typical for applications such as media download, retrieving HTTP objects, and storing sensor data. Utilizing the value of our evaluation metric, we also see that our scheduler can substantially reduce the cost of state transitions by increasing the ratio of sleep

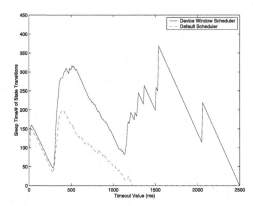

Fig. 3. Disk Access Performance Benefits.

time to the number state transitions. Combined with the energy results from the previous evaluation scenarios, this illustrates that device window scheduling can indeed provide significant power benefits on realistic platforms, by reducing the amount of power consumed by devices.

6 Conclusions and Future Work

System-wide methods for reducing the energy usage of mobile devices remain an active topic of research [7]. The approach taken in this paper is to have the OS scheduler exploit information about processes' devices usage patterns to enhance device usage behavior, particularly, to increase the burstiness of device usage and of device idle times. The device window scheduling algorithm presented in this paper conserves energy by improving processes' inter-device usage distributions.

Device window-based scheduling is implemented in the Linux operating system kernel for the Sitsang XScale evaluation platform for future embedded devices produced by Intel Corporation. Performance measurements on this platform with representative application benchmarks evaluate the potential of device window-based process scheduling, demonstrating substantial improvements in both power and time spent in low power modes. We also analyze access traces of disk devices to project the benefits of our approach with varying timeout values.

Our future work is threefold. First, we plan to implement device window scheduling for a real-time process scheduler in order to avoid the limitations of extending idle periods suffered by using an epoch-based implementation. Second, we will investigate the use of dynamic frequency/voltage scaling in our scheduling approach to further reduce platform power consumption. A third direction of future work is to generalize the single platform scheduling technique presented in this paper to an entire distributed system, comprised of many power-constrained devices. Initial ideas on how to conduct that work appear in [23], demonstrating the importance of gathering and exploiting system-wide information about application and device power behaviors.

References

1. Kravets, R., Krishnan, P.: Application-Driven Power Management for Mobile Communication. In Proceedings of the Fourth ACM International Conference on Mobile Computing and Networking (MOBICOM) (1998) 263–277
2. Lu, Y., Chung, E., Simunic, T., Benini, L., Micheli, G.: Quantitative Comparison of Power Management Algorithms . In Design Automation and Test in Europe (2000) 20–26
3. Ellis, C.: The Case for Higher-Level Power Management. In Proceedings of the Seventh IEEE Workshop on Hot Topics in Operating Systems (HotOS-VII) (1999)
4. Lu, Y., Benini, L., Micheli, G.: Operating System Directed Power Reduction . In International Symposium on Low Power Electronics and Design (2000) 37–42
5. Weiser, M., Welch, B., Demers, A., Shenker, S.: Scheduling for Reduced CPU Energy. In Proceedings of the First Symposium on Operating Systems Design and Implementation (1994) 13–23
6. Swaminathan, V., Chakrabarty, K.: Real-time task scheduling for energy-aware embedded systems. In Proceedings of Real-time Systems and Symposium (Work-in-Progress Session) (2000)
7. Swaminathan, V., Schweizer, C., Chakrabarty, K., Patel, A.: Experiences in Implementing an Energy-Driven Task Scheduler in RT-Linux. In Proceedings of the Real-time and Embedded Technology and Applications Symposium) (2002) 229–239
8. Chou, P., Liu, J., Li, D., Bagherzadeh, N.: IMPACCT:Methodology and Tools for Power-Aware Embedded Systems. Kluwer Design Automation of Embedded Systems (2002)
9. Poellabauer, C., Schwan, K.: Power-Aware Video Decoding using Real-Time Event Handlers. In Proceedings of the 5th International Workshop on Wireless Mobile Multimedia (WoWMoM) (2002)
10. AbouGhazaleh, N., Mosse, D., Childers, B., Melhem, R., Craven, M.: Collaborative Operating System and Compiler Power Management for Real-Time Applications. In Proceedings of the IEEE Real-Time and Embedded Technology and Applications Symposium (RTAS) (2003)
11. Zeng, H., Fan, X., Ellis, C., Lebeck, A., Vahdat, A.: ECOSystem: Managing Energy as a First Class Operating System Resource. In Proceedings of the Tenth International Conference on Architectural Support for Programming Languages and Operating Systems (ASPLOS X) (2002)
12. Zeng, H., Ellis, C., Lebeck, A., Vahdat, A.: Currentcy: A Unifying Abstraction for Expressing Energy Management Policies. In Proceedings of USENIX (2003) 43–56
13. Bellosa, F.: The Benefits of Event-Driven Energy Accounting in Power-Sensitive Systems. In Proceedings of the 9th ACM SIGOPS European Workshop (2000)
14. Shih, E., Bahl, P., Sinclair, M.: Wake on Wireless: An Event Driven Energy Saving Strategy for Battery Operated Devices . In Proceedings of ACM MobiCom (2002) 160–171
15. Krashinsky, R., Balakrishnan, H.: Minimizing Energy for Wireless Web Access with Bounded Slowdown. In Proceedings of ACM MOBICOM (2002) 119–130
16. Weissel, A., Beutel, B., Bellosa, F.: Cooperative I/O-A Novel IO Semantics for Energy-Aware Applications. In Proceedings of the Fifth Symposium on Operating Systems Design and Implementation (OSDI) (2002)
17. Swaminathan, V., Chakrabarty, K., Iyengar, S.: Dynamic I/O Power Management for Hard Real-time Systems. In Proceedings of International Symposium on Hardware/Software Codesign (2001) 237–243

18. Lu, Y., Benini, L., Micheli, G.: Low-Power Task Scheduling for Multiple Devices. In 8th International Workshop on Hardware/Software Codesign (2000) 39–43

19. Lu, Y., Benini, L., Micheli, G.: Power-Aware Operating Systems for Interactive Systems . In IEEE Transactions on Very Large Scale Integration Systems (2002) 119–134

20. Squillante, M., Lazowska, E.: Using Processor-Cache Affinity Information in Shared-Memory Multiprocessor Scheduling. In IEEE Transactions on Parallel and Distributed Systems **4** (1993) 131–143

21. Havinga, P., Smit, G.: Energy-Efficient Wireless Networking for Multimedia Applications. Journal on Wireless Communications and Mobile Computing (2001)

22. Poellabauer, C., Schwan, K.: Energy-Aware Traffic Shaping for Wireless Real-Time Applications. In Proceedings of the Real-Time and Embedded Technology and Applications Symposium (2004)

23. Poellabauer, C., Schwan, K.: Energy-Aware Media Transcoding in Wireless Systems. In Proceedings of the Second IEEE International Conference on Pervasive Computing and Communications (PerCom 2004) (2004)

Implementing Control Algorithms Within a Multithreaded Java Microcontroller

Uwe Brinkschulte and Mathias Pacher

Institute for Process Control, Automation and Robotics,
University of Karlsruhe, Germany
{brinks,pacher}@ira.uka.de

Abstract. Our aim is to investigate if it is possible to control the throughput (IPC rate) of a thread running on a multithreaded Java processor by a closed feedback loop. We implemented a Proportional/Integral/Differential (PID) controller in the processor simulator of the Komodo microcontroller developed at the universities of Karlsruhe and Augsburg to simulate the PID controller as an additional hardware module. It uses the GP (Guaranteed Percentage) scheduling to control the thread. Evaluations show that the aimed IPC rate of a thread is achieved by the controller thus improving the real-time capabilities of the Java processor.

Keywords: Komodo microcontroller, multithreaded Java microcontroller, PID controller, GP scheduling, IPC rate

1 Introduction

In today's microprocessors it is hard to hold real-time bounds because of various reasons. One reason is branch prediction which is implemented in most modern long-pipelined microprocessors. If there is a misprediction the pipeline has to be flushed which costs a lot of penalty clock cycles. For the Pentium III processor this penalty is e.g. at least 11 clock cycles [2]. So it is not possible to guarantee a certain throughput (*Instructions Per Cycle*, IPC) within a small time slice.

Another problem for microprocessors in guaranteeing real-time abilities is the usage of caches because it is hard to give an estimation for the access time to the data. If the required data is in the L1 cache or trace cache the access time is very small, but if it is not in the caches it has to be fetched from the memory which also costs several clock cycles.

This paper describes an approach to compensate these penalties and thus improving the real-time features by applying closed control loops. Our testbed is the Komodo microcontroller developed at the universities of Karlsruhe and Augsburg [16, 17]. Komodo is a multithreaded Java microcontroller. Key features are very rapid context switching realized by hardware multithreading and the real-time scheduling algorithms integrated deeply within the pipeline.

In order to guarantee the handling of hard real-time events on time, the runtime of the event-handling algorithm must be countable in processor cycles. In the Komodo microcontroller this is realized by a scheduling strategy called *Guaranteed Percentage* (GP) which has been newly designed for real-time scheduling

M. Beigl and P. Lukowicz (Eds.): ARCS 2005, LNCS 3432, pp. 33–49, 2005.

on multithreaded processors [2]. The idea is that every thread gets a certain percentage of the processor time and to guarantee this percentage for every thread in a small time slice, e.g. 100 clock cycles in case of the Komodo microcontroller. As an advantage this scheduling strategy ensures a strict isolation of real-time threads against each other and there is a predictable behaviour in time for every thread.

In order to test the Komodo microcontroller a processor simulator was implemented in the Java programming language. So we are able to modify the processor architecture with low costs and to test the changes.

As a scalar processor, the Komodo microcontroller normally needs one clock cycle for the execution of one opcode, but depending on the executed operation latencies can appear. An example are conditional branches where it firstly has to be computed if the branch is taken or not. To bridge the latencies induced by this computation, the multithreaded processor switches to another thread to keep the overall processing performance. But the real-time behaviour of the single thread is affected by the latencies. Similar latencies appear on singlethreaded processors in case of a branch misprediction. More latencies can arise by atomic locks, which can take thousands of clock cycles.

Therefore we implemented a PID controller in the processor simulator allowing to control the IPC rate of a single thread by varying the GP values of the threads. By monitorig the current IPC rate of a thread and comparing it to the aimed IPC rate, the GP value of the thread is adapted in a closed feedback loop.

The goal is to balance the anomalies in the IPC rate which are caused by latencies and locks. This makes the time behaviour more predictable, because the execution time of a piece of code can be calculated based on the balanced IPC rate.

Because of the multithreading property the Komodo microcontroller is well suited for this task and due to the implementation of the PID controller in the simulator this corresponds to a hardware implementation of the PID controller. In this way it is possible to control the threads within *zero clock cycles*.

The idea of controlling is obviously not limited to the Komodo microcontroller. It also works for microcontrollers with similar properties like the Komodo microcontroller which e.g. support GP scheduling.

2   State of the Art

Several approaches use closed control loops in real-time systems to limit communication overhead or to perform admission control (e.g. [9, 10]). These approaches are purely software based. At the time we wrote this paper, to our knowledge no other work is done using control theory approach to compensate latencies for real-time applications on a hardware level.

Only in IBM's Power5 Chip which supports *simultaneous multithreading* (SMT), enhanced SMT features are offered. They make a step towards controlling by e.g. reducing the priority of a thread if resources getting rare [7].

Furthermore, our approach is completely different to adaptive microprocessors, where resources like caches or queues are adapted at runtime [1, 5, 6, 8, 15]. No control theory nor real-time is addressed there.

3   The Komodo Microcontroller

The Komodo microcontroller consists of a processor core attached to typical devices as e.g. a timer/counter, capture/compare, serial and parallel interfaces via an I/O bus [16]. In the following we explain details about the processor core which is kept at a simple hardware level because of its real-time applications.

3.1   The Pipeline of the Komodo Microcontroller

Figure 1 shows the pipeline enhanced by the priority manager and the signal unit. The pipeline consists of the following four stages: instruction fetch (IF), instruction window and decode (ID), operand fetch (OF) and execute, memory and I/O-access (EXE). These stages perform the following tasks as described in [17]:

Instruction Fetch: The instruction fetch unit tries to fetch a new instruction package from the memory interface in each clock cycle. If there is a branch executed in EX the internal program counter is set and the instruction package is fetched from the new address.

Instruction Window and Decode: The decoding of an instruction starts after writing a received instruction package to the correct instruction window. Hereby, the priority manager decides which thread will be decoded by ID every clock cycle.

Operand Fetch: In this pipeline stage operands needed by the actual operation are read from the stack. It has to be marked that the OF is not realized in the processor simulator because the runtime does not matter for the simulator [4].

Execution, Memory and I/O-Access: There are three units in the execution stage (ALU, memory and I/O). All instructions except of load/store are executed by ALU. The result is send to the stack and to OF for forwarding. In case of load/store instructions the memory is addressed by one of the operands. An I/O-access is handled in the same way like a memory access [14, 17].

3.2   GP Scheduling

The priority manager implements several real-time scheduling schemes [2, 4, 17]. For the concern of controlling, only GP scheduling is important. In GP scheduling, the priority manager assigns a requested number of clock cycles to each thread. This assignment is done within a 100 clock cycle period. Figure 2 gives an example of two threads with 20% and 80%. This means, thread A gets 20 clock cycles and thread B gets 80 clock cycles within the 100 clock cycle interval. Of course, these clock cycles may contain latencies. So thread A might not be able to execute 20 instructions in its 20 clock cycles. Here our approach starts. By monitoring the real IPC rate, the GP value is adjusted in a closed feedback loop. If there are e.g. 3 latency clock cycles within the 20 clock cycles of thread A, its percentage needs to be adjusted to achieve the desired 20 instructions in the 100 clock cycle interval.

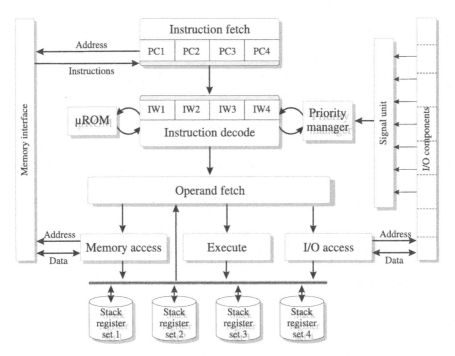

Fig. 1. The pipeline of the Komodo microcontroller.

4   PID Controller

One goal of automation is to affect an output to achieve a reference value. Often this cannot be made directly but by affecting an input. The problem is that the correlation between input and output is not well-known in most cases. So it is necessary to control the input by continuously observing the output and comparing it with the reference value in order to minimize their difference by varying the input [3, 11]. This process is shown in Figure 3. The controller in this closed feedback loop is responsible for generating the control signal $y(t)$ from the difference signal $x(t)$. A well known and popular controller is the **P**roportional/**I**ntegral/**D**ifferential controller (PID controller). The functional equation of a continuous PID controller is as follows:

$$y(t) = \underbrace{K_P * x(t)}_{\text{P element}} + \underbrace{K_I * \int_0^t x(\nu)d\nu}_{\text{I element}} + \underbrace{K_D * \frac{d}{dt}x(t)}_{\text{D element}} \tag{1}$$

Thereby x describes the difference between output and reference value at time t, and y describes the controller signal at time t. K_P, K_I and K_D are constants which have to be adjusted.

In the P element, the difference between output and reference signal is multiplicated by the constant K_P. A controller which only uses a P element is not

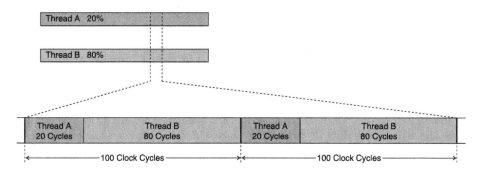

Fig. 2. Example for GP scheduling.

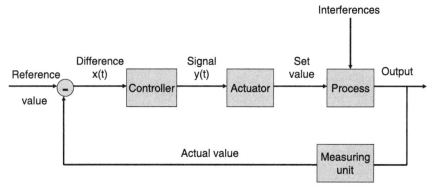

Fig. 3. PID controller.

able to eliminate the difference to zero, because K_P would have to be increased if the difference is too small.

The P element can be improved by adding an I element. It integrates over the past differences and is able to eliminate the difference to zero.

The behaviour of an I element is like a memory because the last differences are saved. A disadvantage of an I element is its slowness if there are changes.

To make the controller reacting faster on changes a D element is added. Descriptively seen the D element acts like a predictor for the future difference:

If the absolute amount of the derivative of x at time t is small, the variation of the difference will be also small. But if the absolute amount of the derivative of x at time t is big, the variation of the difference will be big.

When using a D element one has to pay attention with the choice of K_D, because the controller can overshoot if the constant is too big.

When working with digital systems it's not possible to use a continuous controller because the controller gets the difference only at certain points in time. Therefore it is necessary to modify the formula above allowing to handle with discrete values:

$$y_n = K_P * x_n + K_I * \sum_{\nu=1}^{n} x_\nu * \Delta t + K_D * \frac{x_n - x_{n-1}}{\Delta t} \qquad \text{n = 2, 3, 4...} \qquad (2)$$

Hereby x_n is the difference at the point of time n and y_n is the controller signal at the point of time n. K_P, K_I and K_D are constants again while Δt is the duration between the measurement of x_n and x_{n+1}.

5   Implementation of the PID Controller

As mentioned above the PID controller is implemented in the processor simulator and it controls the GP value of a single thread. First we start with some preconditions:

 - We assume that the sum of the percentages of all threads is less or equal than 100 in order to start the threads *without* using the controller.
 - The main thread is a non real-time thread responsible to start all other threads. So we always assign 1 percent of computing time to the main thread to guarantee progress of the threads.

Figure 4 shows a schematic diagram of the Komodo pipeline with an implemented PID controller.

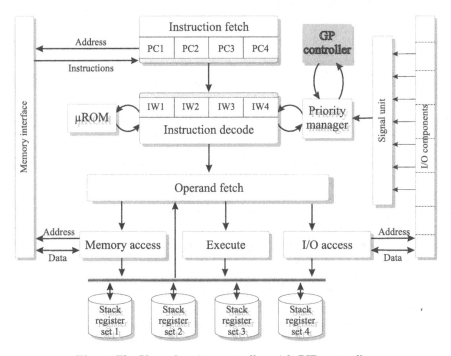

Fig. 4. The Komodo microcontroller with PID controller.

5.1 Measurement of the IPC Rate

In general, the IPC rate of a thread is defined as:

$$IPC = \frac{Number\ of\ instructions\ executed\ within\ time\ slice}{Duration\ of\ time\ slice\ (in\ clock\ cycles)} \tag{3}$$

Since Komodo is scalar processor, each instruction takes one clock cycle, except there is a latency. If we distinguish between active clock cycles, where an instruction of a thread is really executed, and latency clock cycles, we can refine the definition of the IPC rate for the Komodo microcontroller:

$$IPC = \frac{Number\ of\ active\ clock\ cycles\ within\ time\ slice}{Duration\ of\ time\ slice\ (in\ clock\ cycles)} \tag{4}$$

Hereby the number of active clock cycles of a thread means the number of clock cycles executed by a thread without the clock cycles used by latencies. Therefore it's obvious that both latencies and locks interfere the IPC rate. So it's the function of the controller to minimize these interferences in the IPC rate.

We use this formula for various measures: We compute short- and long-term IPC rates. Short-term IPC rates are measured over a constant time slice of e.g. 400 clock cycles. As longtime IPC rate, the cumulative IPC rate is used. Here, we compute the IPC rate from the beginning of thread execution up to now. This means, the duration of the time slice is increasing. While the short-term IPC rate gives information about variations in the current IPC rate, the cumulative IPC rate shows the overall behaviour.

5.2 Details of the Implementation

As mentioned above, the priority manger assigns the requested percentage within a 100 clock cycles interval. This is why we implemented a discrete PID controller,

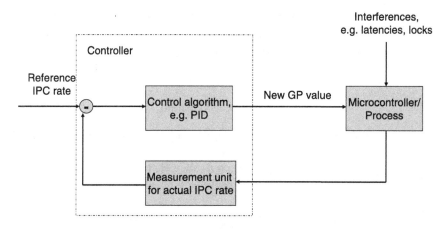

Fig. 5. Schematic diagramm of the control loop.

which recomputes the GP value for all threads every 100 clock cycles. Due to the 100 clock cycle alignment of the priority manager, shorter intervals would have no effect.

The PID controller is implemented as a part of the priority manager (see Figure 4). Its control loop is shown in Figure 5: At the end of a time slice the IPC rate of the controlled thread is measured, and the new GP values of the threads are computed and updated in the same clock cycle. This procedure is repeated every 100 clock cycles.

The user has the choice to control a thread by an IPC rate as to a constant time slice or as to an increasing time slice. So he can choose if the IPC rate should be achieved within short time or if the IPC rate should be stable as to a longer time slice.

It's clear that the controller is only activated if the controlled thread exists and is hardware-active and software-active, where a thread is hardware-active if it does not wait for an external signal, e.g. an user input. A thread is software-active if it does not wait for a resource which, for example, exists only once and is hold by another thread.

Namely if the controller is active while the controlled thread is in a lock section, this would increase the GP value of the controlled thread and therefore the GP values of other existing threads could have to be decreased. So this could lead to starving of the other threads, including the one who holds the lock.

Therefore if the controlled thread is not software- and hardware-active the controller is deactivated and the controlled thread gets a minimum amount of 1 percent in this time slice.

The controller uses a slightly modified formula compared to the formula 2 for computing the new GP value of the controlled thread:

$$y_n = \left\lfloor K_P * x_n + K_I * \sum_{\nu=n-k+1}^{n} x_\nu * \Delta t + K_D * \frac{x_n - x_{n-1}}{\Delta t} \right\rfloor \qquad (n \geq 2) \quad (5)$$

The I element of the controller now integrates about a bounded history because it's not always useful to incorporate the whole history, and the results are rounded off to an integer because it's only possible to assign a whole number.

Because of the value of y_n can be negative, it is the *changing* of the GP value. This means that the new GP value of the controlled thread is computed by adding y_n to the old GP value of the controlled thread:

$$\text{New GP value} = \text{Old GP value} + y_n \qquad (6)$$

The maximum GP value of the controlled thread is 99 because main thread always keeps 1 percent as mentioned above.

After the new GP value is set for the controlled thread and the main thread, the GP values of the remaining threads are set. They share the remaining computing time thread by thread as follows:

$$\text{New GP value}_i = \left\lfloor \frac{(100 - \text{New GP value}_{crl.\ Th.} - 1) * \text{Origin GP value}_i}{100} \right\rfloor \quad (7)$$

If there is not enough computing time for a thread in this chain it either gets the rest or, if there is no rest of computing time the thread will be deactivated. After all, controlling is deactivated if the controlled thread is finished.

6   Evaluation Results

Below we present several evaluation results. There are two diagrams for every test. In each case the first diagram shows two graphs:

- One graph shows the short-term IPC rate of the controlled thread computed over a 400 clock cycle time slice. This graph is dashed.
- The other graph shows the cumulative IPC rate. This graph is drawn black.

Seen by the processor these two values are the output of the system.

In each case the second diagram shows the graph which represents the GP value of the controlled thread. Seen by the processor this value is an input which is computed based on the IPC rate.

As mentioned above the controller is executed in a 100 cycle loop. Therefore the unit plotted on the abscissa always amounts 100 clock cycles.

6.1   First Test Benchmark

In the first test benchmark two real-time threads are generated. Each of them executes some loop cycles and in each loop cycle an output is generated. The initial GP value of thread 1 amounts 30 percent, and the initial GP value of thread 2 amounts 70 percent.

As a comparison we present a measurement *without controlling* first, shown in Figure 6. Only the values of thread 1 are represented because we always controll this thread.

The GP value of thread 1 constantly amounts 30 percent but none of the IPC rates achieves the value of 0.3. The IPC rate as to 400 cycles nervously varies around 0.22 which can probably be explained by the branches caused by the loops. Due to the uniform distribution of the IPC rate around 0.22 the cumulative IPC rate precisely swings into this value.

In the second test we controlled thread 1 by the IPC rate as to 400 cycles. The IPC rate reference value was set to 0.3 and the controller parameters were set as follows:

- $K_P = 30$
- $K_I = 20$
- $K_D = 0.1$
- The I element integrated about the last 50 history entries.
- $\Delta t = \frac{1}{400}$

The IPC rate as to 400 cycles strongly varies around the aimed IPC rate of 0.3 which leads to a strong variation of the GP value. Mostly the GP value is about

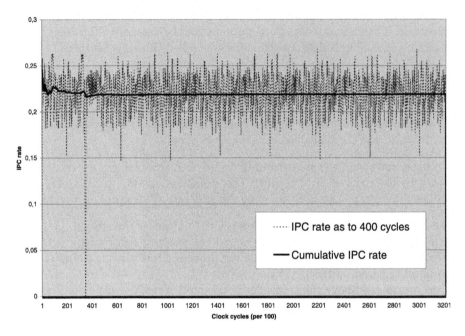

Fig. 6. Test without controlling.

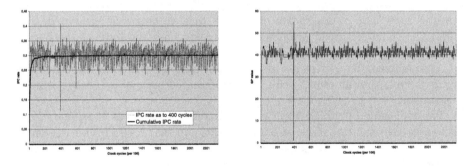

Fig. 7. Controlling as to a short time slice.

40 percent and is sometimes amplituding above in order to balance the latencies. Probably the problem of the latency-caused oscillations cannot be solved because the controller is not able to predict the branches, and therefore it can only react belatedly. The cumulative IPC rate achieves 0.3 fast which has the reason in the absence of locks and the uniform distribution of the IPC rate as to 400 cycles. In comparison to the first test the controller is well able to achieve an IPC rate of 0.3.

In the third test we controlled thread 1 by the cumulative IPC rate. The IPC rate reference value was set to 0.3 and the parameters were set as follows:

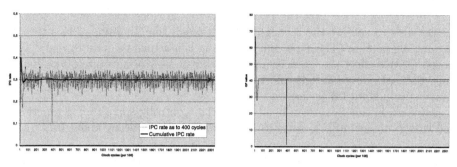

Fig. 8. Controlling as to the cumulative IPC rate.

- $K_P = 70$
- $K_I = 100$
- $K_D = 0.01$
- The I element integrated about the last 50 history entries.
- $\Delta t = \frac{1}{400}$

In this test the IPC rate as to 400 cycles is also amplituding around 0.3 but more smoothly compared to test 2. The reason is the stabilization of the cumulative IPC rate from what results the stabilization of the GP values. In fact they are constant almost all the time.

The most significant difference to the second test can be seen at the beginning. In the second test the cumulative IPC rate is growing up to 0.3 and in the third test cumulative IPC rate shortly swings around 0.3 and is then stabilizing on this value.

To explore the limits of the control loop, in the last test we set the reference value to the impossible IPC rate of 1.0. The thread is controlled by the cumulative IPC rate. The controller parameters were set as follows:

- $K_P = 60$
- $K_I = 100$
- $K_D = 0.01$
- The I element integrated about the last 50 history entries.
- $\Delta t = \frac{1}{400}$

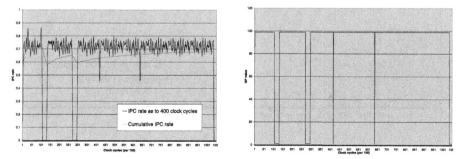

Fig. 9. Controlling as to throughput 1.

It is interesting to see that the IPC rate as to 400 clock cycles swings around 0.7 not able to achieve the throughput 1 although the GP value of this thread amounts 99 percent (The 1 percent remaining is assigned to main thread). The reason for this effect are latencies and locks which now occur quite often. Especially the locks devastatingly affect on the cumulative IPC rate which does not achieve throughput 0.7 at least.

After all, in this test it can be observed that controlling of a thread functions well with both sort of IPC rates if the reference value is below about 0.7.

6.2   Tests with a Producer Consumer Benchmark

In this test two real-time threads are generated. The producer thread generates a picture and puts it to a container object. Then the producer waits in an empty loop as long as the consumer takes up the picture. Then the producer produces a picture again and the whole procedure is repeated. As long as there is no picture the consumer also waits in an empty loop. The initial GP value for the producer amounts 49 percent and the initial value for the consumer amounts 50 percent. In this test the producer thread is controlled. So we only present the results of this thread, starting again with a diagram (Figure 10) showing the IPC rate of the producer *without controlling*. Although the GP value of the producer amounts constantly 49 percent its IPC rate amounts at most 0.44. Besides the IPC rate falls down at regular intervals which can be explained by the empty loops which

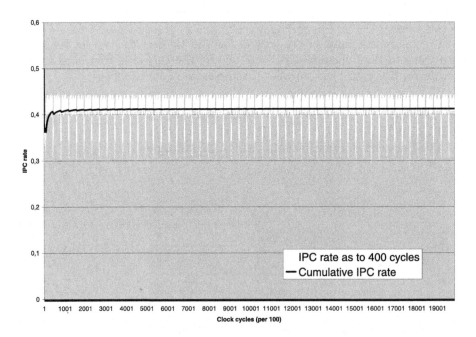

Fig. 10. Test without controlling.

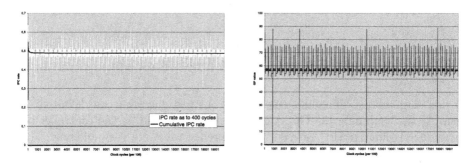

Fig. 11. Controlling as to a short time slice.

are executed by the producer when it waits for the consumer. That's why the cumulative IPC rate also amounts at most 0.41 from the beginning.

In the second test we controlled the producer by the IPC rate as to 400 cycles. The IPC rate reference value was set to 0.49 and the controller parameters were set as follows:

- $K_P = 60$
- $K_I = 30$
- $K_D = 0.01$
- The I element integrated about the last 50 history entries.
- $\Delta t = \frac{1}{400}$

Here the IPC rate swings around 0.49 with a variation of 0.03 and the down peaks are compensated by the controller by short and strong increases of the GP value (see Figure 11). Also in this case this uniform behaviour leads to a well achievement of 0.49 by the cumulative IPC rate.

At last we tested controlling of the producer thread by the cumulative IPC rate. The reference value was also set to 0.49. Here it was necessary to strongly adjust the controller parameters to get an agreeable control behaviour shown in Figure 12:

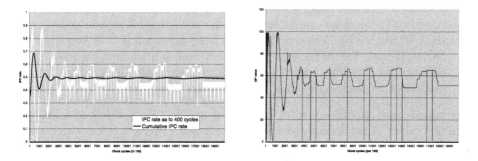

Fig. 12. Controlling as to the cumulative IPC rate.

- $K_P = 60$
- $K_I = 160$
- $K_D = 98$
- The I element integrated about the last 500 history entries.
- $\Delta t = \frac{1}{400}$

In this diagram the differences to the previous two diagrams can definitely be seen. At the beginning the GP values are strongly varied by the controller because the cumulative IPC rate and the reference value are very different. This leads to the effect that the IPC rate as to 400 clock cycles differs strongly from the reference value at the beginning. By-and-by the variations of the GP values are decreasing, reasoned by the stabilization of the cumulative IPC rate. Besides the time intervals, in which the controller varies the GP values, are increasing also because of stabilization of the cumulative IPC rate.

There were two further ideas which we wanted to test:

1. The computation effort of the controller is strong. Therefore it is possible that the controller is too slow to compute and update the new GP value within zero clock cycles. Therefore we decided to update the GP values of the threads with a delay of 100 clock cycles. This means that the GP values are computed by the actual values of the IPC rate of the controlled thread. Then they are saved and updated 100 clock cycles later which is a kind of pipelining implemented in the controller. In this way some problems occur e.g. it is possible that a thread is starting which had not existed 100 clock cycles before. This problem is solved by deactivating this thread as long as it is not incorporated in the computation.

2. Branch prediction is a technique used in modern superscalar microprocessor to ensure continuous instruction fetching. If a branch occurs the branch predictor is used to predict if the branch is taken or not and fetching is continued in this way. It is not supported by Komodo since a misprediction would cost several penalty clock cycles and could harm the real-time applications [2, 12]. Nevertheless we were interested if it would be possible to control a thread on a processor supporting branch prediction.

   The ID stage inserts three NOPs after a branch due to the pipeline structure of Komodo. So we modified the ID stage to accidentally insert further NOPs in order to simulate mispredictions. Precisely if a branch is recognized by ID stage in 90 percent we simulated a correct branch prediction by inserting only three NOPs, and in 10 percent we simulated misprediction by inserting 20 NOPs. We decided for 90 percent of correct branch prediction because of the high quality of today's branch predictors, and we decided for a misprediction penalty of 20 clock cycles in order to simulate a long pipeline.

We tested both modifications of the PID controller. Both delay of updating the GP values of the threads and simulating branch prediction succeeded with the two test programs. In fact tests with the combination of the modifications succeeded even by using the same controller parameter as in the tests without the modifications. Figure 13 and 14 show examples of controlling the producer

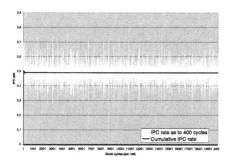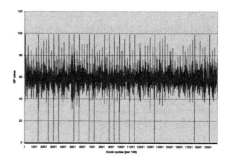

Fig. 13. Controlling by a short time interval with delay of 100 clock cycles and simulation of branch prediction.

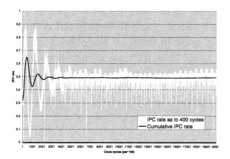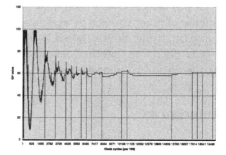

Fig. 14. Controlling as to the cumulative IPC rate with delay of 100 clock cycles and simulation of branch prediction.

consumer benchmark incorporating both modifications. The reference value is also 0.49 and the controller parameters are the same as in the tests without the modifications. Figure 13 shows controlling by the IPC rate as to 400 clock cycles and figure 14 shows controlling by the cumulative IPC rate. It can be seen that the delay of 100 clock cycles does not matter whereas simulation of branch prediction results in a greater variation of the IPC rate as to 400 clock cycles which has the reason in the great misprediction penalty of 20 clock cycles.

In this two examples the controller is also well able to achieve the desired reference value of 0.49

7   Conclusions

We presented an approach to control the IPC rate of a processor by a closed feedback loop. The multithreaded Komodo microcontroller served as our testbed. The evaluation showed that the controller is mostly well able to achieve the desired reference value even when we tested it with some extensions like a delayed update of GP values or simulating of branch prediction.

The goal of GP scheduling is to provide real-time abilities for the threads. In fact, these real-time abilities of a simple thread can by improved by the controller by balancing the oscillations of the IPC rate. This makes the execution time of a piece of code more predictable, it can be calculated based on the reference value for the IPC rate. A balanced IPC rate is especially very useful when data rates have to be guaranteed. The tests also showed the limits of controlling when the reference value gets above 0.7. Then the appearance of interleaves like latencies and locks is too strong to achieve the aimed reference value.

Until now we tested the techniques of controlling. But in fact it is very difficult to find controller parameters (K_P, K_I, K_D) by which the controlling process becomes stable. Therefore, our next step will be to find rules for the parameter choice with the end goal to give guaranteed upper and lower bounds for the IPC rate.

A problem is that we improve the real-time behaviour of one thread at the expense of other threads by assigning them less clock cycles if there is not enough computing time. So it is possible that the real-time abilities of the other threads is lost. Therefore, another next step is to control the IPC rate of all threads to guarantee and to improve the real-time abilities of all threads.

References

1. R. BAHAR, G. ALBERA AND S. MANNE, "Power and performance tradeoffs using various caching strategies", *Proceedings of the 1998 ISLPED*, ACM Press, 1998
2. UWE BRINKSCHULTE AND THEO UNGERER, "Mikrocontroller und Mikroprozessoren", *Springer-Verlag*, 2002
   http://ipr.ira.uka.de/perso/brinks/books/microcontroller/
3. RICHARD DORF AND ROBERT BISHOP, "Modern Control Systems", *Addison-Wesley*, 2000
4. JOCHEN KREUZINGER, "Echtzeitfähige Ereignisbehandlung mit Hilfe eines mehrfädigen Java-Mikrocontrollers", Dissertation, *Logos Verlag Berlin*, 2001
5. R. GONZALEZ AND M. HOROWITZ, "Energy dissipation in general purpose microprocessors", *IEEE Journal of Solid-State Circuits 31*, 1996
6. C. HUGHES, J. SRINIVASAN AND S. ADVE, "Saving energy with architectural and frequency adaptations for multimedia applications", *Proceedings of the 34th MICRO*, 2001
7. RON KALLA, BALARAM SINHAROY AND JOEL M. TENDLER, "IBM Power5 Chip: A Dual-Core Multithreaded Processor", *IEEE micro*, March/April 2004, pages 40-47
8. *Intel Corporation : Intel SpeedStep^{TM} Technology*, 2002
9. C. LU, J. A. STANKOVIC, G. TAO AND S. H. SON, "Design and Evaluation of a Feedback Control EDF Scheduling Algorithm", Real Time Systems Symposium (RTSS) 1999, Phoenix, USA
10. C. LU, J. A. STANKOVIC, T. F. ABDELZAHER, G. TAO, S. H. SON AND M. MARLEY, "Performance Specifications and Metrics for Adaptive Real-Time Systems", Real Time Systems Symposium (RTSS) 2000, Orlando, USA
11. HOLGER LUTZ AND WOLFGANG WENDT, "Taschenbuch der Regelungstechnik", *Verlag Harri Deutsch*, 2002

12. SCOTT MCFARLING "Combining Branch Predictors", *WRL Technical Note TN-36, Western Research Laboratory*, 1993
13. MATHIAS PACHER, "Einsatz von Regelalgorithmen in mehrfädigen Prozessoren", Studienarbeit, *University of Karlsruhe*, 2004
14. MATTHIAS PFEFFER, "Ein echtzeitfähiges Javasystem für einen mehrfädigen Java-Mikrocontroller", Dissertation, *Logos Verlag Berlin*, 2004
15. R. SASANKA, C.J. HUGHES AND S.V. ADVE, "Joint local and global hardware adapations for energy", *Proceedings of the ASPLOS-X*, ACM Press, 2002
16. M. PFEFFER, TH. UNGERER, S. UHRIG, U. BRINKSCHULTE, "Connecting peripherial interfaces to a multithreaded java microcontroller", In *Workshop on java in embedded systems, ARCS 2002, Karlsruhe*, April 2002
17. S. UHRIG, C. LIEMKE, M. PFEFFER, J. BECKER, U. BRINKSCHULTE, TH. UNGERER, "Implementing Real-time Scheduling Within a Multithreaded Java Microcontroller", 6th Workshop on Multithreaded Execution, Architecture, and Compilation MTEAC-6, Istanbul, Nov. 2002, in conjunction with 35th International Symposium on Microarchitecture MICRO-35, Workshop proceedings

Adaptivity for Quality
and Timeliness Flexible Real-Time Systems

Thomas Schwarzfischer

Institute of Computer Architecture (Prof. Dr.-Ing. W. Grass),
Faculty of Mathematics and Informatics, University of Passau
Innstr. 33, 94032 Passau, Germany
schwarzf@fmi.uni-passau.de

Abstract. The basis for this work is a model for fine-granular flexibility of applications in two directions. These are the quality of computations on the one hand and their timeliness on the other hand. Dynamic scheduling of quality- and timeliness-flexible tasks on the same hardware platform as the application itself exhibits two obvious sources of trade-offs. The first one exists between the desired quality levels for individual tasks (depending on the processing time awarded to them) and the ability of these tasks to meet timing constraints. The second one can be found between the overall distribution of processing time between the application tasks and the scheduling algorithm. A high processing time allowance granted to the scheduler may leave too little resources for the actual application; however, a small scheduling allowance might prevent finding good schedules according to the given objective function. We use a control-theoretic approach to allow the scheduler to adapt to the current characteristics of the application in terms of workload and frequency and regularity of task releases automatically at run-time.

1 Introduction

Whereas traditional real-time scheduling schemes emphasize on meeting timing constraints for a set of tasks, flexible computation models generalize this simple objective by trading off the compliance of an application with temporal constraints for the quality of the computations. In many cases, the semantics of a problem allow a scheduler to degrade the accuracy, granularity or likelihood of correctness of tasks; this property is called *quality-flexibility*. Other (soft real-time) applications can tolerate late completion of component tasks to a certain extent; these problems are *timeliness-* or *utility-flexible*. Models for both of these directions of flexibility have been investigated. In our work we deal with sets of tasks which are both quality- and utility-flexible and call the problem class quality/utility scheduling. Dynamic quality/utility scheduling is especially interesting, because we do not need complete knowledge of an application before run-time. The meta scheduling problem of finding an optimal allocation of the available processing time for the scheduling algorithm itself is typical for

M. Beigl and P. Lukowicz (Eds.): ARCS 2005, LNCS 3432, pp. 50–64, 2005.

dynamic scheduling. The behaviour of the application and environmental parameters may change and make adaption of the scheduling allowance and other scheduler parameters necessary.

In the beginning we will present the formulation of the quality/utility scheduling problem and the basic ideas for schedulers working on this problem class. Meta scheduling, the simulation environment and some experimental results are the topics of the following sections.

2   Basic Quality / Utility Scheduling Problem

In this section we will describe the basic problem of trading off the quality of computations for their timeliness. For the time being, an application consists of a set of independent tasks to be executed on a single processor.

Consider a set of tasks $\mathbb{T} = \{T_1, T_2, \dots\}$ with

- release times

$$r_{T_1}, r_{T_2}, \dots$$

- monotonically increasing quality functions

$$q_{T_1}, q_{T_2}, \dots : \mathbb{N}_0 \to \mathbb{R}_0^+$$

- monotonically decreasing utility functions

$$u_{T_1}, q_{T_2}, \dots : \mathbb{N}_0 \to \mathbb{R}_0^+$$

Quality functions express the progress of tasks depending on their processing time, utility functions rate the timeliness of the computations. Figure 1 shows example quality and utility functions. The two kinds of functions are defined on different time domains: utility functions are based on a global time common to all tasks. Quality functions are defined on the local time of tasks, i.e., the amount of processing time allocated to the task.

Schedules for a set of tasks can be written as a collection of local time functions $\tau_{T_1}, \tau_{T_2}, \dots$ mapping global time to local time for each task, as demonstrated for a set of three tasks in figure 2. For the remainder of this work, $\vec{\tau}$ denotes the vector of all local time functions and hence represents a schedule for the task set. Likewise, $\vec{q}$ and $\vec{u}$ are the vectors of the quality and utility functions for the current task set, respectively.

Objective functions

$$v_{\vec{q}, \vec{u}}(\vec{\tau}, t)$$

for the scheduling algorithm are defined on the vectors of quality and utility functions, the vector of local time functions and the global time and yield real values.

Schedulers try to approximate the optimal schedule

$$\max_{\vec{\tau}} \arg \lim_{t \to \infty} v_{\vec{q}, \vec{u}}(\vec{\tau}, t).$$

We propose a set of properties we assume all prospective objective functions to hold. These are

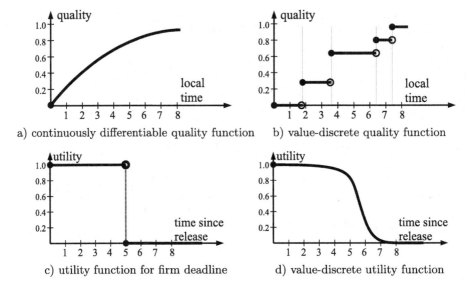

a) continuously differentiable quality function   b) value-discrete quality function

c) utility function for firm deadline   d) value-discrete utility function

Fig. 1. Example quality and utility functions

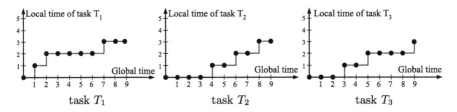

Fig. 2. Functions mapping global time to local times of tasks

Global time monotony: The objective function must be monotonically increasing in the global time.

Allocation history monotony: The objective function must be prefix monotonic in the vector of local time functions.

Allocation amount monotony: The objective function must be monotonically increasing in every local time function.

Allocation time monotony: The objective function must be monotonically decreasing in the inverse of each local time function.

Utility monotony: The objective function must be monotonically increasing with any utility function of tasks.

Quality monotony: The objective function must be monotonically increasing with any quality function of tasks.

One possible objective function obeying above conditions is the following:

$$v_{\vec{q},\vec{u}}(\vec{\tau},t) := \sum_{T\in\mathbb{T}} \max_{t'\leq t} u_T(t') \cdot q_T(\tau_T(t'))$$

3 Scheduling Algorithms

As mentioned above, we primarily developed dynamic scheduling algorithms for the presented problem class, because we want to be able to apply the methods to time-variable task sets with possibly no or incomplete knowledge of the release times. The dynamic scheduler is invoked repeatedly; these invocations are called scheduling phases and compute partial schedules for a limited window of time into the future, starting from current time. The scheduler works on a set of tasks either released before the beginning of the phase or likely to be released in the near future (i.e., within the scheduling window). Figure 3 shows that consecutive windows may (and in fact usually do) overlap, because imprecise estimates of the release times of tasks may make it necessary to adapt partial schedules before the end of the window.

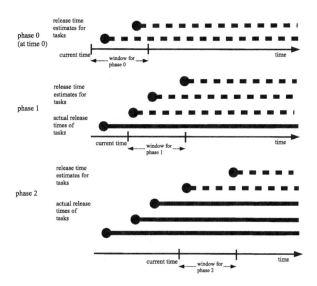

Fig. 3. Scheduling phases

As an example application, consider a set of three tasks with the following release times and quality and utility functions:

$$r_{T_1} = 0 \quad u_{T_1}(t) = \begin{cases} 0 & \text{if } t - r_{T_1} < 0 \\ 1 & \text{if } 0 \le t - r_{T_1} < 6 \\ 0.6 & \text{if } 6 \le t - r_{T_1} < 13 \\ 0.1 & \text{if } t - r_{T_1} \ge 13 \end{cases} \quad q_{T_1}(n_1) = \begin{cases} 0 & \text{if } 0 \le n_1 < 4 \\ 0.3 & \text{if } 4 \le n_1 < 8 \\ 0.4 & \text{if } 8 \le n_1 < 12 \\ 0.8 & \text{if } n_1 \ge 12 \end{cases}$$

$$r_{T_2} = 2 \quad u_{T_2}(t) = \begin{cases} 0 & \text{if } t - r_{T_2} < 0 \\ 1 & \text{if } 0 \le t - r_{T_2} < 8 \\ 0.2 & \text{if } 8 \le t - r_{T_2} < 12 \\ 0 & \text{if } t - r_{T_2} \ge 12 \end{cases} \quad q_{T_2}(n_2) = \begin{cases} 0 & \text{if } 0 \le n_2 < 2 \\ 0.1 & \text{if } 2 \le n_2 < 4 \\ 0.2 & \text{if } 4 \le n_2 < 6 \\ 0.3 & \text{if } n_2 \ge 6 \end{cases}$$

$$r_{T_3} = 5 \quad u_{T_3}(t) = \begin{cases} 0 & \text{if } t - r_{T_3} < 0 \\ 1 & \text{if } 0 \le t - r_{T_3} < 8 \\ 0.7 & \text{if } 8 \le t - r_{T_3} < 10 \\ 0.1 & \text{if } t - r_{T_3} \ge 10 \end{cases} \quad q_{T_3}(n_3) = \begin{cases} 0 & \text{if } 0 \le n_3 < 2 \\ 0.4 & \text{if } 2 \le n_3 < 8 \\ 1.0 & \text{if } n_3 \ge 8 \end{cases}$$

t is the global time, $n_1, n_2, n_3 \in \mathbb{N}_0$ the local times for T_1, T_2 and T_3.

A first set of schedulers divides the scheduling window into elementary intervals, during which no task changes its utility. For the example task set and a window size of 16, we receive elementary intervals as in figure 4.

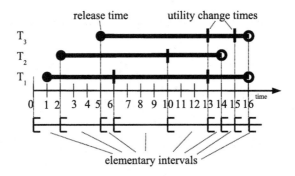

Fig. 4. Calculation of elementary intervals within interval $[t_0; t_0 + ws[= [1; 16[$

For the (non-optimal) distribution of units of processing time among the tasks in the elementary intervals of table 1, we receive the objective function values of table 2.

We implemented scheduling algorithms based on both simulated annealing and tabu search working on the search space formed by elementary intervals as described above. An approach using Lagrangian optimization is applicable to a slightly modified formulation of the problem. Furthermore, we investigated a

Table 1. Non-optimal distribution of processing time for example

	$[1;2[$	$[2;5[$	$[5;6[$	$[6;10[$	$[10;13[$	$[13;15[$
T_1	1	1	0	1	2	0
T_2	0	2	0	1	0	0
T_3	0	0	1	2	1	2
sum	1	3	1	4	3	2

Table 2. Objective function value for example distribution

	$[1;2[$	$[2;5[$	$[5;6[$	$[6;10[$	$[10;13[$	$[13;15[$
$\max\limits_{J'\leq J} u_{T_1}(J')\cdot q_{T_1}(\tau_{T_1}(J'))$	0	0	0	0	0.18	0.18
$\max\limits_{J'\leq J} u_{T_2}(J')\cdot q_{T_2}(\tau_{T_2}(J'))$	0	0.1	0.1	0.1	0.1	0.1
$\max\limits_{J'\leq J} u_{T_3}(J')\cdot q_{T_3}(\tau_{T_3}(J'))$	0	0	0	0.4	0.4	0.4 0.68
$\sum\limits_{T\in\{T_1,T_2,T_3\}}\max\limits_{J'\leq J} u_T(J')\cdot q_T(\tau_T(J'))$	0	0.1	0.1	0.5	0.68	

scheduler considering possible sets of ready tasks in the near future and computing strategies for a Markov decision process to act on the various situations that can be encountered; this method is a reasonable alternative to computing partial schedules if the release times of tasks cannot be predicted with high accuracy.

4   Generalization of Model

Instead of executing a set of independent tasks on a single processor, we now introduce a series of modifications to our original model. The first one is the target architecture now being a heterogeneous multiprocessor system.

The task set is structured in a hierarchy of tasks and subtasks, as shown in the upper part of figure 5b). This has the advantage of a more natural modelling of many applications in an increasingly more detailed level. Furthermore, we can build the application on top of a library of reusable basic algorithms called methods. Depending on the type of scheduling algorithm, rescheduling may take place on subgraphs of the entire application graph, and partial solutions to prior problems can be reused at a later time. Caching mechanisms were introduced for this purpose, increasing the efficiency of scheduling algorithms significantly. Finally, different semantics of the nodes of the hierarchy graph can be expressed by assigning different local objective functions to them; the overall value is passed on from the leaf nodes to the root in bottom-up manner. For example, in an and/or graph, child nodes can be interpreted as components or alternatives of

the parent node and (depending on the logical type of the parent) translated
into different local objective functions.

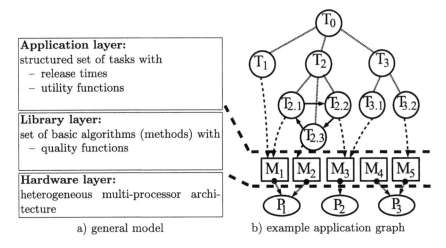

Application layer:
structured set of tasks with
  – release times
  – utility functions

Library layer: set of basic algorithms (methods) with   – quality functions
Hardware layer: heterogeneous multi-processor archi- tecture

a) general model   b) example application graph

Fig. 5. General model for the quality / utility scheduling problem

In addition to the hierarchy graph, a second graph structure is introduced
between tasks (for example, the subtasks of task T_2 in figure 5b)). This graph
can be seen as a value-based equivalent to precedence constraints. The execution
order of tasks influences the objective function. However, execution of tasks in
the wrong order is not prohibited, but only penalized.

5 Scheduling / Execution Tradeoff

As mentioned before, our dynamic schedulers encounter a tradeoff between the
amount of processing time allowed for the scheduler and the one remaining for
the actual application.

Consider a set of three tasks T_A, T_B, T_C with release times $r_{T_A} = r_{T_B} = r_{T_C} = 0$ and quality and utility functions

$$q_{T_A}(n) = \begin{cases} 0 \text{ if } n < 4 \\ 1 \text{ if } n \geq 4 \end{cases} \quad q_{T_B}(n) = \begin{cases} 0 \text{ if } n < 5 \\ 2 \text{ if } n \geq 5 \end{cases} \quad q_{T_C}(n) = \begin{cases} 0 \quad \text{ if } n < 2 \\ 0.5 \text{ if } n \geq 2 \end{cases}$$

$$u_{T_A}(t) = \begin{cases} 1 \text{ if } t < 11 \\ 0 \text{ if } t \geq 11 \end{cases} \quad u_{T_B}(t) = \begin{cases} 1 \text{ if } t < 9 \\ 0 \text{ if } t \geq 9 \end{cases} \quad u_{T_C}(t) = \begin{cases} 1 \text{ if } t < 11 \\ 0 \text{ if } t \geq 11 \end{cases}$$

For scheduling allowances of 0, 0.3, 0.5, 0.8, and 1, optimal schedules (with a
prefix in each row reserved for the scheduler) are as in the table below. The size
of the search space (ss) is calculated with the simple rule that allocating cpu
time units to tasks with zero utility should be avoided. If the search algorithm

can make 10 steps in unit time (sut), we receive the percentage of the search space which can be visited by the scheduling algorithm in the final row.

sa	optimal schedule									value of optimal schedule	search space size (ss)	$\frac{sa \cdot ws \cdot sut}{ss}$
0	B	B	B	B	B	A	A	A	A	3	$3^8 \cdot 2^2 = 26244$	0
0.3	–	–	–	B	B	B	B	B	C	C	2.5	$3^5 \cdot 2^2 = 972$	0.03
0.5	–	–	–	–	–	A	A	A	A	–	1	$3^3 \cdot 2^2 = 108$	0.46
0.8	–	–	–	–	–	–	–	–	C	C	0.5	$3^0 \cdot 2^2 = 4$	20
1	–	–	–	–	–	–	–	–	–	–	0	$3^0 \cdot 2^0 = 1$	100

The scheduler can cover the entire search space in the last two cases. We can assume that an optimal schedule will be calculated for a scheduling allowance of 0.8 or 1 and with a reasonably high probability can be found for a scheduling allowance of 0.5, but with a considerably smaller probability for a scheduling allowance of 0.3. This is expressed by the suboptimal schedule in row 2 of the following table. Finally, it is extremely unlikely that the (presumably arbitrary) solution found for a scheduling allowance of 0 is anywhere close to optimal.

sa	schedule										value of found schedule	relative value
0	A	B	C	A	B	C	A	B	C	B	0	0
0.3	–	–	–	A	B	A	A	A	C	C	1.5	0.6
0.5	–	–	–	–	–	A	A	A	A	–	1	1
0.8	–	–	–	–	–	–	–	–	C	C	0.5	1
1	–	–	–	–	–	–	–	–	–	–	0	–

The relative value is highest for partial allocation of the processor time to the scheduler.

We use a PID controller to decide on appropriate settings for the scheduling allowance at run-time. Let $sa_i \in [0; 1]$ denote the scheduling allowance for the i-th scheduling phase. The scheduling allowance is the manipulated variable of the PID controller. Further, let $\Delta_i \in \mathbb{N}$ denote the length of the i-th phase (scheduler phase and partial schedule).

We define the start times of the i-th phase as follows:

$$t_1 = 0 \qquad\qquad t_{i+1} = t_i + \Delta_i$$

In the i-th scheduling window, the scheduler is awarded a computation time of $sa_i \cdot \Delta_i$, the application tasks receive an allocation of $(1 - sa_i) \cdot \Delta_i$ time units.

As the controlled variable of the controller, we use the change in value density (the slope of the respective value functions) between two consecutive phases, expressed by

$$slope_i := \frac{v_{\vec{q},\vec{u}}(\vec{\tau}, t_{i+1}) - v_{\vec{q},\vec{u}}(\vec{\tau}, t_i)}{\Delta_i}$$

$$\Delta slope_i := slope_i - slope_{i-1}$$

where t_i is the start time of a new scheduling phase (figure 6b)).

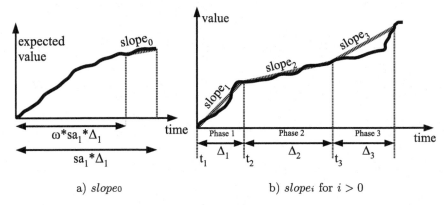

a) $slope_0$ b) $slope_i$ for $i > 0$

Fig. 6. Change in value density

Obviously, above definition for $\Delta slope_i$ is valid only for $i > 1$. Therefore, as a starting point, we use a different definition for $slope_0$ based on the development of value during the first scheduling phase. For this purpose, we need a parameter $\omega \in]0; 1[$ to mark one certain point of the scheduling phase during its lifetime, namely after reaching a certain percentage of its allowance.

We then define $slope_0$ as the terminal gain between the values after $\omega \cdot \Delta_i$ time units of scheduling and the final value of the schedule for the first phase:

$$slope_0 := \frac{v_{\vec{q},\vec{u}}(\vec{\tau}, sa_1 \cdot \Delta_1) - v_{\vec{q},\vec{u}}(\vec{\tau}, \omega \cdot sa_1 \cdot \Delta_1)}{(1-\omega)\Delta_1}$$

The definition for the special case of the first scheduler phase is shown in figure 6a).

As the set point, we choose a slope of 0, such that the error function for scheduling phase i is

$$err_i := \Delta slope_i.$$

The set point of 0 is chosen due to the following motivation:

- If the slope is negative, too much effort has been spent on scheduling in the preceding phase, taking too much of the computation time from the application tasks; the scheduling allowance should be decreased.
- If the slope is positive, it is likely that an even higher allocation of computational resources could result in even better schedules. To exploit this potential, the scheduling allowance should be increased.

The integral and derivative parts of the controller measure over a distance of $spi, spd \in \mathbb{N}_0$ phase numbers; $C_d, C_p, C_i \in \mathbb{R}_0^+$ are user-defined constants. Error terms err_i are defined to be 0 for negative i.

Finally, we can define the control function as follows:

$$sa_{i+1} = sa_i - C_d \cdot \frac{err_i - err_{i-spd}}{spd} - C_p \cdot err_i - C_i \cdot \sum_{j=0}^{spi} err_{i-j}$$

The initial scheduling allowance, sa_1, must be provided by the user.

6 Simulation Environment

An integrated specification and simulation environment called PaSchA (Passau Scheduling Analysis) for scheduling problems was implemented for the purpose of modelling real-time applications and testing the scheduling algorithms for such example applications as well as for generic loads. PaSchA was designed as a set of tools communicating via message-passing mechanisms and shared files.

6.1 Application Model

A PaSchA application model contains specifications of both a software application and the target hardware architecture on which to execute it. Both of these components are stored within an application graph.

PaSchA allows applications to target heterogeneous multiprocessor architectures as their execution platform. Further attributes of processors are their speed modes and their power consumption. Non-processor resources contain information on how many units of the resource are available and whether units can be returned to the pool of resources after use or they are consumed and never become available again.

The software model comprises two kinds of nodes, namely methods and tasks. Methods can be thought of as basic algorithms available to the application designer as an algorithm library. Both the run-to-completion assumption and the anytime execution paradigm have been implemented in PaSchA. Based upon the library of methods, applications are defined by the application developer as a hierarchical task network consisting of a set of task nodes and two distinct graph structures on them, namely a task hierarchy and a dependency graph. Both precedence constraints and quality dependencies exist in the PaSchA model. Of the many possibilities to specify stochastic distributions for release times, geometric and uniform distributions were implemented in PaSchA, as they appeared to be sufficient for many scheduling problems.

There are two possibilities for timing constraints in PaSchA. The first one is by traditional *deadlines* posed on the tasks, i.e., by specifying either in absolute time or relative to the release time of a task the latest time when it must finish. The second one is the more fine granular specification of *utility* by means of pointwise constant functions of the time passed since the release of a task.

The two ways to create application graphs for PaSchA are the graphical editor and specialized graph generators. Figure 7 shows the main window of the graphical editor with a complete application graph.

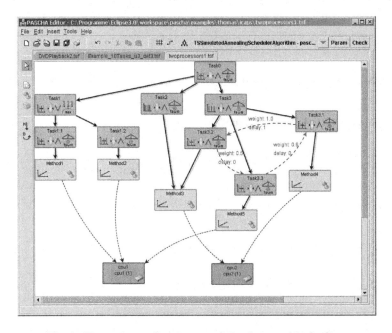

Fig. 7. Example application graph in the graphical editor

The simulator component itself can be accessed via a graphical user interface and an application programming interface.

The visualization components receive their input from the simulator or log player and display relevant data from the event streams resulting from the (live or recorded) interaction between the simulation of the behaviour of an application and the decisions made by the scheduler. As examples, we show two of the view modes in the following: The time view mode (figure 8) is an extended form of Gantt charts, displaying the state of the task set on a common time line. Information like the release and termination of tasks, their activation and usage of resources and processors as well as the quality values achieved by individual nodes can be shown over a rather wide time range. The statistics view mode (figure 9) gives the user the opportunity to derive secondary data on the application and the schedule. Among the quantities that can be included here are processor utilization, residence time or waiting time of tasks, or the number of ready or working tasks at any time. From any individual quantity, several additional pieces of information can be recorded, e.g., arithmetic and geometric mean, standard deviation, etc.

Scheduling algorithms for the PaSchA system must be implemented in Java and extend the scheduler base class provided by the system. As a minimum requirement, a scheduler class must implement three methods:

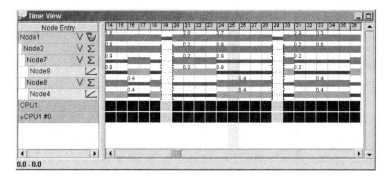

Fig. 8. Time view mode

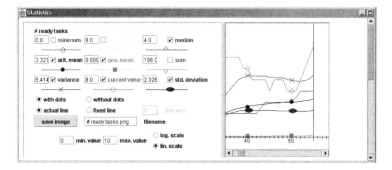

Fig. 9. Statistics view mode

- a compatibility test for application graphs
- an initializing method for the scheduler
- a method for execution at each point in simulator discrete time

Among the optional components of a scheduler class is a scheduler-specific graphical user interface to edit the parameters. Numerous dynamic and static scheduling algorithms have successfully been implemented in PaSchA.

In order to perform automatic benchmark tests for scheduling algorithms, the appropriate application graph or generator configuration along with the necessary parameter sets are defined within Java test cases. The input data as well as the results produced by scheduler and its interaction with the simulator are stored in a database for later evaluation.

7   Results

Our experimental work included a test series with a family of graphs with 10 tasks [1] with a processor utilization between 1.3 and 7.6 (the algorithms are primarily intended to work in overload situations), and quality and utility functions

---

[1] the term *family* referring to the fact that the graphs have the same topology, i.e., hierarchy graph, dependency graph, and processor specification

in the tests were piecewise constant with $q_T(n) = 0$ for $n < n_{q,1}$, $q_T(n) = c \in \mathbb{R}_0^+$ for $n \geq n_{q,2}$, $u_T(n) = 1$ for $n < n_{u,1}$ and $u_T(n) = 0$ for $n \geq n_{u,2}$ and a finite number (with given maximum) of constant sections in between.

The settings for the controller parameters were as follows:

C_p	C_i	C_d	spi	spd
0.3	0.6	0.1	5	5

Tests showed that the controller was able to stabilize after a small number of scheduling phases (figure 10a)) and that the flexible setting of the scheduling allowance outperforms most runs with fixed values for the scheduling allowance (figure 10b)). Although there are clearly cases where this is not true, remember it is virtually impossible to find the optimal scheduling allowance by offline analysis. Furthermore, obviously no fixed setting of the scheduling allowance can be appropriate for applications with task release frequency changing dramatically with time (e.g., intervals with few long-running tasks taking turns with larger numbers of short tasks).

Simulation results also showed [1] that in non-overloaded situations traditional dynamic scheduling mechanisms outperform the techniques described in this work, primarily due to a smaller computational overhead at runtime. In non-overloaded settings, the control mechanism could be used for adapting the parameters of the scheduling algorithm rather than the scheduling allowance; however, this remains work still to be done.

Finally, the decision for one of several available alternative scheduling algorithms may also be made online. [1] demonstrates the sensitivity of the scheduling results to the chosen algorithm at verying side conditions, especially with load and the predictability of release times.

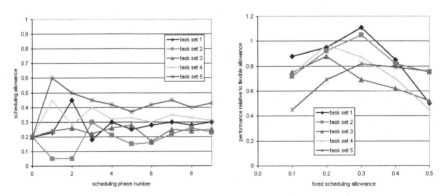

a) stabilization of PID controller   b) fixed vs flexible scheduling allowance

Fig. 10. Tests for meta scheduler

8   Related Work

Probably the first work on timeliness-flexible scheduling was by Locke and Jensen [2, 3], who developed a repair-based method and called it best-effort scheduling. It estimates the probability of a future overload situation and uses heuristics to reduce the load. Heuristics for this purpose were also suggested by Aldarmi and Burns [4], by Mossé et al. [5] and by Morton and Pentico [6]. Tokuda, Wendorf et al. [7] investigated the problem of run-time costs for deliberation in the best-effort scheme. Chen and Muhlethaler [8] took a constructive approach to timeliness-flexible scheduling. Unlike the best-effort model, their ideas assume tasks to be non-preemptive.

Among the best-known quality-flexible models are anytime tasks described by Dean and Boddy [9] and further investigated by Zilberstein [10]. A very similar idea is that of flexible computations by Horvitz [11]. Imprecise computations (Burns, Bernat et al. [12]) take the two-stage approach of guaranteeing a basic service level offline and optimizing an objective function for optional components at run-time. IRIS tasks (Dey, Kurose et al. [13]) are similar to anytime tasks, but do not necessarily have an upper bound on their result quality.

The control-theoretic feedback mechanism was adopted from the work of Lu, Stankovic et al. [14] on feedback-controlled EDF (FC-EDF); however, the system model and the objectives in their work are different from the ones described in this article. Whereas FD-EDF assumes fixed execution times for tasks and emphasizes on admission or rejection of new tasks by means of a PID controller, in our context the controller operates on the processing allowance for the scheduling algorithm.

The basic model of quality/utility scheduling was presented in [15]. Experimental results and extensions to the basic model can be found in more detail in [16] and [17].

9   Conclusion

In this work we were able to demonstrate the feasibility of scheduling algorithms for task sets exhibiting both the properties of quality and timeliness flexibility. We were also able to describe the much more general simulation environment with which all our experimental results were gained. The tradeoff between the effort of scheduling and execution of the resulting schedules could be shown. We suggested a control-theoretic mechanism to find appropriate levels of the scheduling allowance at run-time and found that the controller was able to stabilize after a small number of scheduling phases. The scheduling techniques presented are suitable for flexible firm and soft real-time applications, but do not easily extend to hard real-time systems, as guarantees on timing or precedence constraints cannot generally be given for individual tasks.

References

1. Schwarzfischer, T.: Quality and Utility - On the Use of Time-Value Functions to Integrate Quality and Timeliness Flexible Aspects in a Dynamic Real-Time Scheduling Environment. PhD thesis, Fakultät für Mathematik und Informatik, Universität Passau (2005)
2. Locke, C.: Best-Effort Decision Making for Real-Time Scheduling. PhD thesis, Carnegie-Mellon University (1986)
3. Jensen, E., Locke, C., Tokuda, H.: A time-driven scheduling model for real-time operating systems. In: Proceedings of the IEEE Real-Time Systems Symposium. (1985)
4. Aldarmi, S., Burns, A.: Dynamic value-density for scheduling real-time systems. In: Proceedings of the 11th Euromicro Conference on Real-Time Systems. (1999)
5. Mossé, D., Pollack, M., Ronén, Y.: Value-density algorithms to handle transient overloads in scheduling. In: Proceedings of the 11th Euromicro Conference on Real-Time Systems. (1999)
6. Morton, T., Pentico, D.: Heuristic Scheduling Systems. John Wiley (1993)
7. Tokuda, H., Wendorf, J., Wang, H.: Implementation of a time-driven scheduler for real-time operating systems. In: Proceedings of the IEEE Real-Time Systems Symposium. (1987) 271–280
8. Chen, K., Muhlethaler, P.: A scheduling algorithm for tasks described by time value functions. Real-Time Systems **10** (1996) 293–312
9. Dean, T., Boddy, M.: An analysis of time-dependent planning. In: Proceedings of the Seventh National Conference on Artificial Intelligence. (1988) 49–54
10. Zilberstein, S.: Operational Rationality through Compilation of Anytime Algorithms. PhD thesis, University of California at Berkeley (1993)
11. Horvitz, E.: Reasoning about beliefs and actions under computational resource constraints. In: Proceedings of the Third Workshop on Uncertainty in Artificial Intelligence. (1987)
12. Bernat, G., Burns, A.: Three obstacles to flexible scheduling. In: Proceedings of the 13th Euromicro Conference on Real-Time Systems. (2001)
13. Dey, J., Kurose, J., Towsley, D., Krishna, C., Girkar, M.: Efficient on-line processor scheduling for a class of IRIS (inreasing reward with increasing service) real-time tasks. In: Proceedings of 1993 ACM SIGMETRICS Conference on Measurement and Modeling of Computer Systems. (1993) 217–228
14. Lu, C., Stankovic, J., Tao, G., Son, S.: Design and evaluation of a feedback control EDF scheduling algorithm. In: Proceedings of the IEEE Real-Time Systems Symposium. (1999)
15. Schwarzfischer, T.: Quality and utility - towards a generalization of deadline and anytime scheduling. In: Proceedings of the 13th International Conference on Automated Planning and Scheduling. (2003)
16. Schwarzfischer, T.: Using value dependencies to schedule complex soft-real-time applications with precedence constraints. In: Proceedings of the 1st Multidisciplinary International Conference on Scheduling: Theory and Applications (MISTA). (2003)
17. Schwarzfischer, T.: Application of simulated annealing to anytime scheduling problems with additional timing constraints. In: Proceedings of the 5th Metaheuristics International Conference (MIC2003). (2003)

Apricot Agent Platform
for User-Friendly Mobile Service Development

Petteri Alahuhta[1], Henri Löthman[1], Heli Helaakoski[1],
Arto Koskela[2], and Juha Röning[2]

[1] VTT Electronics, Kaitoväylä 1, 90571 Oulu, Finland
{Petteri.Alahuhta,Henri.Lothman,Heli.Helaakoski}@vtt.fi
[2] University of Oulu, Linnanmaa, PL 4500, 90014 Oulun yliopisto, Finland
{Arto.Koskela,Juha.Roning}@ee.oulu.fi

Abstract. The trend of increasing mobile services has set a new challenge for service providers: how to develop more advanced and user friendly, context-aware and personalized mobile services for the users. Apricot Agent Platform is an agent-based software platform designed for developing context-aware and personalized mobile services. Apricot Agent Platform supports the development of user-friendly mobile services by providing tools for combining various mobile and Internet-based services. Apricot agent architecture consists of an agent platform, agents and agent containers. For the developers of mobile services, it provides built-in functionality and communication mechanism. Furthermore, this paper describes four demonstrators that are built up on the Apricot Agent Platform to evaluate the usability and efficiency of the platform in processes of building mobile services. The results of the evaluation indicate relatively promising results and the further target for development is revealed.

1 Introduction

Mobile applications and services have been considered an important era of the information and communications technology [1]. The development of mobile network technologies as well as mobile terminals has offered users, developers and businesses new opportunities to access information, communicate or be entertained. Person-to-person communication has been the main service for the end users of mobile terminals. In addition to traditional voice communication and voice mail, the Short Message Service (SMS) has been dominating the mobile service area, at least in Finland [2].

Manufacturers of mobile devices as well as network operators have been promoting mobile data services such as Multimedia Messaging, Mobile Browsing and Mobile Email. However, the growth in mobile data services hasn't been as fast as operators in the market expected. Since the technology is mature enough to produce mobile services, there must be other reasons that prevent large-scale use of the services. From the regular user's viewpoint, three factors can be identified that make the use of mobile services complicated:

- Mobile data services are hard to find
- Mobile data services are not easy to use
- Mobile data services do not provide added value [3].

M. Beigl and P. Lukowicz (Eds.): ARCS 2005, LNCS 3432, pp. 65–78, 2005.

Users know how to use PC and network-based services for viewing, searching, extracting and maintaining information, they are able to store and process digital content and share it with other people and communities. In the mobile context the situation is quite the contrary. An average user of mobile phones has just learned how to benefit from mobile phone calls and short messages. Neither the technology nor the culture for using mobile data services have developed enough that mobile applications and services could be considered a real choice for using digital information services.

In current SMS-based mobile service markets, the customer first needs to know about the existence of the service; and secondly he needs to remember the phone number of the service and a defined format of SMS message for achieving a certain service. For example, in order to acquire a weather forecast, you type the SMS message "WEATHER OULU" and send it to the number 12345, and you get weather information as a return message. In order to be beneficial to the user, the user should be able to get more advanced and versatile mobile services in a simpler way. We believe that this can be realized by integrating several mobile or internet services to create one combined service that meets the needs of users better than many simple services alone. The mobile service would be even more prospective and user-friendly if it would automatically deliver the integrated, personified services. However, if the idea is to support the users in their tasks when on the move, easier ways to find services should be available. Possible solutions might be the use of context information or personal preferences to automate the use of search engines [4].

Several researchers have proposed the use of intelligent agents for developing software applications [5, 6]. Agent systems are also considered suitable for systems that integrate existing software systems and therefore assist the users of those systems [7, 8]. The first version of Apricot Agent Platform [9] focused mainly on the agent-based component of the intelligent environment, which manages services on behalf of the user. Since the use of mobile devices has increased, the demand on agents accompanying users in such devices is inevitable. Mobility has set new requirements for agent systems, either the agents or agent platforms must run on small devices like mobile phones and PDAs. Or the mobile terminal must be devised with an application that provides a user interface to the personal agent running on the server side. One of the first lightweight agent platforms is JADE-LEAP [10], a FIPA-compliant agent platform that runs on small devices. The CRUMPET [11]-project has made an extension to the FIPA-OS agent platform called MicroFIPA-OS [12]. MicroFIPA-OS has been proposed as a framework for nomadic agent-based applications [13].

The Apricot research rises to the challenge set by the availability and usability of mobile services for the user. Since there is an obvious need to assist users of mobile services, the service developers must be able to easily produce user-friendly mobile services. Apricot research approaches the development of user-friendly services step by step. As a first step, we have developed an Apricot Agent Platform for mobile service developers, through which the mobile services can be produced to provide added value for regular users of mobile handsets. The second step will be integrating several existing services in a way that is most convenient for the user.

The aim of Apricot research can be summarized as follows:

1) Support for developing mobile services in order to help users.
2) Integration support to combine mobile and web-based services to respond to the user preferences in the most convenient way.

In our approach to research, we have made several iteration rounds of developing, starting from the basic features of the agent platform, such as functionality of the agents and mobility.

This paper introduces the basic architecture of the Apricot platform and gives a short description of the implemented demonstrators that has been used for evaluating the usability and efficiency of the Apricot Agent Platform for service development.

The rest of the paper is organized as follows. The next section defines the mobile environment and mobile services discussed in this paper. The Apricot platform is presented in the next section. The following section describes the implemented demonstrators. Discussion about the findings of this research will be given after the description of demonstrators and the paper will conclude with a glance at the future work.

2   Mobile Environment and Services

The main advantage in mobile services compared to stationary information processing is the mobility itself. Mobile technology enables people to access digital information located in the Internet or be entertained outside the reach of stationary Internet access. The mainstream focus of mobile service researchers is called the anytime-anywhere principle: requests for services by mobile users should be always satisfied in an unchanged and transparent way, regardless of the time at which the service is requested and the place from which it is requested [14].

In this paper *mobile service* refers to the use of a mobile terminal, such as mobile phones or personal digital assistants (PDA), and mobile telecommunication network for delivering an electronic service for the customer. The service can be a delivery of information (such as news, timetables, tickets, etc,) or entertainment content (like video clips, ring-tones, images). The service can also be an operation of an actuator controlled using a mobile terminal (remote control, activating lighting, controlling heating, etc). The mobile service is typically part of a larger system. In addition to the mobile end of the service, there are other components in the service as well. Server implementations, networking and databases are typically needed in order to produce a feasible mobile service. The mobile service is often a complementary service to other electronic services. For example, there may be a downscaled mobile version of an Internet site.

Mobile application refers to program code executed in a mobile terminal. A mobile application may use networking capabilities which makes it a part of the mobile service. It may also be a stand-alone application. For example, a data collection application may in many cases be a stand-alone application. Single-player games, calculators and alarm clocks in mobile terminals can also be considered mobile applications.

In addition to the benefits of mobile technology, there are also great challenges in mobile communication and computing. The environment of a person on the move is highly dynamic. Restricted computing power and bandwidth, limited memory as well as constricted input/output capabilities in the mobile devices make it challenging for the mobile service providers to produce services that really benefit the user in her tasks and in information needs when one is on the move. Context awareness and personalization have been studied [15] extensively in order to develop technology to help the users consume electronic services while on the move. Personalization and context awareness are also close to the focus of the Apricot project.

3 The Apricot Platform

The Apricot platform is a distributed software platform, which provides different tools for service development, maintenance and monitoring purposes. The design of the Apricot platform is a combination of several different approaches, which are familiar from the Internet and from the computer systems and their designs. The main technologies utilized in the design of the Apricot platform are: Web Services [16], Enterprise Java Beans (EJB) [17], FIPA Agent Architecture [18], Semantic Web [19], and FIPA Agent Communication Language (ACL) [20].

3.1 The Apricot Architecture

The architecture of the Apricot platform follows the FIPA agent architecture. It specifies the main components and system agents, which are the mandatory parts of an agent platform. The architecture also specifies the structure of the messages and the communication protocol between the agents which are implemented into the platform accordingly. The content language used in the agent messages is a XML version of the RDF (Resource Description Framework) languages N-Triplets [21]. This conversion is the result of a requirements posed by the mobile terminals MIDP (Mobile Information Device Profile) 2.0 Java implementation and the PC's Java environment. Both of these environments lack the build to support RDF parsing, which is not the case with XML. N-Triples is a line-based, plain text format for representing the RDF abstract syntax. It is a small subset of Notation3 [22]. When N-Triplets are combined with the task model of the Apricot agent, it creates a simple and effective framework to create and use the services that are deployed into the Apricot platform. The referred agent task model is inherent to the Apricot agent model. It is a programming paradigm that is derived from a model of how the Apricot agent processes information. It also defines how the services that they provide are constructed. The Apricot architecture is presented in Fig 1.

The Apricot architecture is very similar to Internet architecture and to the basic client-server-model. Agent services act as servers, which provide the routing services, information repositories and network applications. The agent containers act as peers of the network, also providing different kinds of information services. The agent model provides the building blocks for realizing information services. The Apricot terminal is a window to this network and its services, such as a web browser, serve as a window to the World Wide Web.

3.2 The Agent Service

The Agent service is a server side component of the Apricot platform. It provides services to the network as follows:

- Directory services: Yellow Pages, and White Pages.
- Application deployment services: Application/Service upload and removal.

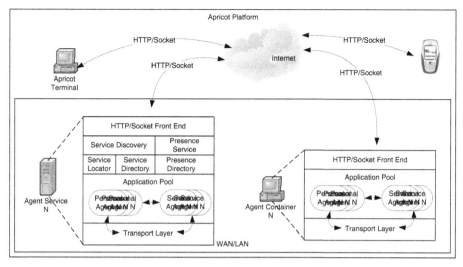

Fig. 1. The Apricot Architecture

- Message routing services: A routing table for connected agent services and agent containers.
- System Database Services: access to vocabulary, task, profile and midlet resources.
- Authentication services: Access control for system resources and user identification.

The Directory Services implementation follows the FIPA Abstract Architecture specification [17] by providing the core services defined for the agent platform. However, in the Apricot platform these services have been extended with additional features. These features enable the platform to perform basic presence services [23] so that the developer can create different kinds of services that use the presence framework. Another noteworthy feature of these directory services is the Apricot platforms core feature, which provides support for dynamic adaptation of new services. A high-level overview of the structure of the Apricot agent service is presented in Fig 2.

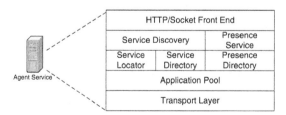

Fig. 2. The Apricot Agent Service

3.3 Apricot Agent Container

The Apricot agent container is a lightweight version of the Apricot agent service. It is an application container that provides the application and service deployment/removal functions. It is designed to be an application repository for support application/service distribution which gives the system scalability - the service network can be extended dynamically, robustness- the services can be duplicated and distributed around the network and processing power - a service can be a composite service where parts of it are distributed around the network. The Apricot agent container is presented in Fig 3.

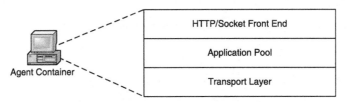

Fig. 3. Apricot Agent Container

Both the agent service and the agent container contain three layers, which are the same in both implementations (The HTTP/Socket front end, Application Pool and Transport Layer). These three components form functionality similar to a simplified EJB framework where there is a container component, which contains the Java beans, and the application part, which is implemented with Java beans. In the Apricot platform, these two main components of the EJB paradigm correspond to the agent container as the environment and Apricot agent as the Java bean. The major difference in these implementations can be found in the functional implementation of the developed application.

3.4 The Apricot Agent

According to the Java bean model, Apricot agent can be described as an entity bean, which describes the functionality most accurately. However, it is still not a comprehensive definition for an Apricot agent. The main difference comes from the design of the Apricot agent, which encloses the session bean functionality and also partially enfolds the functionalities of the message-driven object. This is due to the process-like nature of the task instances. These tasks are run concurrently and they form the applications by themselves or they are sub-units of another application. The design of the apricot agent model, illustrated in Fig 4, has been influenced by the UNIX architecture, and the functional model in particular.

The development of the Apricot agent model was guided by the goal to hide some of the peculiarities of the agent technology and to develop tools that ease the application development for developers who are not familiar with agent technology. The outcome of this was the Apricot agent model, which uses the EJB model and leans on the task and process model of the UNIX architecture. The EJB model is used because of its design, which encapsulates and defines the entities and their capabilities from each other to form an easily manageable object model. The EJB model is extended in the Apricot agent model by introducing a task paradigm for the service and application construction. These tasks are the building blocks of the different application. They conceal some of the agent-related concerns from the developer, such as the language, ontology, protocol and content language processing. This approach is simi-

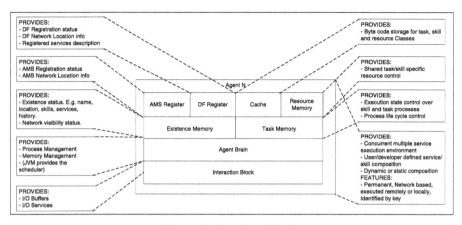

Fig. 4. Apricot Agent Model

lar to what is described by Berger et al. [24]. They named these components generic service components. The comparison between the characteristics of Apricot agents and Java beans is presented in Table 1.

Table 1. Comparison of the Features of an Apricot Agent and EJB Objects

The Apricot Agent	Corresponding EJB-Object
1) Concurrent multiple service/skill task execution environment.	-
2) Static developer defined or dynamic service/skill composition.	-
3) Can act as a client and/or a server.	-
4) Provides an object view of data in the database.	*Entity Object*
5) Allows shared access from multiple users.	*Entity Object*
6) Identified by a unique key.	*Entity Object*
7) Can be long-lived	*Entity Object*
8) Is asynchronously invoked.	*Message-Driven Object*

3.5 The Apricot Service Model

The Apricot platform is an environment for developing and deploying heterogeneous services into the IP network. These services are consumed by the end user via his personal agent, which acts as an interface to the service network composed of heterogeneous service agents.

The Web Services model is used and extended in the service discovery and the consumption of the discovered services. The personal agents adapt themselves to the service, which is described using the RDF format [25]. These descriptions are published in and queried from the Yellow Pages service. These service descriptions contain information about the service itself, service provider, service location, language, protocol, ontology, the location and names of the Java classes that implement the functionality, and also the names of the Midlet UI classes and their locations.

According to the service descriptions, the personal agent loads the Java classes and starts using the service accordingly. These service descriptions made in RDF format remotely follow the Semantic Web [26] approach where the research focus is on describing the web resources and pages to enable the use of the web content by computers. The service usage is presented in Fig 5. The figure describes the sequence of events in an example scenario where Mike's personal agent has already adapted itself to a news service and is now providing the service for him.

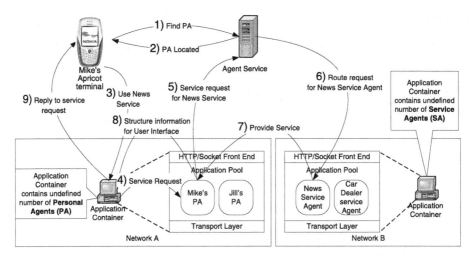

Fig. 5. Apricot Service Usage Model

The EJB framework was used here to illustrate the similarities between the designs of these two systems and to give a solid cornerstone for comparison of the Apricot platform. The motivation to create an Apricot system came from the mobile world where the mobile users needed to be served with services that have some degree of personalization and context awareness. The common Personal Agent (PA) model was the most suitable for this scenario. However, this scenario posed a handful of design issues that had to be solved accordingly.

1. The system should be able to facilitate a large number of PA's.
2. This should be done in a manner in which the maintenance would not become an issue.
3. The PA's should be able to adapt new services dynamically.
4. How the services should be designed so that they could be dynamically adaptable.
5. How the terminal represents the new services adopted by PA's and how they are consumed by the end user.

The first two issues of the PA paradigm will not pose a problem for the EJB implementation, but the last three are somewhat out of the scope of the EJB intended application area.

4 Implementation of Mobile Applications Using Apricot Agent Platform

This section briefly describes the demonstrators built on the Apricot platform. The original assumption was that using Apricot Agent Platform would make the development of multi-user applications and services easier and faster that without the help of such tools.

The demonstrators have been realized to validate features in the platform that support person-to-person communication, community communication, content management and multi-agent coordinated tasks. Moreover, these demonstrators aim to prove that development of mobile services using the Apricot platform is relatively easy and fast and, furthermore, take advantage of the capabilities of the agents. These demonstrators were built in a short time by exploiting the features provided by Apricot Agent Platform.

The descriptions of demonstrators introduce the main features and advantages of each application. The four demonstrators are *Mobile Instant Messenger*, *Mobile Car Salesman*, *Location- and user preference-based messaging application* and *Service Viewer*.

4.1 Mobile Instant Messenger

The Apricot Mobile Instant Messenger (IM) is a demonstrator built on Apricot Agent Platform. The main purpose of building the demonstrator was to test the basic features of the platform. These features include content sharing, networking, management of personal agents and communication between personal agents.

The main features of Mobile Instant Messenger are:

- Private instant messaging between different registered users.
- Public chatting between registered users of the chat channels.
- Management of different chat channels.
- Sharing of textual content within a community.

The functionality of the demonstrator can be realized using existing technology like Short Message Service (SMS), which might have been an even more robust means of realizing previously-mentioned functionality. There are also other instant messaging services available for mobile terminals e.g. in [27]. However, the purpose of realizing the instant messaging service using Apricot Agent Platform was to assess the viability of the platform. The communication concept of the mobile instant messenger demonstrator has been illustrated in Fig 6.

Mobile instant messenger clients were implemented in a Symbian environment on a Nokia 6600 mobile phone. In figure 6, the messenger clients can be considered to be the users called Lisa, Mike, Pekka and Joe. The terminal client was implemented using Java Mobile MIDP version 2.0. Networking was done over GPRS connections.

Mobile Instant Messenger was implemented in a couple of weeks by a programmer who was not involved in the development of the platform. During the course of developing the demonstrator, the Apricot platform proved to be a useful tool for realizing this kind of mobile service. Despite the claim of usefulness of the platform, it must be stated that an alternative implementation was not realized. Therefore, we can only assume that when using an Apricot platform the implementation was effective, since the platform takes care of basic mobile service routines such as networking and message routing.

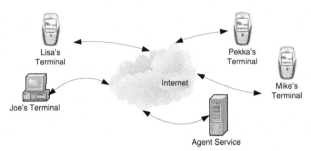

Fig. 6. Components of Mobile Instant Messenger Demonstrators

4.2 Mobile Car Salesman Application

The Mobile Car Salesman application was built up to prove the reusability and flexibility of services and applications previously implemented on top of an Apricot platform. The Apricot Instant Messenger application existed at the time the design and implementation of the Car Salesman-demonstrator was started. The other point of interest was the next generation mobile services, in which there will be a high level of interactivity in B2C markets. In particular, mobile marketing is a growing area of business and the demand for user-friendly, flexible mobile service development tools will grow.

Dealer end features of the Mobile Car Salesman application are:

- A duplex communication channel between the dealer and customers for customer approved conversation initiation.
- A view of users' requirements for the car
- A way for the dealer to update the cars-for-sale information.
- A channel for sending advertisements.

Customer end features:

- Browsing through the list of cars for sale.
- Update the watcher's information concerning requirements for cars.
- Modifying the alert routines and channels.
- Browsing and responding to received advertisements.

All communication in this application was built on the existing instant messenger (IM) software. This application uses the IM software for carrying the messages concurrently while the other user uses the IM for its original purpose. The development time used on the Car Salesman application was reduced due to the high reusability of the existing IM software.

This experiment does not give an accurate result regarding how flexible the platform actually is or what the actual reduction of development time is. However, it states the benefits of developing new applications on top of others. It also proves that the platform design supports the expandability of the applications as planned. This feature also raises questions on what will happen if the underlying application is updated. This kind of situation is handled by the Apricot platform if the Apricot agent design guides have been followed during the implementation of application.

The Apricot platform has a built-in feature, which automatically updates those clients that are trying to use the recently updated service. This update operation is done dynamically and does not require any manual work by the system administrator. The update sequence is in fact almost the same procedure as the service adaptation done by the Apricot Agent when they adapt a service for the first time.

4.3 Location- and User Preference-Based Messaging Application

An application for context-aware messaging was built to test and demonstrate the possibility of combining the Apricot platform and a reactive, event-driven control system in order to achieve a reliable and fast compound system. The basic idea was to design robust control architecture for context-based applications such as context-sensitive message delivery. For instance, context-sensitive message delivery can be used for location-dependent communication between family members or workmates.

In order to enhance the reliability and robustness of the system depicted, a two-level architecture has been developed. The system is distributed into intelligent and reactive domains. In the intelligent domain, the Apricot platform is used for high-level reasoning. In the reactive domain, independent state machines are used for message delivery.

The reactive level components of the system are independent state machines capable of using contextual information during their execution. Reconfigurable state machines are constructed on–the-fly from RDF-based State Machine Markup Language descriptions [28]. The reactive system is used for delivering messages based on the contextual information, such as location information from a Position and Navigation System (PANS). Messages are received via an IMAP4-compliant email server and presented with the terminal device most suitable for the user's current context. Communication between the components is arranged through a simple CORBA-based interface called Property Service, also introduced in [28].

Apricot platform agents are used for controlling and configuring the reactive system. The intelligent agent acquires contextual information to make high-level control decisions. Based on the decisions, the agent configures the reactive components by supplying new SMML-descriptions for the state machines. In the actual implementation depicted in Fig 7, decision-making is made by the user via the agent's configuration interface.

The intelligent and reactive domains can be physically separated into a logical system, where reactive components are executed in-house and intelligence is provided by an external party. Loose cohesion between the intelligent and reactive domains enables continuous system functionality even during network disruptions. The idea of using an agent system to control self-reliant applications is thus applicable.

4.4 Service Viewer

A Service Viewer application evaluates the support of Apricot platform in the adaptation of mobile services in the user's mobile terminals. In this application, the user's

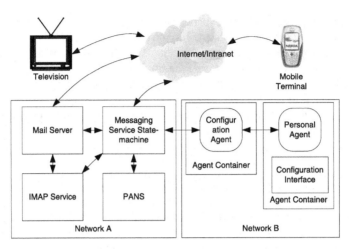

Fig. 7. Control Architecture Implementation

personal agent (PA) dynamically adapts the terminal user interface according to the variable services. The Service Viewer has mechanisms to deliver the services built in the Apricot network (E.g. Instant Messenger, Mobile Car Salesman, etc.) to the users of these services. Service descriptions define the appearance of services in terminal. The Viewer also provides the user with an execution frame for the GUIs and the delivered information.

The Apricot terminal deals with this problem by regenerating the terminal application-midlet every time the user wants to start using a new service provided by the Apricot network. This regeneration is supervised and carried out by the users PA, which knows the current composition of the user's terminal. It also receives the information about services the user would like to use. According to this information, it prepares and delivers a new Service-midlet into the user's mobile phone.

This approach to implementation of the terminal-application gives the service developer the opportunity to freely and independently design the service GUI's and their functionalities. This is not the case, for example, if the developer is using a terminal platform that uses some UI description language, such as the user interface markup language (UIML) or extensible user interface language (XUL). Despite the benefits in the Apricot terminal application, there are also drawbacks. The main drawback is that the use of the service viewer requires a lot of bandwidth, because the terminal software easily grows to more than 1mb in size. Most likely it will continue to grow even larger. Another problem we encountered was the unstable implementation of the Java Over the Air (OTA) specification by some mobile terminal manufacturers. A lot of features specified in the OTA specification were missing from the mobile phone implementations. Due to this problem, there are no guarantees that the software developed for one Java MIDP 2.0 enabled mobile phone will work in another. Furthermore, there are even fewer guarantees of compatibility between software and the program code in the actual mobile phone. This problem will probably diminish over time as the implementations of the OTA specification get better.

5 Conclusions

The vision behind this research was the requirement to assist the use of mobile services by integrating several services in a way that is convenient and transparent for the user. Our research approached the solution step by step, first by developing technology enablers for mobile service providers and secondly by making demonstrators, the aim of which is to solve the usability and availability problems of mobile services. As our work continues, we will be able to produce user-friendly mobile services with the help of Apricot platform.

This paper has shown how agent-based systems can be used for developing software systems, particularly for producing user-friendly mobile services. We also show how Apricot Agent Platform facilitates the implementation work of mobile services by providing an agent platform and agent frames with basic functionality. We have built several demonstrators for evaluation purposes of Apricot platform, we have used less hours for building up the demonstrators than ever before for producing mobile services.

We have been able to show that Apricot system provides an easy way to produce mobile services, since the agents have basic features already built-in, such as functionality and communication mechanism. In other words, agents can be considered partially reusable software components.

As the tendency for mobility grows all the time, we have also introduced a lightweight version of the Apricot platform. Apricot Agents are able to provide an interface on mobile phones with Java Virtual Machine support. In the demonstrators, so called Smart Phones-type mobile phones were used as they provide relatively good processing power as well as memory capacity. We believe that it would also be possible to implement Apricot systems in mobile environments with more limited resources; however, this kind of test was not carried out during the experiments described in this paper.

These results of Apricot research can be extended in a number of directions. We have two major targets for development: to further develop Apricot platform to fully rise to the challenge set by the mobile environment and to develop Apricot-supported applications for real business cases to benefit users. Technically, the development of the platform has to improve usability, stability and performance in order to test it in real-life business cases.

Acknowledgment. The Apricot project gratefully acknowledges the funding and support provided by Tekes (National Technology Agency of Finland), Infotech Oulu, and the companies associated with this project: Nokia Oyj, Pohjanmaan PPO Oy and DNA Finland.

References

1. Senn, J.A., The Emergence of M-Commerce, Computer, vol. 33 (12), pp. 148-150, 2000.
2. Snellman, K., Mobiilipalvelumarkkinat Suomessa 2003 (In Finnish), Liikenne-ja viestintäministeriön julkaisuja 24/2004.
3. Anckar, B.; D'Incau, D.; Value-added services in mobile commerce: an analytical framework and empirical findings from a national consumer survey, System Sciences, 2002. HICSS. Proceedings of the 35th Annual Hawaii International Conference on, 7-10 Jan. 2002

4. Antoniou, G., Van Harmelen, F. A Semantic Web Primer, MIT Press, ISBN 0-262-01210-3, April 2004b

5. Jennings, N.R. and Wooldridge, M.J. 1998. Applications of Intelligent Agents. Agent Technology: Foundations, Applications, and Markets. Jennings, N.R. and Wooldridge, M.J (Eds.), Springer, pp. 3-28.

6. Aylett R., Brazier, F., Jennings, N., Luck, M., Preist, C., and Nwana, H., Agent Systems and Applications, The Knowledge Engineering Review, 13(3), 303-308, 1998.

7. Helaakoski, H., Feng, S.C., Jurrens, K.K., Ojala, K., and Kipinä, K., Collaborative Software Agents in Steel Product Industry, The IASTED International Conference on Artificial Intelligence and Applications, Innsbruck, Austria, February 16-18, 200

8. Stroulia, E., and Hatch, M.P., An Intelligent Agent Architecture for Flexible Service Integration on the Web, IEEE Transactions on Systems, Man and Cybernetics-Part C. Applications and Reviews, vol.33,no.4,November 2003.

9. Riekki, J., Huhtinen, J.; Ala-Siuru, P.; Alahuhta, P.; Kaartinen, J.; Röning, J., Genie of the net, an agent platform for managing services on behalf of the user, Computer Communications.Vol.26(2003) Nr:11,pp.1188 - 1198

10. M. Berger, M.,et al., "Porting Distributed Agent-Middleware to Small Mobile Devices," Proc. First Int'l Joint Conf. Autonomous Agents and Multi-Agent Systems (AAMAS '02), Workshop 16 (Ubiquitous Agents on Embedded, Wearable, and Mobile Devices), 2002.

11. Poslad, S., et al., "CRUMPET: Creation of User-Friendly Mobile Services Personalised for Tourism," Proc. Second Int'l Conf. 3G Mobile Comm. Technologies (3G 2001), 2001.

12. Tarkoma, S., and Laukkanen, M., "Supporting Software Agents on Small Devices," Proc. First Int'l Joint Conf. Autonomous Agents and Multi-Agent Systems (AAMAS-02), 2002.

13. Laukkanen, M., Helin, H., and Laamanen, H., "Supporting Nomadic Agent-Based Applications in the FIPA Agent Architecture," Proc. First Int'l Joint Conf. Autonomous Agents and Multi-Agent Systems (AAMAS '02), 2002.

14. Maamar, Z., Dorion, E., Daigle, C., Toward Virtual Marketplaces for E-Commerce, Communications of the ACM, 44(12):35:38, Dec. 2001.

15. Mäntyjärvi, J., Sensor-based context recognition for mobile applications. Espoo, VTT Electronics, 2003. 118 p. + app. 60 p. VTT Publications; 511, ISBN 951-38-6253-4; 951-38-6254-2, http://www.vtt.fi/inf/pdf/publications/2003/P511.pdf

16. Web services http://www.w3.org/2002/ws/

17. Enterprise JavaBeansTM Specification,, http://java.sun.com/products/ejb/ Version 2.1

18. FIPA Abstract Architecture Specification, http://www.fipa.org

19. W3C Semantic Web Activity: www.w3.org/2001/sw/

20. FIPA ACL Message Structure Specification http://www.fipa.org

21. N-Triples W3C RDF Core WG Internal Working Draft.
    http://www.w3.org/2001/sw/RDFCore/ntriples/

22. Notation 3 by Berners-Lee http://www.w3.org/DesignIssues/Notation3

23. Nokia, Mobile Internet Technical Architecture, "Solutions and tools", IT Press

24. Berger M., Bouzid M., Buckland M., Lee H., Lhuillier N., Olpp D., Picault J., and Shepherdson J., "An Approach to Agent-Based Service Composition and its Application to Mobile Business Processes" IEEE Transactions on Mobile Computing Vol. 2, No. 3, July-September 2003

25. Resource Description Framework (RDF): Concepts and Abstract Syntax,
    http://www.w3.org/RDF/

26. Berners-Lee T., Hendler J. and Lassila O. (2001) The Semantic Web. Scientific American, May.

27. http://my-symbian.com

28. Mäenpää T., Tikanmäki A., Riekki J., Röning J. (2004) A Distributed Architecture for Executing Complex Tasks with Multiple Robots. The 2004 IEEE International Conference on Robotics and Automation (ICRA), New Orleans, USA, April 26 - May 1, 2004.

Support of Reflective Mobile Agents in a Smart Office Environment

Faruk Bagci, Holger Schick, Jan Petzold, Wolfgang Trumler, and Theo Ungerer

Institute of Computer Science,
University of Augsburg,
86159 Augsburg,
Germany
{Bagci,Petzold,Trumler,Ungerer}@Informatik.Uni-Augsburg.DE
HolgerSchick@web.de

Abstract. Ubiquitous systems will integrate computers invisibly and unobtrusively in everyday objects. Information will appear in new forms, i.e. data will be catched from single or multi-sensor devices and will be used for context extraction. New location-based services will be adapted to user preferences. For this the ubiquitous system needs to know user profiles, likings, and habits. As the user moves these information have to be sent to the new location of the user. Either the user carries her data on wearable or portable computers or the ubiquitous environment takes responsibility for transporting them. The amount of new devices and services makes an efficient use by centralized systems very difficult. The idea presented in this paper is that a virtual reflection of the user represented by a mobile agent accompanies her in the ubiquitous environment. Mobile agents offer a possibility to encapsulate information of a person and her preferences and perform location-based services of the ubiquitous system in the name of the user. Because of the personal data security and privacy are major concerns of such an agent system. This paper describes a ubiquitous mobile agent system named UbiMAS which has security extensions to provide high protection of agents and significant personal data. UbiMAS is used in a smart office environment with smart doorplates.

1 Introduction

Future computers will be integrated in objects of everyday life. The user shouldn't perceive these computers in his familiar environment. Ubiquitous systems should be invisible and unobtrusive. A further fundamental feature is their knowledge of context information. Context is the situation arising by realization and interpretation of environmental information. Single or multi-sensor boards [14] are developed to be used in smaller and more powerful intelligent environments. These devices can build a sensor-network and communicate with each other over wireless media. To include the location of a person into the context information different location-tracking systems can be used [5]. Additionally personal

M. Beigl and P. Lukowicz (Eds.): ARCS 2005, LNCS 3432, pp. 79–92, 2005.

information like profiles, preferences, likings, and habits are indispensable. Ubiquitous systems can use this data to adapt to the respective situation and react to changes without active user interventions. In case of location changes of the person the personal information has to be sent to the current location. The Mobile Computing field provides here various computing devices, like Tablet PCs, PDAs, notebooks, or even wearables. The person could carry portable devices to store these information. These devices are usually dedicated to a single person, so that security and privacy issues are on responsibility of the user. The disadvantage of these devices is that they need to be carried always by the person who owns them. The power consumption of wearable devices is an additional problem. It can lead to a loss of availability. Often it is inconvenient for users to carry such devices and users are inclined to forget the devices in their offices or at home.

We propose in this paper that the ubiquitous environment takes care for storing and sending the personal information. The person is always accompanied by a mobile virtual object in the ubiquitous environment. So location-based services adapted to personal profiles can be offered. Certainly the ubiquitous system could be realized as a server-centric approach. But concerning personal movements and data this would lead to a big-brother-is-watching-you scenario where entities that gain access to the server would have access to all personal information. Regarding ubiquitous environments a central server could rapidly become a bottleneck because of the amount of clients and services running on the system. Moreover, a failure on the server would endanger the whole system.

The paradigm of mobile agents ideally fits into the decentralized approach. The mobile agent constitutes a virtual reflection of the user and carries personal information which enables the agent to perform various services for the user. Additionally the mobile agent can use the environmental information which is provided by the local ubiquitous system. Personal context of users need to be secured on foreign nodes to anticipate spying out personal data. Therefore security is an essential factor for the acceptance of ubiquitous mobile agents. This paper describes an ubiquitous mobile agent system called UbiMAS [1] with new communication and security extensions. The agent system is applied in an office building where electronic doorplates offer flexible office services. Mobile user agents accompany the person who is tracked by a location tracking system and can instruct service agents to perform tasks for the user. We implemented three applications using UbiMAS: a direction scenario where a visitor is navigated with arrows displayed on electronic doorplates, an e-mail application where an employee can assign her user agent to inform her about expected e-mails at each doorplate in the office building, and a file access application where the employee can securely read or download files which are placed on a PC where she has read access. The next section deals with related work. The subsequent section describes the idea of reflective agents in the Smart Doorplate project [2] and explains the system architecture of UbiMAS with its communication and security extensions. Section 4 presents some applications and evaluation results. The paper ends with the conclusion.

2   Related Work

Several research projects exist for smart office and home environments. The Active Badge system described in [19] is an IR-based location tracking system. It is used in an office scenario, where phone calls are redirected to the current location of the user. The Aware Home project [11] aims to built a ubiquitous house to create a living laboratory for research in ubiquitous computing for everyday activities. Using various sensors new applications are implemented like the identification of person over a Smart Floor or finding Frequently Lost Objects (FLO). Mozer [13] proposes an Adaptive Control of Home Environments (ACHE). ACHE monitors the environment, observes the actions taken by inhabitants, and attempts to predict their next actions. All of these projects are one-server-centric. We chose with our reflective mobile agents a distributed approach obviating central point storage of information.

The idea of using mobile agents in ubiquitous environments appears in several projects. In [9] a flexible mobile code approach is described which is used in a ubiquitous and active augmented reality system. The user inspects the world through this AR system and is tracked by a location-tracking system. When she enters a space of a real object which has an active tag, a mobile code is downloaded on the user's device and is executed by a Mobile Code Engine (MCE). The mobile code contains executable information, e.g. appropriate user interfaces, but it is not a mobile agent system because the mobile code isn't autonomously performing a service.

The Hive system [12] is a distributed agent platform for building applications by networking local system resources. Agents are used to control devices in ubiquitous computing environments. Hive also supports agent migration. However the agents here are simply remote objects, e.g. buttons, without an agent communication infrastructure.

[16] and [17] describe a framework which is very similar to our approach. The framework provides a way for mobile agents to follow their users as they move around and to adhere to places as virtual post-its. However the papers describe only a framework and shift the security issues to the used agent system and the Java Virtual Machine.

Security in mobile agent systems is examined in multiple research projects. [3] describes a security concept where mobile agents only migrate to trustful nodes. [15] replaces the concept of trust by a concept of reputation. Agents can increase or decrease the reputation of nodes dependent on the experiences that they make with the nodes. To protect against occupation of node resources by agents [10] defines a restriction on the number of times an object can be accessed. These projects influenced our security approach which more specifically targets the requirements of ubiquitous environments.

3   Reflective Agents on Smart Doorplates

Reflective agents accompany persons in the ubiquitous environment and carry user specific data. In order to examine this idea in a real scenario we mounted touch screens at each door of an office building replacing fixed doorplates. These

Smart Doorplates [2] offer a platform for several services. Users of the services are employees, i.e. the office owner, and visitors of the building. Employees have their personal reflective agent, which resides in the environment and contains data about the employee. The data consists of basic user information like name, office room, etc. and security data like private and public keys, user names and passwords of the owner used for communication, data security, and access operations. Furthermore the agent stores context information belonging to the user and updates these data automatically.

The doorplates serve also as interface between user and agent. The user can instruct her reflective agent to perform services in her name. The reflective agent communicates with service agents and passes on the instructions. If the user moves to a new location the reflective agent migrates to the doorplate next to the user. The user location is determined by an RFID tracking system. The user must only carry an RFID tag.

This mobile agent model is implemented in UbiMAS. The UbiMAS architecture is described in the following subsection.

3.1 UbiMAS Architecture

The ubiquitous mobile agent system UbiMAS is implemented as a service running on top of middleware systems. Currently, UbiMAS is based on the Autonomic Middleware for Ubiquitous eNvironments named AMUN [18]. UbiMAS services run on top of AMUN besides other services like a location tracking service.

AMUN is designed with the goal in mind to foster the device independent application of autonomic computing demands proposed by IBM in ubiquitous environments [7]. AMUN uses the peer-to-peer system JXTA [8] as communication infrastructure. Communication in JXTA is realized by three kinds of pipes: propagate, input and output pipes. If two JXTA peers want to exchange messages directly they arrange input and output pipes for unlimited and bidirectional communication. AMUN uses an event-based approach for message delivery. It offers services the interfaces needed to exchange messages over middleware pipes. Each service defines its own message type. When a message arrives AMUN analyzes the message type and generates an event for the registered services. An Event Dispatcher offers services the functionality to send messages and to register themselves as listeners to specified types of messages. In this manner the services can register for different message types and get informed when one of these messages arrive. So each application decides if it wants to receive sensor, location, middleware or other kinds of messages. UbiMAS defines an own message type. UbiMAS nodes that are implemented as AMUN services register for this UbiMAS message type.

UbiMAS consists of two parts: the UbiMAS basic platform and the UbiMAS extensions. The UbiMAS basic platform defines abstract agent nodes and the interface for agent implementations. It realizes the basic communication functions between nodes and agents and several security concepts.

The UbiMAS extensions part implements the application specific components, i.e. the reflective user agents and the service agents. Furthermore the communication functions are extended here with secure agent-agent and agent-node methods to fulfill the requirements of the Smart Doorplate application.

This separation in a basic and an extensions part makes a broad usage of UbiMAS possible.

3.2   The UbiMAS Node Service

To host UbiMAS agents each peer has to start at least one UbiMAS agent node as service on top of the middleware (see Figure 1).

UbiMAS implements additional communication protocols for agent and node communication and for agent migration. All messages are acknowledged in Ubi-MAS what is not implemented by the base middleware.

If a middleware peer receives a UbiMAS type message it informs the node sending an event on which the node listens. UbiMAS nodes implement a Message Delivery component which receives the events sent by the middleware and processes the incoming messages. If the node wants to send a message it forwards it to the Message Delivery where the appropriate header information are set.

If the receiver of a message is an agent the Message Delivery hands it on to the PoBox. The PoBox has for each agent an interface called PoBoxAdder where the agents can send and receive messages. This is the only connection of

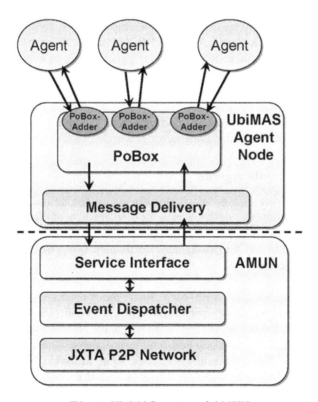

Fig. 1. UbiMAS on top of AMUN.

an agent to a node. All communication between agents and nodes is handled over the PoBox using the PoBoxAdder. The PoBoxAdder describes the interface for putting messages into the queues. Besides the **addMessage** method of the PoBoxAdder there are no method references between nodes and agents.

The PoBox installs for each agent a queue for incoming messages. In the same manner each agent has a queue for messages sent by the PoBox. The queue lengths are managed dynamically by the possessing entity. This approach offers various security features which are described in the UbiMAS security section below.

3.3   Agent Node Peer Groups

The agent nodes can form alliances in form of peer groups independent from the middleware peer groups. If two peers want to build a peer group they have to arrange new pipes which are built using a pipe advertisement. The advertisement contains a unique pipe ID. Only the peers which know this ID can receive the messages sent over this pipe. Figure 2 shows an example for UbiMAS peer groups. Each agent node which wants to join a peer group must send a request. The peer group members can decide if this request will be accepted or rejected. Inside of a peer group the agent nodes communicate over a secure communication protocol. Messages to foreign nodes outside the peer group are still possible but are not secured.

Different peer groups can build a partnership. Applied to an office building each floor could build a peer group, and floors of the same institution could form an alliance. This makes it possible for agent nodes to communicate with nodes from other peer groups. Besides UbiMAS there are other services, e.g. Location Services, using the same middleware for communication. Mobile Agents can register for events of these services and will be informed when new events occur. In this way agents can be notified by sensor events from the environment or location events of particular persons.

3.4   UbiMAS Mobile Agents

Agents in UbiMAS are started as single threads on the actual node. An agent reacts to messages, i.e. the agent is in a loop where it waits for incoming messages. A UbiMAS node can host several agents. There are two types of agents in UbiMAS: user-agents and service-agents. Both agent types descend from an abstract agent that defines different basic methods for communication and security functions.

Agents can communicate with each other using messages. An agent must implement functions which are performed when a specific message is received. If an agent doesn't know the message type it ignores the message. The abstract agent defines methods for creating and sending messages. The agent nodes serve here as mediators. Messages addressed to a local available mobile agent are forwarded directly to the recipient agent by the local PoBox. If the agent is on another node the message is transferred first to this node.

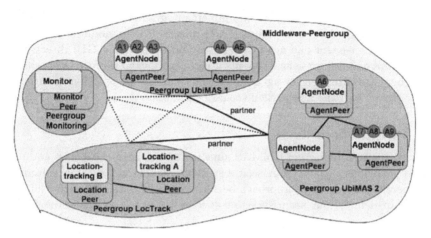

Fig. 2. UbiMAS Peer Group Example.

Each agent is identified over a unique ID. UbiMAS supports message encryption. Each node owns a certificate, a public and a private key. Each agent has an own key pair for message encryption. The abstract agent defines further data structures for security keys of the agent and the public key of the actual host. Furthermore there are methods for requesting public keys of other agents or nodes.

Below are some methods of the abstract agent described. To send a message an agent performs:

- `createAgentMessage` is called by an agent when it wants to send a new message. It returns an prepared UbiMAS message where the ID of the calling agent is set into the sender information by the PoBoxAdder.
- `encodeAgentMessage`: The agent can encode the contents of the message using the coding methods RSA or DES. As key the agent uses the public key of the receiver agent or node.
- `sendToAgent` and `sentToHost` are called by an agent when it wants to send a message to another agent or to a node. The PoBoxAdder puts the message into the queue of the PoBox.

Moreover if an agent receives a new message the following methods are called:

- `addMessage`: The PoBoxAdder calls this method to put a message into the queue of an agent.
- `decodeAgentMessage`: If the message is encoded the agent can decode the contents of the message with his private key.

For migration the agent calls:

- `sendAgent`: If an agent wants to migrate to another host it calls this method. The agent code is serialized and packed as a byte stream into a message and is sent to the PoBox. The PoBox sends the message to the receiver node and destroys the agent after receiving an acknowledgement.

Extending this abstract agent we implemented a user-agent that can receive location messages concerning its user and migrate to the node next to this location. The user-agent can get instructions and data over a GUI directly from the user and can ask for service-agents assigning them to perform a specific service. There are three service-agents implemented. The last section describes the service-agents and the application scenarios in detail.

3.5   UbiMAS Security

The security architecture of UbiMAS aims to protect both the agents and nodes against malicious behaviors. A secure system is essential for the acceptance of the reflective mobile agent approach because personal data is sensitive [6]. In [4] the author defines four security issues specific to mobile agent systems. These are:

- protection of the host against agents,
- protection of agents against other agents,
- protection of agents against host, and
- protection of the underlying network.

Each involved entity of the mobile agent system can be regarded as a potential intruder. Malicious agents could be used to forward confidential information or to attack other entities. Nodes have full access to the agent code and therefore could clone agents, manipulate the migration path or attack the host PCs. The host PCs and the communication network offer a broad basis for attacks on the agent communication and migration. There are other entities who could endanger the agent system, like administrators, authors, owners, and agent users. The administrator installs, configures, and maintains the mobile agent system. He could arbitrarily manipulate the system. The author develops the mobile agents and could build a Trojan horse or hidden functions. In some cases the owner and the user of mobile agents are different persons. The owner describes the person who feeds the system with agents. He could consciously bring malicious agents into the system. The user can't bring new agents into the system but utilizes the agents and could apply many agents trying to start a Denial-of-Service attack. To stem the potential attacks UbiMAS realizes various security approaches which are described below.

Protection of Agents Against Hosts: UbiMAS assumes only trustful nodes. The nodes are installed by an administrator. We assume here social protection mechanisms. The administrator and author of the agent nodes are known. It is supposed that these persons will act trustful in their own interest. Infiltration of foreign nodes is not possible because of certificates and keys for each service. Furthermore only UbiMAS peers of the same application can form a peer group. Each peer group has its own certificate which is validated during communication. All messages in UbiMAS are coded using Public Key Infrastructure (PKI) approaches. If the sender node doesn't know the public key of the receiver it first asks for it and stores it for future communication. The main point therefore is to protect the agent node and agents against malicious mobile agents.

Protection of Agents and Hosts Against Rogue Agents: The first step in this direction is to secure the message exchange between agents and nodes. Our solution is the PoBoxAdder which has several protection functionalities. Protection against impersonating is realized through the property that the sender of messages isn't set by the agent but by the PoBoxAdder. This means that an agent can't describe as another agent. Furthermore the PoBox has a limited queue for messages. The node can change the length of each queue dynamically. Agents can only send until the queue is full. Besides this the node can set a timer. The agents have to wait until the timer is expired before they can send a new message. The messages of all different PoBox queues are served by a fair scheduling algorithm, e.g. FIFO. This makes denial of service attacks by agents against nodes more difficult. In the case of an attack the node can set the queue-length of the concerning agent to zero blocking further sendings.

One more protection approach results by avoidance of references. This means that no mobile agent knows direct references on the node or other agents, i.e. the agent can't call external functions or access external data. The only interface for communication is the PoBoxAdder. Each agent reaching the actual node gets the public key of this node. All messages which the agent sends to the PoBoxAdder are coded with the public key of the node. In the same way the node codes messages to an agent with its public key. So even if an other agent gets this messages it has no possibility to decode the information. With this approach UbiMAS can allow all kinds of agents, even malicious ones.

To provide platform independence UbiMAS is implemented in Java. To execute an agent the node has to know its class. The agent usually migrates with its class. The node has the responsibility for securing that the agent code won't be manipulated during migration. This is done by encryption. However, here a security gap may arise because agents could be started with the wrong class which have the same name as the agent class. UbiMAS ensures that mobile agents are always loaded with the right class. If the class isn't known the node requests it from the sender node. Since in UbiMAS there is no limitation for agents and agent authors it is impossible to avoid name conflicts through a name convention. To avoid name collisions each agent has its own class loader. This enables separation of name spaces. Since generic classes could be loaded redundantly we differentiate between standard and non-standard agent classes. The agent node implements a standard class loader that loads the communication classes. Remaining agent-specific classes are loaded by the agent class loader. In that way the communication classes are loaded only once on the node.

UbiMAS disallows cloning of agents. All user-agents are loaded only once per person. During migration the nodes observe that the agents are deleted after acknowledged transfer. The same service-agent can be loaded several times but each agent becomes its own unique ID, so there are no clones of service-agents, too.

In our office scenario service-agents are allowed to access resources on hosts. This access needs to be secured. This is done using the Security Manager of Java. The problem here is that the Security Manager protects the system only against applications. However mobile agents are not applications but implemented as threads. If the Security Manager would give permissions to an agent as application all agents on this node would get the same access. This is naturally not acceptable. What we need here is a permission system for single threads. The problem on threads is that the thread ID changes after agent migration, because each node starts a new thread for each received agent. To guarantee that only a specific agent gets the access rights on chosen resources it needs an access approach based on a unique identification technique independent from the thread ID. UbiMAS realizes a security extension of the Java Security Manager where rights on system resources can be applied for agent threads. The Security Manager requires several attributes like username, password, permission name, permission parameters, and a permission ID. To ensure that this permission ID is unique it is calculated using the agent ID and is decoded using public/private key mechanisms. Therefore the calculated ID is independent from the thread ID and is unique because all agent IDs are unique.

Besides the nodes the agents have their own private/public keys. To secure the message exchange the agents can encrypt the information in the messages with the public key of the receiver agent or node which subsequently decrypts it with its private key. Furthermore agents always store encrypted personal data of its user. There is no possibility to access this data because the only access to agents is by messages over the PoBox.

If an agent wants to migrate to another node it asks the node to send the agent to the destination. There are two methods for migration. The agent can ask for transfer directly to a node or it can ask for transfer to the node where a specific agent resides. For the second method the actual node may start a finding procedure for the destination agent. In both cases the agent that wants to be transferred waits for migration by sleeping. In that time the agent can still receive messages. The sender node tries to build a bidirectional connection to the receiver node. If this was possible, the node begins with transfer preparations. The node also uses private/public key encryption for agent migration. It serializes the agent code, uses the public key of the recipient node for encryption, and packs it into a message. Additionally the messages received for the current agent are attached to this message. The destination node realizes that the message has a mobile agent type. It decrypts the message with its private key, deserializes the agent, and wakes it up. After that the node delivers the messages to the agent which were received in meantime.

4   Application Scenarios and Evaluation

To evaluate UbiMAS we have implemented several Smart Doorplate scenarios and present here one user-agent scenario and three service-agent scenarios. For each user (employee or visitor) exists a user-agent as reflective agent, which is fed into the system when the person physically enters the building. The smart doorplates offer an interface between user-agent and the user. If a user wants to utilize a service, she stops in front of the next doorplate. The location tracking system based on RFID recognizes the user and fires an event containing the user ID. The user-agent catches this event and migrates to this smart doorplate. After authenticating herself the user can choose a service. If the user wants to go to an office and don't know the way she can ask her user-agent for navigating her. The user-agent then displays arrows in the direction the user has to go. Knowing the next doorplates the user will pass, the user-agent jumps ahead and shows the right direction. If the user reaches the destination the agent displays a reached message. Figure 3 shows a picture of one smart doorplate and figure 4 shows the floor of our institution with a smart doorplate at each door.

Fig. 3. Smart Doorplate.

Besides this scenario we have implemented three service-agents: an e-mail agent, a file reader agent and a file fetcher agent. In the e-mail scenario an employee uses her office PC to retrieve e-mails and can arrange to be notified if she expects a special e-mail. Because of security reasons she doesn't want to receive all her incoming mails on a foreign smart doorplate. She instructs her user-agent to check the e-mails appropriate to a special filter and to inform her when matching e-mails were found. The user-agent calls an e-mail service-agent and gives it the filter in coded form. At the same time it applies for the required rights on the host PC for checking e-mails. The service-agent moves now to the agent node on the host PC. There the host can validate the ID of the agent and can set the rights, which were requested by the user-agent before. Now the service-agent can search the received e-mails using the filter. If the agent finds a matching e-mail it migrates to the node where the user-agent is and gives the results to the user-agent. The file reader agent and the file fetcher agent perform in the same way. The first one only reads out a file, e.g. a log-file which the employee wants to see, and displays the contents on the doorplate. The file fetcher agent brings a specific file to a desired doorplate and stores it into a public folder.

Fig. 4. Floor with Smart Doorplates.

The movement of the mobile agent should be faster than the movement of the person. Usually the migration of the agent has some delay because the location tracking system takes some time to recognize the person and to fire an location event. In [1] we performed preliminary tests with Bluetooth and WLAN connected PDAs which showed insufficient transfer performance already for the basic system without encryption. As result, we based the doorplate system on ethernet connected PCs. In order to evaluate UbiMAS with its security extensions we measured the ping time (PT), i.e. the time an agent needs to jump from a node to another and back on the PC-based system. We increased the size of data carried by the mobile agent. The measurement is taken once with encryption/decryption the agent code during migration and once without encryption. Figure 5 describes the evaluation results. The results show that using security encryption increases the agent transfer time. Encryting more agent data needs more processing time. However the migration time is still acceptable for the reflective agent scenario.

5   Conclusion

This paper presented the Ubiquitous Mobile Agent System UbiMAS. UbiMAS grabs the idea that ubiquitous systems are responsible for storing personal user data and sending them to the actual location of the person where the system offers user specific services. This transfer of private information is the reason why UbiMAS cares much for security aspects. Mobile agents carry user specific information and perform services in the name of the person. It is essential that agents and nodes are protected against malicious agents. For this UbiMAS offers various security features. The PoBox is one of these used to ensure that no agent has references to other agents or nodes. We described the UbiMAS node

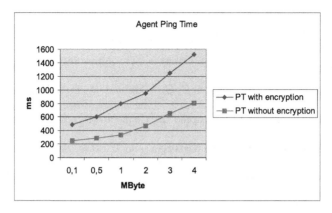

Fig. 5. Agent Ping Time with/without encryption.

peer infrastructure where new communication protocols are used for secure message exchange between agents and nodes. We implemented different scenarios for flexible office buildings with smart doorplates where we differentiated between user-agents and service-agents. The agent system bases on an autonomic middleware which provides additional application possibilities for the agent system. We currently explore how mobile agents can support the self-monitoring and self-configuring features of the autonomic middleware system. UbiMAS is designed in a generic way ensuring broad application possibilities.

References

1. F. Bagci, J. Petzold, W. Trumler, and T. Ungerer. Ubiquitous Mobile Agent System in a P2P-Network. In *UbiSys-Workshop at the Fifth Annual Conference on Ubiquitous Computing*, Seattle, October 2003.
2. F. Bagci, J. Petzold, W. Trumler, and Th. Ungerer. Smart Doorplate. In *The First International Conference on Appliance Design (1AD), Bristol, UK*, May 2003.
3. W. Farmer, J. Guttmann, and V. Swarup. Security for Mobile Agents: Authentication and State Appraisal. In *Proceedings of the Europea Symposium on Research in Computer Security (ESORICS), LNCS 1146*, pages 118–130. Springer-Verlag, 1996.
4. R. S. Gray. Agent Tcl: A Flexible and Secure Mobile-Agent System. In *Proceedings of the Fourth Annual TCL/Tk Workshop (TCL 96)*, 1996.
5. J. Hightower and G. Boriello. Location Systems for Ubiquitous Computing. *IEEE Computer*, pages 57–66, August 2001.
6. F. Hohl. Mobile Agent Security and Reliability. In *Proceedings of the Ninth International Symposium on Software Reliability Engineering (ISSRE '98). IEEE Computer Society*, page 181, Paderborn, Germany, November 1998.
7. P. Horn. Autonomic Computing: IBM's Perspective on the State of Information Technology. http://www.research.ibm.com/autonomic/, October 2001.
8. Project JXTA. http://www.jxta.org, August 2004.

9. K. Kangas and J. Roning. Using code mobility to create ubiquitous and active augmented reality in mobile computing. In *Proceedings of Conference on Mobile Computing and Networking (MOBICOM '99)*, pages 48–58, Seattle, August 1999.

10. G. Karjoth, D. B. Lange, and M. Oshirma. The Aglet Security Model. In *IEEE Internet Comp.*, July–Aug 1997.

11. C. D. Kidd, R. Orr, G. D. Abowd, C. G. Atkeson, I. A. Essa, B. MacIntyre, E. D. Mynatt, T. Starner, and W. Newstetter. The Aware Home: A Living Laboratory for Ubiquitous Computing Research. In *Cooperative Buildings*, pages 191–198, 1999.

12. N. Minar, M. Gray, O. Roup, R. Krikorian, and P. Maes. Hive: distributed agents for networking things. In *Proceedings of Symposium on Agent Systems and Applications/Symposium on Mobile Agents (ASA/MA '99)*, IEEE Computer Society, Palm Springs, CA, October 1999.

13. M. C. Mozer. Lessons from an adaptive house. In *Smart environments: Technologies, protocols, and applications*. J. Wiley & Sons, 2004.

14. The ScatterWeb Platform. http://www.scatterweb.net, August 2004.

15. L. Rasmusson and S. Jansson. Simulated Social Control for Secure Internet Commerce. In *New Security Paradigms '96*. ACM Press, 1996.

16. I. Satoh. Spatialagents: integrating user mobility and program mobility in ubiquitous computing environments. *Wireless Communications and Mobile Computing*, 3(4), June 2003.

17. Y. Tanizawa, I. Satoh, and Y. Anzai. A mobile agent framework for ubiquitous computing environments. In *Information Processing Society Journal*, pages 3774–3784, 2002.

18. W. Trumler, F. Bagci, J. Petzold, and T. Ungerer. AMUN - Autonomic Middleware for Ubiquitious eNvironments applied to the Smart Doorplate Project. In *International Conference on Autonomic Computing (ICAC-04)*, pages 274–275, New York, NY, May 2004.

19. R. Want, A. Hopper, V. Falcao, and J. Gibbons. The Active Badge Location System. In *ACM Transactions on Information Systems*, pages 91–102, January 1992.

Learning Action Sequences Through Imitation in Behavior Based Architectures

Willi Richert, Bernd Kleinjohann, and Lisa Kleinjohann

University of Paderborn / C-Lab, Germany
{richert,bernd,lisa}@c-lab.de

Abstract. In this paper a new architecture for learning action sequences through imitation is proposed. Imitation occurs by means of observing and applying sequences of basic behaviors. When an agent has observed another agent and applied the observed action sequence later on, this imitated action sequence can be seen as a meme. Agents that behave similarly can therefore be grouped by their typical behavioral patterns. This paper thus explores imitation from the view of memetic proliferation.

Combining imitation learning with meme theory we show by simulating agent societies that with imitation significant performance improvements can be achieved. The performance is quantified by using an entropy measure to qualitatively evaluating the emerging clusters.

Our approach is demonstrated by the example of a society of emotion driven agents that imitate each other to reach pleasant emotional state.

1 Introduction

Much effort has already been put into the study of "imitation" ([2], [4], or [6]). Yet, imitation has been studied so far mainly in terms of learning by demonstration, where the role of the teacher and the student, or demonstrator and imitator, are fixed, e.g. a robot arm equipped with a computer and a camera that has to learn the exact movement of a human arm playing tennis. However, in many application fields these basic movements, also called *basic behaviors*, are already known, and instead the proper sequence of these behaviors has to be learnt. The information describing which action sequences improve the performance can thus be seen as a crucial information entity that can possibly be obtained by observing other agents. What can be learnt by observing others does not have to be learnt with great efforts by oneself using trial and error.

When one subject copies an information unit from another one, the object that is being transferred underlies several rules. Dawkins was the first one to state that ideas or information units that can be transferred evolve according to similar rules that govern biological evolution [9]. The Oxford English Dictionary describes this information unit, called "meme" according to the biological counterpart "gene", as follows [1]:

> **meme, n.** *An element of a culture or system of behaviour that may be considered to be passed from one individual to another by non-genetic means, esp. imitation.*

M. Beigl and P. Lukowicz (Eds.): ARCS 2005, LNCS 3432, pp. 93–107, 2005.

This way, an action sequence or episode can also be seen as a meme that is transferred from one agent to another at every observation. After a while, groups of agents performing different action sequences should emerge, because different agents will have observed different behavioral patterns at different times. The more benefit a meme offers to the possible hosts the more it will be spread following a *survival of the fittest* pattern. An action sequence in the general sense is an output sequence that manipulates the environment.

In this paper a simulated environment is described in which agents perform action sequences. These action sequences correspond to physical actions in the real world. The agent's perception is simulated also and is not a research topic in this paper, which concentrates on imitation. The performance improvement is measured by means of the agents' utility functions. This is a heuristic composed of emotions and drives, which are the driving force behind the agent's behavior. Our emphasis is on adapting this heuristic to solve technical problems and not on the discussion about the *real* emotional model of human beings. Every agent strives for feeling good emotions and avoiding bad ones. According to Plutchik [15] emotions have the following important features: 1) Emotions are aroused by external stimuli. 2) Emotions are directed towards those stimuli. 3) Emotions are aroused after the subject has perceived and interpreted the stimulating object. 4) Emotions are volatile and decay over time.

Since their emotions are the consequence of external stimulation the agents have to modify the cause for this stimulation – either by neutralizing the stimulus in case it aroused bad feelings or by supporting it in the other case. To accomplish this they have to find out and select the proper sequence of actions or behaviors in their behavior repertoire that will be applied by the behavior system. In our approach this selection is learned by the imitation system of an agent which strives to imitate action sequences that have been observed with other agents in the past and have been considered to be successful, meaning that the agent *felt better* afterwards, as registered by its emotion system. Contrary to the established learning approaches this architecture does not contain any sophisticated learning algorithm like e. g. Reinforcement Learning [18] or evolutionary algorithms [19].

2   Related Work

Gatsoulis et al. show how foraging can be trained via learning through imitation [13]. In their experiments they point out, that the imitator can generalize beyond its training data. Billard looks at the imitation learning problem from the biological point of view, when presenting a model for motor skills imitation [6]. The modules of this architecture correspond to brain regions responsible for the control of movement in primates. Demiris and Hayes distinguish active and passive imitation [10] to handle the situation, in which the demonstrated action is already known to the observer and that one, in which the observer has to imitate completely new actions, differently. In the passive case, the motor systems are only involved during the *reproduce* phase in the *perceive – recognize – reproduce* process, whereas in the active case the motor systems are involved throughout the whole process. This is necessary for the imitation architecture to learn completely new actions for the first time. These two cases are combined in their *dual-route architecture*. Schaal showed how demonstrated trajectories can be described as sequences of action units that are formalized as stable nonlinear attractor systems, called *Dynamic Movement Primitives* [16]. These research papers focus mainly on how individual behaviors of a demonstrator can be exactly imitated. The problem how sequences of such behaviors can be imitated is not addressed. Borenstein and Ruppin developed a framework called *imitation enhanced evolution* (IEE) to explore, how imitation can be utilized in evolutionary processes of agent populations [11]. By leveraging the knowledge possessed by members of the population they concentrate on the horizontal imitation (imitation between members of the same generation) as opposed to the vertical or cultural imitation. Thus, in IEE only innate behaviors can be imitated. It prevents an imitated behavior from being imitated once more. Thereby, IEE does not allow an exploration of meme dispersion. Moreover, the framework always clearly constitutes who is the teacher in the society, which is taken randomly but proportionally to fitness value. This contradicts to the aim of our work that memes in the form of action sequences spread through imitation processes more freely, in which the teacher is chosen by the memes themselves.

3   Architecture

Our imitation learning approach adapts the triple tower architecture [14] from the robot head MEXI [12] and extends it with an imitation system that enables agents to imitate each other. To achieve this it provides an interface by which agents can read from other agents their executed action and emotional state. The overall architecture has to perform the following tasks:

- *Imitation System*: Observe agents and apply previously observed episodes appropriate for the improvement of the current emotional situation.
- *Emotion System*: Choose a behavior that should be applied if the imitation system has no better episode to offer. The calculation of the behavior is based only on the current emotional state.
- *Behavior System*: Map the chosen behavior to more detailed action instructions (e. g. Behavior $X \rightarrow$ "turn 10°, move forward 5mm, open gripper").

Combining these three systems *imitation system*, *emotion system*, and *behavior system* the architecture is designed as shown in Fig. 1.

   In this data flow graph the perception module delivers the data directly to every system in the middle tower. Thus, all these systems work on the same data basis and no perception filtering between them is applied.

   Using the perception data the *emotion system* consisting of emotions and drives, which will be described in detail later on, calculates which action should be executed so that every emotion will be perceived affirmatively as an effect. Together with its action choice it delivers the current emotional state to the *imitation system*. The imitation system evaluates the emotional state and switches into one of three modes, which are represented by according behaviors in the behavior system:

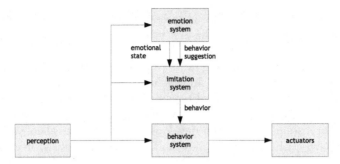

Fig. 1. The agent's model. The emotion module gives hints about which actions should be favored. But, the imitation module has the right to veto if the agent has observed in the past an action sequence that could be better for the agent's actual emotional state.

OBSERVE: Look at the nearest agent and record its emotional state together with the executed action for a similar situation in the future, where it might be applied.

APPLY: Find in the episode memory an episode which matches the current situation and execute it.

OTHERWISE: Perform some random action like e. g. foraging.

In the *OBSERVE* and *APPLY* mode the action selection by the emotion system has no influence. The behavior system is entirely controlled by the *imitation system*. In the mode *OTHERWISE*, the *emotion system* takes over the control. If the *imitation system* has decided which action to execute it forwards this choice to the *behavior system* which has the task to transform it into a set of detailed action commands that can be passed to the actuators. Arkin showed how this can be straightforwardly accomplished using *Motor Schemes* [3].

The *behavior, emotion,* and *imitation system* will now be described in more detail using an example application for illustrating and evaluating the concepts: A two-dimensional simulation environment has been set up, in which ten agents are simulated for 10,000 time steps per simulation run, with the aim to feel good emotions and avoid bad ones. To achieve this they have to collect flags which are distributed over the whole simulation field and carry them to one of four bins which are located in the corners of the field. The agents dispose of a gripper which they can open, close or put into trigger mode, i. e. it is open until the agent has moved onto a flag. Furthermore, they can move in every direction.

3.1   The Behavior System

The task of the behavior system is to translate the abstract behaviors into more detailed atomic actions that can be executed by it's actuators: the motor and the gripper. To the emotion and imitation system it offers a repertoire of ten complex behaviors. The behavior repertoire can be grouped into two different behavior classes: normal behaviors and imitation behaviors, which are triggered only on behalf of the imitation system. All behaviors are modeled using the Motor Schemes architecture enhanced by application specific utility functions like usage of the gripper or using the imitation interface. Using Motor Schemes simplifies the behavior system to a high degree: Given a two-dimensional field with obstacles $O_1 \ldots O_n$ and one goal G, the Motor Schemes approach calculates a vector field for the agent that shows the agent the way to the goal without interfering with the obstacles. This can be easily achieved by having a vector field for each obstacle O with vectors pointing diametrically away (`AvoidObstacle`) and one vector field for the goal where all vectors point toward the goal (`MoveToGoal`). Now, all the vector fields which are atomic behaviors can be simply combined by superposition. In addition, at each time step the calculation has only to be performed for the agent's current position and not for each point in the whole two-dimensional field. Combining atomic behaviors, the basic behaviors are constructed, which will be introduced in the following.

Normal Behaviors. The normal behaviors are *STOP, WANDER, ACQUIRE, DELIVER1* to *DELIVER4*, and *DROP* and have the following function:

STOP: Stand still and do nothing with the gripper.

WANDER: Wander around in random direction to find some flags. Gripper is opened.

ACQUIRE: Approach the nearest flag with gripper in trigger modus, i. e. that it closes its gripper if the flag is in the gripper.

DELIVER(1-4): Move toward bin 1, 2, 3, or 4. Only applicable if the agent holds a flag in its gripper.

DROP: Lie down the flag in the gripper and move away from the flag's position.

Imitation Specific Behaviors. The imitation system's functionality has been implemented by the two behaviors *OBSERVE* and *APPLY*. They have the possibility to access the agent's episode memory and to read the observed agent's emotion system's state directly.

OBSERVE: An agent can observe any agent within a predefined radius. This behavior takes care of keeping close distance to the observed agent so that the observation is not interrupted. While observing, the executed behavior and emotional state change of the observed agent is recorded at every time step. Every time the observing agent has to make a decision on the following three possibilities:

- Observe further since the collected data is useful so far.
- Stop observation, because the recorded data contains no valuable information.
- Stop observation and refine the recorded data for storing into the episode memory.

Its result is based on the emotional change of the observed agent. If the quality (cf. equation (1)) has changed significantly ($\Delta G \geq \Delta_S$, $\Delta_S = 0.2$) in the considered time frame the episode will be extracted and saved in the episode memory. Otherwise, it will be forgotten. The episode's start is set to the behavior immediately preceding the first rise of quality. Its end is set to the behavior immediately succeeding the last rise of quality. Then, the episode is compressed, meaning that only behaviors that at least increase the quality by Δ_B ($\Delta G \geq \Delta_B$, $\Delta_B = 0.09$) are left in the episode. The episode memory is limited to ten memory entries. If it is already full, an episode with a lower quality value than the newly observed episode is abandoned, and the new episode is ready to be used the next time the agent executes the *APPLY* behavior. The values Δ_S, Δ_B, and the size for the episode memory have been determined empirically.

APPLY: In this behavior the agent has to choose which one of the previously collected episodes is the best one to apply in the current situation. To solve this problem the agent looks at the G values of every episode and at the individual emotion's changes. But, these values have been observed only with another agent. It does not mean that these emotion changes will appear if the observing agent is applying the episode's behavior by itself. To tackle this problem the emotional differences are adjusted after every application. This way, the agent can filter out badly observed episodes or correctly observed episodes that do not work for it. Let ΔE_k be the observed episode's difference for the emotion k before and after the application, and ΔEA_k its difference at the actual application. Then the emotional difference is adjusted as follows: $\Delta E_k \longleftarrow 0.9 \cdot \Delta E_k + 0.1 \cdot \Delta EA_k$ Using this adjustment, also the problem of "eternal episodes" could be solved, which occurs, when an observed episode specifies certain emotional increases which are never perceived when the agent applies the episode the first time.

3.2 The Emotion System

The driving force behind the propagation of memes in this work is the agent's emotion system: memes will only be copied from one agent to another if they serve the well being of the imitating agent, i. e. the execution of its behavior sequence proved as being advantageous.

MEXI [12] and Kismet [8] have successfully shown how emotions can be modeled and expressed using an algorithmic approach. In this work, MEXI's emotion architecture has been adopted, offering a triple-tower architecture with its middle tower (the behavior system) enhanced by an emotion system. This is responsible for setting the action selection bias towards actions that will result in a better emotional feeling. Differently from MEXI, the emotion system in this work does not directly affect the behavior system in action selection. Instead, the output of the emotion system works only as an advice for the imitation system which has been inserted between the behavior system and the emotion system (cf. Fig 1). Ultimately, the imitation system chooses which actions are executed.

At the beginning, when no episodes have been observed yet, the emotion system's choices for behavior are accepted by the imitation and forwarded directly to the behavior system. In the long run, when the imitation system has gathered many beneficial episodes these episodes are preferred to the emotional system's choices.

The emotion system controls the emotions and drives. The emotions can be positive or negative ones and are real values in the range $[0, 1]$ having a threshold value. In this work we distinguish the positive emotion "joy" and the negative emotion "anger". If the positive emotion's threshold is exceeded or the value for the negative emotion falls below the threshold those emotions are said to be satisfied and the agent "feels good". Otherwise, the emotions system tries to get back to the satisfied area. In this work only one drive is used – the drive *Imitation*, which controls the recurrent phases *OBSERVE* and *APPLY*. The drive's value ranges in the interval $[-1, 1]$ and has two thresholds – a positive and a negative. The area between those thresholds is called the homeostatic area, meaning that the drive is satisfied. The drive is connected to the *OBSERVE* and *APPLY* phases with their corresponding behaviors. If the value for *Imitation* exceeds the positive threshold it is an indicator that the emotion system has the bias to observe other agents. In the other case, if the value crossed the negative threshold, the imitation system would try to apply some previously observed episode. In both cases the emotion system is not obstinately switching to the corresponding behavior. Instead, it only modifies its inclination toward the behavior by means of its configuration, as with MEXI. It is important to note that the choice of behaviors is no discrete action. Instead, as modeled in the MEXI architecture, emotions *configure* the individual behavior weights. In the end, the final configuration is calculated by the configuration suggestions of each emotion [12].

The internal state of an agent is completely described by its emotions. To ease the comparison between two emotional states, which is necessary in the *OBSERVE* phase, the quality G describing the desirability of an emotional state is introduced. Let P and N be the number of positive and negative emotions, respectively. Further, let $E_{k,p}$ denote the positive and $E_{l,n}$ the negative emotions with $k \in [1, \ldots, P]$, $l \in [1, \ldots, N]$, and w_i the individual emotion weights denoting its impact on the overall quality. Then the quality G is calculated as defined in Formula (1).

$$G = \sum_{k=1}^{P} w_k \cdot E_{k,p} + \sum_{l=1}^{N} w_l \cdot (1 - E_{l,n}) . \tag{1}$$

Now, an episode Q lasting from time t_1 to t_2 can be easily classified depending on the quality value before t_1 and after t_2:

$$G_{t_2} > G_{t_1} \Rightarrow \text{Episode } Q \text{ is favorable}$$
$$G_{t_2} \leq G_{t_1} \Rightarrow \text{Episode } Q \text{ is not favorable}$$

How do external stimuli affect the emotions? Emotions in real life have interesting time dependent properties. E. g. the emotion *anger* decays over time if the initial anger evoking stimulus has ceased. This behavior is modeled with the help of excitation functions. Combining emotions with excitation functions and external stimuli, Fig. 2 shows exemplarily how the emotion anger develops. In this diagram the diagonally hatched areas stand for negative stimuli, the horizontally hatched areas for positive ones. At $t = 2$ a small negative stimulus arouses anger to a small degree. At $t = 3$ the stimuli has increased its intensity resulting in a

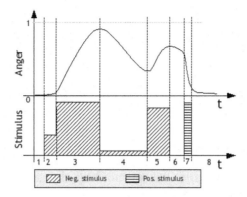

Fig. 2. Example: The responsiveness of anger at negative and positive stimuli.

steep rise of the emotion anger. At the time step 4 still a negative stimulus is perceived by the agent. However, since the excitation function is stronger than the small stimulus, the anger is decreased. Finally, at $t = 7$ a positive stimulus results in a steep decrease of anger's intensity.

3.3   The Imitation System

The act of imitation is made up of the following three processes [7]:

1. **Recognition** of successful action sequences.
2. **Transformation** of these sequences from the perspective of the *demonstrator* into the perspective of the *imitator*.
3. **Generation** of the according action sequence.

Recognition and transformation is the task of the *OBSERVE* behavior. Generation is the domain of *APPLY*. The question, when to observe other agents and when to apply the observed episodes is addressed by the emotion system and its cyclic property of oscillating between the according two phases.

Because the agents have no possibility to see some kind of gesture or facial expression of the observed agent they need another means by which they can judge the outcome of the recently executed episode. Because the agent society is run in a simulation environment a direct interface to the observed agent's "mind" was implemented into the architecture, enabling reading of the recently executed action and emotional state.

As in real life the human interpretation of emotional expression is always faulty, some noise in the interface readings is needed to be more realistic. However, the noise has not been added to the readings directly. Instead the agents have to find out the beginnings and ends of observed episodes in a stream of observed behaviors by themselves. In this way, uncertainty has been added and mutation of memes is enabled. The observer has three data entities at his disposal: The observed emotion state prior to an action, the action itself, and the observed emotion state immediately after the behavior execution. To quantify an emotional state to make it comparable the quality G that is computed out of the emotional state's components as described in section 3.2 is used. The more favorable an emotional state is the higher is the value of G. Taken an episode that lasts from time step t_1 till t_2 an episode is said to be favorably if $G_{t_2} > G_{t_1}$. In this case the agent has to process the episode's data and save it for the according emotional state. While executing the OBSERVE behavior the quality of the observed agent's emotions is monitored at every time step. In case that it is not increasing over a predefined period of time the OBSERVE behavior is canceled. It does not suffice to record only the executed behaviors. If, e. g., an agent only records the action sequence (A_1, A_2, A_3) it does not know when the state changes $A_1 \rightarrow A_2$ and $A_2 \rightarrow A_3$ have occured. In addition, the events that triggered the behaviors have to be saved. Here, the changes of the emotions are treated as event triggers. If an emotion has increased or decreased more than a predefined value this change is considered as being a trigger for the following executed behavior of the observed agent. If the observer is executing this episode in the future, it will not switch to the next episode step or behavior until it is registering at least the same emotional changes.

The episode memory Z consists of up to z_{max} memory entries $Z_i = (E, O, T)$, which stands for episode, originator, and time-stamp, respectively. The triggers or preconditions that must be met before the next behavior in that episode can be executed are stored together with the behavior itself. Thus, an episode entry is a tuple (C, b) with C being the emotional preconditions for the behavior b and b the number of the corresponding behavior. Every time the agent has observed an apparently advantageous episode and saves it in its episode memory it also updates its mapping from emotional states to episodes. This way it always knows which episode to execute at the current emotional state.

4   Application Example

As already stated a flag capturing environment is used as an application example (cf. section 3). Since the basic behaviors for this application were already described in section 3.1 this section concentrates on the agent's emotion system. In this example, it controls the positive emotion *joy*, the negative emotion *anger*, and the drive *imitation*. The threshold values of both emotions are fixed, but the drive's thresholds are dynamically adjusted to be more flexible when a more greedy or wacky behavior is needed.

Impact of Stimuli on the Emotions Joy and Anger. The agent's perception system is able to extract the following perceptual predicates out of the environment: *FlagVisible* is true, if a flag outside a bin is visible. *FlagInGripper* is true, if the agent holds a flag. *StayingInBin* is true, if the agent stays in one of the four bins. These predicates' impact on the agent's emotion system is listed in Table (1).

The Role of the Imitation Drive. For simplicity reasons the drive's meaning has been changed compared to Plutchik. In this work, the single drive *imitation* has the only purpose of controlling the *OBSERVE* and *APPLY* phases together

Table 1. *Impact of perceptions on emotions.* Meaning of impact column: "↑": increase, "↓": decrease, "↑↑": strong increase, "↓↓": strong decrease, "⋆": only the first time of occurrence and once more only after a longer period of time.

Perception	true		false	
FlagVisible	Joy	⋆ ↑↑	Joy	↓
	Anger	⋆ ↓↓	Anger	↑
FlagInGripper	Joy	⋆ ↑↑	Joy	↓
	Anger	↓	Anger	↑
StayingInBin	Joy	⋆ ↑↑	—	

with their corresponding behaviors. Its thresholds mark the point where the agent has the possibility to switch to the according behavior. The interval between the positive and negative threshold is called the homeostatic area, where the agent's drive is satisfied. As opposed to Plutchik, the drive is not returning to the homeostatic area when the proper behavior is executed in the *APPLY* mode. Instead, the drive's state is locked until the agent has managed to execute all episode steps contained in the imitated episode.

Impact of the Emotions and the Drive on the Choice of Behaviors. The values of the emotions and drives affect the bias toward their individual preferred behaviors. If an emotion is not satisfied it can strengthen or reduce its bias of a behavior that could satisfy or prevent it. In this work we just reduced the biases of the two imitation related behaviors in favor of the other behaviors that yield a more direct effect. The drive's role is for controlling reasons but works similar via bias adjustments. The impact of the emotions and drives are listed in Table 2.

5   Evaluation

To achieve the goal of demonstrably showing the performance improvement of simple imitation an agent society consisting of ten agents was simulated. For that purpose we used the TeamBots[1] package which provides a full range of simulation supporting software modules. The agent society's learning success can be investigated in two ways: 1) By simply measuring the performance increase,

Table 2. *Impact of the emotions "joy" and "anger" and the drive "imitation" on the choice of behaviors.* ">": exceeding its threshold, "<": falling below the threshold. "∼": the homeostatic area. "↑"/"↓": increase/decrease of the preference of the behavior.

Emotion	Threshold	Impact
Joy	>	*OBSERVE* ↓
	<	—
Anger	>	—
	<	*APPLY* ↓

Drive	Threshold	Impact
Imitation	>	*OBSERVE* ↑
	∼	*OBSERVE* ↓
		APPLY ↓
	<	*APPLY* ↑

---

[1] www.teambots.org

and 2) by analyzing the agent society's diversity, i. e. how the agents disperse to groups using similar behavioral patterns. Each simulation (also called a simulation round) consists of 10,000 steps. To achieve meaningful results, the simulation has been consecutively executed 100 times. After the first round each simulation used the learned episodes from the previous round, but randomized the agents' and flags' positions. This simulation of 100 rounds was repeated 80 times from scratch (called a simulation run). Afterward, an average run is calculated, in which every average nth round is calculated of the average of all the nth rounds in the 80 simulation runs.

In order to screen the learning progress the Wellness-Test has been devised. It calculates the performance measure w for every agent as follows: For every simulation step increase w by one for every satisfied emotion, i.e. if the positive emotion *joy* is above its threshold or the negative emotion *anger* is below its threshold. Since every simulation round consists of 10,000 simulation steps, an agent may collect up to 20,000 Wellness points. This value is reachable only in theory, though, because even the best agent will start its observed action sequences only if one of the emotions is dissatisfied, and this means that it will not get maximum Wellness points for the according simulation step. The average of all ten agents which accounts for the performance of the total agent society is displayed in Fig. 3. The Wellness interval $[0, 20000]$ is transferred to $[0, 1]$. Starting with 0.178 after step 0 the average performance amounts to 0.397 after step 99, which means an increase by approximately 120%.

6   Results

Transferring Shannon's information entropy [17] to the field of society diversity in ethnology (cf. [5]) the overall diversity of the agent society with ten agents in this work can be computed with Formula (2):

$$H(\mathbb{A}) = -\sum_{i=1}^{c} P_i \log_2(P_i) \ . \tag{2}$$

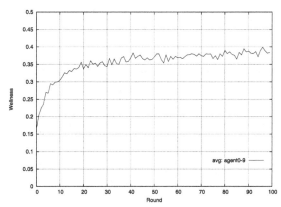

Fig. 3. The average performance regarding to the Wellness-Test over 100 rounds. Every round is the average over 80 runs. The performance increase amounts to $\approx$ 120%.

Here a society $\mathbb{A}$ is subdivided into n clusters $C_1 \ldots C_n$. The proportion of cluster C_i is denoted with $P_i = \frac{|C_i|}{\sum_{j=1}^{n} |C_j|}$. Hence, with ten agents the value for $H(\mathbb{A})$ lies within the interval $[H_{min}, H_{max}]$, where H_{min} denotes the diversity for a totally homogeneous society (all agents in one cluster) and H_{max} is the diversity value if the society is totally diverse, i.e. ten clusters each containing one agent: $H_{min} = 0$, $H_{max} = -10 \cdot (0.1 \cdot log_2(0.1)) \approx 3.322$. The clusters are calculated on the basis of the resemblance of the episode memory of the two agents A_i and A_j, denoted as $D(A_i, A_j)$ in Formula (3):

$$D(A_i, A_j) = \frac{1}{S} \sum_k |\pi_i(k) - \pi_j(k)| . \tag{3}$$

The number of different states is S. $\pi_a(k)$ stands for the episode that agent a is selecting in state k. But how can Episodes be subtracted? The expression $|\pi_i(k) - \pi_j(k)|$ is defined as in Formula (4).

$$|\pi_i(k) - \pi_j(k)| := \begin{cases} 1, & \text{if } E_i \neq E_j \\ 0, & \text{otherwise} \end{cases} . \tag{4}$$

with E_k being the episode memory of agent A_k. Two episode memories are considered different, if there is at least one state for which both agents select different episodes to execute. The state is a two-bit number, with joy corresponding to the higher bit and anger to the lower bit. "1" means that the emotion is satisfied, "0" otherwise. The state $(joy = 1, anger = 1)$ is omitted because in that case the agent is totally content with the actual situation and no episode has to be executed. Having three different states Formula (3) can have the values $1/3$, $2/3$ and 1.0. The grouping into clusters can now be performed for a given resemblance threshold ϵ. That means that two agents are considered to be sufficiently equal for belonging to the same cluster if the following equation is satisfied: $D(A_i, A_j) < \epsilon \iff A_i \equiv_\epsilon A_j$.

In the following the diversity and clustering of the agent society is applied to an example, which is arbitrarily taken from the 80 simulation runs. Diversity and clusters are calculated dependent on the value for ϵ. This has to be set between two possible consecutive values of $D(A_i, A_j)$. In this case we chose the values 0.4, 0.7 and 1.0 for ϵ.

Example. The episodes that the agents have learned after 100 simulation rounds are shown in Table 3. $D(A_i, A_j)$ is calculated in Table 4. Having ϵ set to 0.4 we get the clustering $C = \{\{0, 1, 8\}, \{2\}, \{3, 6, 7\}, \{4, 5\}, \{9\} \}$ and the heterogeneity $H = 2.17095059445$. Comparing this value for H with the heterogeneity interval $[0, 3.322]$ we can say that neither all agents learned the same (then H would be zero) nor learned they very different episodes. Learning has taken place which shows that agents have imitated each other to a certain degree. Doing the calculation for all the values of ϵ the clustering is displayed in Fig. 4 to point out how clusterings are grouped together with an increasing value for ϵ.

Table 3. Example: Learned Episodes of the ten agents after 100 simulation rounds. Legend: W=*WANDER*, A=*ACQUIRE*, D(1-4)=*DELIVER(1-4)*, DR=*DROP*.

Agent	Emotional state k					
	0		1		2	
0	A	D1	A	D1	A	D1
1	A	D1	A	D1	D1	DR
2	D3	DR	D3	DR	A	D2
3	A	D3	A	D3	A	D3
4	D4	DR	D4	DR	D3	DR
5	D4	DR	D4	DR	D3	DR
6	A	D3	A	D3	A	D3
7	A	D3	A	D3	A	D3
8	A	D1	A	D1	A	D1
9	A	D4	A	D4	D1	DR

Table 4. Example: Difference $D(A_i, A_j)$ of the agents' episode memories. $D(A_i, A_j)$ is symmetric, only the triangular matrix is needed.

A	1	2	3	4	5	6	7	8	9
0	1/3	1	1	1	1	1	1	0	1
1		1	1	1	1	1	1	1/3	2/3
2			1	1	1	1	1	1	1
3				1	1	0	0	1	1
4					0	1	1	1	1
5						1	1	1	1
6							0	1	1
7								1	1
8									1

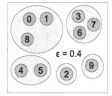 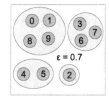

Fig. 4. Example: Clustering with $\epsilon = 0.4$ ($H \approx 2.17$), $\epsilon = 0.7$ ($H \approx 1.85$), and $\epsilon = 1.0$ ($H = 0$). The numbers in the circles denote the agents.

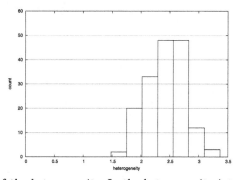

Fig. 5. Histogram of the heterogeneity. In the heterogeneity interval [0,3.322] the average of all runs is $H_{avg} = 2.57$.

Meaning of the Heterogeneity Values. Relating the heterogeneity of all last rounds in the 80 runs, the distribution can be seen in the histogram of Figure 5. It divides the histogram interval in seven non-zero areas. The height of each box stands for the number of runs in which the heterogeneity of the agent society after the last round lied in the area's interval. The average heterogeneity is $H_{avg} = 2.57$. Hence, in this work for the heterogeneity interval [0, 3.322] the average agent society is approximately $\frac{3.322-2.57}{3.322} = \frac{0.752}{3.322} \approx 0.23$, that means 23% homogeneous. How can this homogeneity rate be evaluated? It means that although some measurable amount of the agent society adopted behaviors of other agents, there has been left room for the development of new behaviors.

7   Discussion and Outlook

In this paper an agent architecture has been described that enables agents to learn behavioral patterns also called "action sequences" through imitation. Investigations have been conducted how those agents develop a kind of society by means of similar episodes they execute in the same states. It could be shown that using this kind of architecture the average learning performance of the agent society can substantially be improved, i.e. clusters of agents are emerging, where the individual agent's performance increases with more and more imitated episodes.

In dynamic environments where the future development is not predictable, imitation can pave the way for agent societies to adapt appropriately. Thus, we see imitation as being a cornerstone for organic systems. We plan to investigate how physical agents perform with such an architecture. Equipped with full-colored LEDs expressing emotions it will be both more realistic but also difficult. Future work should also investigate, how goals can be incorporated in an emotion system that is used in technical applications to achieve a truly goal-directed behavior of a complete system. Furthermore, it would be interesting to find out how memes, i.e. the episodes, change in detail when being transferred from one agent to another, if more realistic randomization effects could be deployed.

References

1. *The Oxford English Dictionary*. Oxford University Press.
2. A. Alissandrakis, C. Nehaniv, and K. Dautenhahn. Learning how to do things with imitation, 2000.
3. R. C. Arkin. *Behaviour-Based Robotics*. MIT Press, 1998.
4. Christopher G. Atkeson and Stefan Schaal. Robot learning from demonstration. In *Proc. 14th International Conference on Machine Learning*, pages 12–20. Morgan Kaufmann, 1997.
5. Tucker Balch. *Behavioral Diversity in Learning Robot Teams*. PhD thesis, Georgia Institute of Technology, December 1998.
6. A. Billard. Learning motor skills by imitation: a biologically inspired robotic model, 2000.
7. Susan Blackmore. *The Meme Machine*. Oxford University Press, 1999.
8. C. Breazeal and B. Scassellati. How to build robots that make friends and influence people, 1999.
9. R. Dawkins. *The Selfish Gene*. Oxford University Press, Oxford, 1976.
10. Demiris, J. and Hayes, G. Imitation as a dual-route process featuring predictive and learning components: a biologically-plausible computational model. 2001.

11. Elhanan Borenstein and Eytan Ruppin. Enhancing autonomous agents evolution with learning by imitation. In *Second International Symposium on Imitation in Animals and Artifacts*, 2003.

12. Natascha Esau, Bernd Kleinjohan, Lisa Kleinjohann, and Dirk Stichling. Mexi: Machine with emotionally extended intelligence, 2003.

13. Yiannis Gatsoulis, George Maistros, Yuval Marom, and Gillian Hayes. Learning to forage through imitation. In *Proceedings of the Second IASTED International Conference on Artificial Intelligence and Applications (AIA2002)*, pages 485–491, September 2002.

14. Nils J. Nilsson. *Artificial Intelligence: A New Synthesis*. Morgan Kaufmann Publishers, San Francisco, 1998.

15. R. Plutchik. *The Emotions*. University Press of America, 1991.

16. S. Schaal. Dynamic movement primitives – a framework for motor control in humans and humanoid robotics. *The International Symposium on Adaptive Motion of Animals and Machines*, 2003.

17. C. E. Shannon. A mathematical theory of communication. *Bell System Technical Journal*, 27:379–423 and 623–656, July and October 1948.

18. Sutton and Barto. *Reinforcement Learning: An Introduction*. MIT Press, Cambridge, 1998.

19. Karsten Weicker. *Evolutionäre Algorithmen*. Teubner, 2002.

Self-healing Execution of Business Processes
Based on a Peer-to-Peer Service Architecture

Thomas Friese[1,2], Jörg P. Müller[2], and Bernd Freisleben[1]

[1] Dept. of Mathematics and Computer Science, University of Marburg
Hans-Meerwein-Str, D-35032 Marburg, Germany
{friese,freisleb}@informatik.uni-marburg.de
[2] Siemens AG Corporate Technology, Intelligent Autonomous Systems,
Otto-Hahn-Ring 6, D-81739 München, Germany
joerg.p.mueller@siemens.com

Abstract. The automated execution of business processes that are composed of individual web services has seen a growing importance throughout enterprise computing in the recent years. The Business Process Execution Language for Web Services (BPEL4WS) has become the predominant language to express such business process compositions. In this paper we present the design and implementation of a Robust Execution Layer that acts as a transparent, configurable add-on to any BPEL4WS execution engine to support self-healing execution of business processes. Resilience of the process execution is achieved through service replacement in case of communication failures, by relying on a robust peer-to-peer service discovery and selection mechanism for alternative services.

1 Introduction

The availability of web-service based middleware has opened new possibilities for business process automation. Web service infrastructures and in particular the WSDL [1] and UDDI [2] standards provide a unified way of describing, registering, and looking up services, and of binding service descriptions to service instances. The service-oriented computing metaphor can be applied in a natural way to model business processes as compositions of individual service requests, which can be mapped to web service calls. The Business Process Execution Language for Web Services (BPEL4WS; in the remainder of this paper abbreviated as BPEL for the sake of simplicity) [3] is probably the best known example of an executable business process language.

A shortcoming of today's business process languages is that the runtime infrastructure supporting them does not provide a great deal of flexibility as to how exceptions and errors are handled. Rather, a lot of the underlying logic in how to deal with failures at execution time needs to be defined at design time and programmed into the process description code.

Over the past few years, peer-to-peer (P2P) computing has been emerging as an architectural approach for building distributed software systems (mostly focusing on distributed resource management) that provides built-in, low-cost, and highly scalable mechanisms for ensuring software resilience.

The objective of the research described in this paper is to bring together the strengths of state-of-the-art service-based business process execution languages and

M. Beigl and P. Lukowicz (Eds.): ARCS 2005, LNCS 3432, pp. 108–123, 2005.

infrastructures (exemplified by BPEL) on the one hand, and of P2P architectures on the other. In particular, we present the design and implementation of a middleware framework called Robust Execution Layer (REL) that acts as a transparent, configurable add-on to any BPEL execution engine to support the self-healing execution of business processes that are managed by the engine. By using P2P protocols managing service registration and lookup, REL provides improved service-level resilience without the explicit need of additional dedicated hardware or communication redundancy, reducing the management overhead for centralized components.

In designing the robust execution layer, a number of technical problems needed to be solved, including the management of the execution context of multiple process instances. The paper presents architectural and methodic approaches to solve these problems. The underlying P2P architecture has been developed in the context of the European Integrated Project ATHENA [4]. ATHENA addresses the vision of seamless interoperation of distributed enterprises across and beyond Europe, focusing on the problem of interoperability, but also covering aspects such as cross-enterprise business process modeling and architectures and platforms for business process management and enactment (see also [5]).

The structure of the paper is as follows: In Section 2, we briefly introduce the BPEL language, discuss levels of resilience, and identify basic requirements and problems to be solved in adding resilience to business process execution. Section 3 introduces the REL architecture and outlines the basic components and their interaction. Section 4 presents an example scenario for the usage of REL. Related work is discussed in Section 5. Section 6 concludes the paper and outlines areas of future work.

2 Problem Description

In this section we will give an introduction to the basic principles of BPEL and analyze a number of problems that need to be addressed to provide self-healing execution support in the case of a partner service failure. Throughout the discussion, we will consider RPC style interactions with partner web services using SOAP [6] encoded messages that are transferred via the HTTP protocol. However the principles discussed in this section can also be applied to message or document based interaction with web services.

2.1 BPEL Basics

The Business Process Execution Language for Web Services has emerged from the earlier proposed XLANG [7] and Web Service Flow Language (WSFL) [8]. It enables the construction of complex web services composed from other web services that act as the basic activities in the process model of the newly constructed service. BPEL offers a conceptual distinction between *abstract* processes that describe the external view on the process model and *executable* processes that describe the workflow of the compound service and can be executed by a process execution engine in order to provide the functionality of the compound service to a client. The specification of an executable process basically defines a blueprint that models the stateful interaction and is used by the execution engine to derive a *process instance*. This process instance captures the state of the interaction with all external web services and clients as well as internal state data used throughout the process workflow. Access to the process is exposed by the execution engine through a web service interface, allowing those processes to be accessed by web service clients or to act as basic activities in other process specifications.

In traditional workflow management systems, a business process is represented by a workflow model. This model consists of a number of basic activities and describes their order of execution. Similarly, BPEL models business processes as sequences of basic activities and introduces control constructs such as loops or conditional branches [9]. The most important activities offered by BPEL for the business process specification are the *invoke* and *receive* activities. The invoke activity is used to invoke external services while the receive activity enables the process to collect external input and delay further execution of the process flow until reception of this input. In the web service interface exposed by the execution engine, the receive activity is represented by an operation provided to clients to invoke and pass parameter values to the process instance during its execution.

The state of a business process includes the previously exchanged messages between partners as well as temporary data used in the process flow. To catch this state data, BPEL offers the ability to define and modify *variables* in the workflow of a business process. Variables may be typed as WSDL message types, XML Schema [10] simple types or elements.

A number of different process instances derived from the same process specification may be created by the process execution engine upon service requests received from different clients. Messages from the clients to the business process are directed towards a single web service port. While this addressing is sufficient to determine the process specification corresponding to the port or port type, another mechanism is required to identify the correct process instance that should receive the message. BPEL defines the concept of *correlation sets* in order to enable the engine to carry out instance-level routing of messages.

A correlation set is a group of message properties that are sufficient to identify the process instance a message has to be delivered to during the process conversation. The correlation properties can be regarded as late bound constants that are initiated and assigned by a specially marked message.

Activities in a BPEL process are associated with a surrounding scope that holds definitions for variables and correlation sets as well as *event handlers*, *fault handlers* and a *compensation handler*. Event handlers and fault handlers provide a mechanism to respond to messages or faults emitted by activities or external partner services. They are active process logic embedded in the process specification that allows for the termination of activities and the reversal of effects caused by prior execution of activities.

2.2 Fault Conditions

Consider the process execution environment shown in Fig. 1.An operation f provided by a partner service is invoked by the process P. The call is encoded as a SOAP message and transmitted via HTTP to the service provider where some service middleware decodes the SOAP message and hands the call to the specific implementation

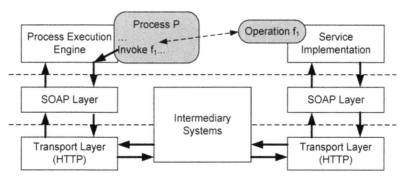

Fig. 1. Process execution environment: The process execution engine encodes service invocations as SOAP messages that are transported via HTTP, received at the service provider after passing possible intermediary systems, decoded and passed to the actual service.

the service. The result of the call is then again encoded as a SOAP reply and transmitted via HTTP to the process engine. Fault conditions can arise at three different levels in this interaction:

- Application specific errors may occur during the processing of the request in the service implementation.
- The service middleware may produce errors during the decoding or encoding of messages if, for example, no suitable serializers are available to encode certain result contents.
- There may be communication failures in the transport protocol. The service provider may not be reachable due to network interruption or system failure.

While errors on the upper two levels are content or application related, a possible recovery from communication failures may be the replacement of the original service by another service that also provides the operation f_1. In this case, the whole process could be successfully finished in spite of communication failures with the originally contacted service provider.

2.3 Realizing of Fault Recovery in the Process Execution Environment

We now present three different ways to realize fault recovery by replacing a service with another service of the same type within the BPEL process execution environment.

The replacement of a service can be seen as a dynamic partner binding that can be addressed at the process specification level and thus can be encoded in the process specification itself. In this case, the activity to invoke $A.f_1$ is preceded by a directory lookup for services that implement the required port type (i.e. the port type of service A). Then, a loop is added to surround the invoke activity that consecutively replaces the invocation target with one of the services returned by the registry lookup operation until the invoke activity can successfully be carried out. The structural changes to the process specification are shown in Fig. 2. Such a change to the specification of invoke activities would have to be explicitly encoded around every service invocation that is intended to be performed in a more robust way throughout the whole process. We will refer to this alteration of the process specification as *intra- process recovery*.

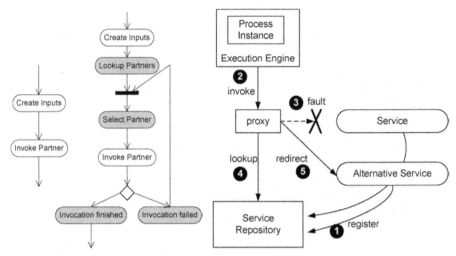

Fig. 2. Structural changes to a process specification when dynamic partner binding is added to an invoke activity.

Fig. 3. Redirection of an invocation message after a communications failure and service lookup.

Similar actions may be implemented in the underlying process middleware (i.e. the process execution engine or the communications infrastructure used to actually transmit the SOAP calls emitted by the execution engine). Communication failures can be detected through expiry of a timeout period. If this event occurs, either (a) the engine or (b) a component in the communication infrastructure may perform registry lookup for alternative invocation targets and reroute the message to an alternative service implementation (this behavior is depicted in Fig. 3). The intermediary system in the communications infrastructure may be implemented as a HTTP or SOAP aware proxy. Therefore, we will refer to the approaches (a) and (b) as *intra-engine recovery* and *proxy recovery*, respectively.

The alteration of the process offers the best way to control the semantics of the compensation action to be associated with an invoke activity. Control of the partner binding can be specified in a very flexible way and the decision to armor certain invocations can be determined on a very fine-grained level. On the other hand, it also poses the need to alter the process specification and introduce additional code at a very fine-grained level. A number of operations need to be introduced for every invoke activity leading to process "code" that contains robustness additions eventually exceeding the size of the original process code.

The realization of the recovery strategy within the infrastructure – either as an intra-engine solution or as a proxy solution – does not require changes to the process specification, therefore no additional code has to be introduced in the process specification. The robust invocation of partner services is an inherent, possibly configurable feature carried out in an autonomous manner by the execution environment. In the case of an engine neutral implementation as a proxy instead of an altered specific engine, one is not bound to the concrete implementation or engine features. Furthermore, the feature might be added to the process execution environment without control of the implementation of the process execution engine.

2.4 Dependencies Between Activities and Process Instances

In the preceding sections we considered only one invoke activity in the flow of the process. We will now look at an extended example process P_1 that specifies the invocation of a sequence of operations (A.f_1, B.g_1, A.f_2) provided by two partner services A and B. If communication with partner A cannot be established and the infrastructure replaces service A by an alternative service A* for invocation of the operation f_1, it is very likely that there is an implicit connection between A.f_1 and A.f_2 that requires the subsequent invocation of f_2 to also be directed towards A* instead of A. If, for example, A is a hotel accommodation service, f_1 represents a booking function of this service and f_2 a payment verification function, both of these operations have to be used within the same instance of the accommodation service.

The recovery mechanism for invocation failures is built on the assumption that there are at least two distinct instances of the service of type A to choose from. BPEL only offers the options of a static binding to a partner or an explicitly expressed dynamic partner binding through additional mechanisms encoded in the process flow. A conservative and safe assumption for an infrastructure solution that provides invocation robustness through replacement of service instances is to assume that the first invocation of an operation on one service instance selects this service instance for every subsequent invocation. While the process specification determines the type of service to be invoked, the infrastructure holds the ability to select among a set of service instances that implement this service type. After selecting a particular instance, this instance has to be used for every interaction occurring throughout the lifecycle of a process instance derived from the process specification.

It might be desirable to explicitly tighten or relax the service instance binding through internal or external annotation of the business process. Situations may occur where subsequent invocations of operations provided by a service are truly independent and can be directed towards different instances of the service. In other cases, a strict binding to the specified service is desired that should under no circumstances be altered to another service instance implementing the same service type. As an example consider a business process to handle the billing and charging of customers. A contract might bind the service requestor to use the credit card service of one particular company. In this case, it is undesirable to replace the service in case of a communication failure, even if other companies provide an equivalent service.

Now consider a situation in which two clients X and Y requested the creation of process Instances I_{1x} and I_{1y} derived from P_1. An implementation of the process execution engine has to hold state information for both instances. It can easily extend this state information to incorporate the binding between the process instance and the service instances used. A proxy implementation which is completely decoupled from the process execution engine only receives the SOAP requests emitted by the process execution engine. This information contains the target endpoint used for the communication as well as the message format and message values encoded in the request. Consider the above scenario where I_{1x} and I_{1y} invoke two operations f_1 and f_2 on service A. If the invocation of f_1 gets redirected to A* for I_{1x} but reaches A in the case of invocation by I_{1y}, the proxy has to identify the process instance that executed the invocation activity in order to determine whether to redirect the call to A* or directly call A when a subsequent request for A.f_2 reaches the proxy. This situation is illustrated in Fig. 4. If another Process P_2 that uses A is instantiated as I_{2x} in the engine,

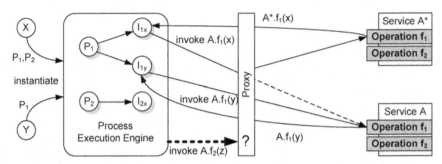

Fig. 4. Two process instances emit a message to operation A.f_1. After redirecting one of the invocations, the proxy has to determine an invocation target for a subsequent invocation to A.f_2.

the proxy must also be able to distinguish this instance from the instances derived from the other process specifications.

Information about the process instance may be either explicitly or implicitly encoded in the messages passing through the proxy. An explicit encoding requires the alteration of the business process to emit some instance identification token. This token must be enclosed in every message exchanges with external partner services, therefore the input message format of these services must be altered. This solution is not satisfactory.

A more transparent solution would require the process execution engine to emit the instance identification token transparently to the process and partner services. It could be attached as a SOAP message header to every message emitted by the process execution engine. This mechanism would allow the development of loosely coupled infrastructure components that are not tied to a specific engine implementation but enable these components to distinguish process instances participating in a business interaction. This solution requires a modification of the communication standard implemented by process execution engines.

BPEL addresses a similar problem of instance routing of inbound messages through the concept of correlation sets (see section 2.1). With the definition of *outbound correlation sets* over message properties used in *invoke* activities, a proxy implementation is in a similar way able to correlate a message with the process instance that is the originator of the message exchange. This approach has some limitations: Since BPEL correlation sets are intended to be used on the messages that are inbound to a process, the developer has much greater control over the message specification used in the conversation. For a given set of external services it might be impossible to find a common set of message properties that can be used as a correlation set throughout the whole conversation. Furthermore, a distinction between instances derived from two process specifications that use the same message for initialization of the outbound correlation set is difficult.

3 Design and Implementation of a Robust Execution Layer

In this section, we present the design and implementation of a peer-to-peer based robust execution layer for business processes, addressing the problems and requirements outlined in Section 2. The basic idea of the REL is to provide handling capabilities for low level communication faults in the interaction of a business process engine with external web service providers. By doing so, the business process is protected from failures due to propagated errors that are caused by the low level communication faults.

P2P systems [11] are designed to be self-healing loosely coupled networks of independent nodes. The nodes of the P2P network collaboratively provide a service to each other – such as item storage, lookup and retrieval – that can dynamically adapt to a large number of nodes as well as withstand frequent node arrivals and departures from the network. P2P systems incorporate mechanisms to handle peak loads of information requests as well as sporadic node failures. To discover services, a service repository is needed. In the case of a centralized repository one party has to provide this repository while in the P2P network all involved partners collaborate to operate the needed service repository reducing the maintenance overhead for centralized components in the system. Additionally, P2P schemes have been developed that allow service providers to retain firm control of the information they publish to a service repository. These inherent design principles of P2P systems are ideal properties to be used as an adaptive and resilient information repository in the REL.

The design of the robust execution layer is intended to avoid the need to alter the implementation of the business process execution engine, the business process specification or the implementation of the partner services. As described in Section 2.3, the intra-process as well as the intra-engine recovery realization impose the need for those changes. Therefore, the REL is designed as an intermediary component in the communications infrastructure that intercepts message exchanges between the process execution engine and external services. This intermediary component is basically a SOAP proxy that receives service calls from the process execution engine for added resilience this proxy could in turn be implemented as redundant failover system. As a first step, the proxy has to determine the primary target service for the message. There are two possibilities for the selection of the primary target service:

1. The target service originally requested by the execution engine, if a strict binding to a specific service instance has been specified or no prior interaction between the process execution engine and the service of a specific type has determined a strict binding to another service instance.

2. A different target service that has been selected during prior interaction between the process instance and a specific service instance chosen as an alternative invocation target due to communication faults.

The REL will then try to pass the message on to the primary target service and relay the results of a successful invocation to the process execution engine. Another component of the REL – the *endpoint mapper* - is used to determine a different target service for invocation if no communication link can be established and a deviation from the original invocation target is allowed. This deviation is only allowed in the first case above, when no strict binding has been specified (e.g. through process annotation). The question whether an alternative target of the invocation is required, allowed or prohibited is answered by the *process instance manager* of the REL. The attempt to contact different implementations of a specific service type may be repeated upon subsequent communication faults. If no link can be established at all, the error condition is passed on to the process execution engine where fault handling mechanisms specified for the business process have to ultimately deal with the error.

The purpose of the endpoint mapper is the discovery of alternative services for a given target endpoint. It first needs to determine the type of the target service (i.e. the port types implemented by the service that is associated with the original target endpoint). Afterwards, it must query a service repository to find other services that implement the same port types. A centralized service repository is a single point of failure in the overall system. Therefore, the endpoint mapper of our robust execution layer is implemented on top of a P2P system that provides mechanisms for the storage and retrieval of key-value-pairs in a robust way even under node failure.

For the purpose of instance identification and the initial identification of partner services associated with the business process specifications we use a *process repository connector* to realize access to the set of process specifications that have been deployed in the business process execution engine. Access to the process specifications is optional and only needed to allow an implementation of the *process instance manager* to determine the process instance that is the originator of a specific service call.

The resulting component design of the REL with an embedded business process execution engine as well as some partner service providers is illustrated in Fig. 5. The core interfaces of the central components used by the REL proxy are illustrated in Fig. 6. Supporting classes as well as the factories for the process instance manager as well as the process repository connector components are omitted for brevity.

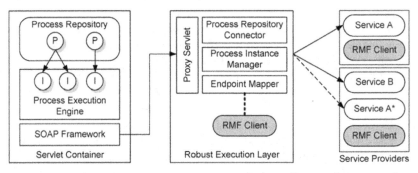

Fig. 5. Components of the Robust Execution Layer acting as an intermediary system between the process execution engine and the service providers.

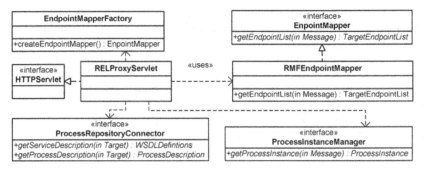

Fig. 6. Core interfaces used by the REL proxy. The factory pattern is used for all components in analogy to the EndpointMapperFactory.

We use the IBM Business Process Execution Language for Web Services Java Run Time (BPWS4J) [12] as the process execution engine with our implementation of the REL. The engine is deployed in a Tomcat servlet container [13] that is configured to use the REL implementation as a proxy for HTTP requests. This is simply achieved by passing the `http.proxyHost` and `http.proxyPort` options to the java virtual machine that is used to load the Tomcat server.

The functionality of the REL is provided to the process execution engine by an implementation of an HTTPServlet. This `RELProxyServlet` works as a transparent HTTP proxy when all robust execution support is disabled. In order to provide the additional functionality, the `RELProxyServlet` uses Factories to instantiate the needed components. The concrete implementation of the corresponding interfaces of these components is configurable by specifying the implementing classes as run time properties. The basic algorithm used by the RELProxyServlet to handle a client request is shown in Fig. 7.

```
receive message

pi = processInstanceManager
      .getProcessInstance(message)

if ( pi.mustRedirect(message.target) )

mesage.changeTarget(
            pi.getRedirectionTarget(message))

deliver(message)

if ( ! message.delivered() )

    targetServiceList = endpointMapper
                    .getEndpointList( message )

while ( pi.allowRedirect(message.target)
        AND
        targetServiceList.hasMoreTargets()
        AND
        ! message.delivered() )

{

        message.changeTarget(
            targetServiceList.getNextTarget() )

        deliver(message)

}
```

Fig. 7. Core message handling algorithm used by the REL proxy servlet.

3.1 P2P Based Service Discovery

A robust lookup component for partner services is a key concept of the REL. In a classical service-oriented implementation of the system, this functionality is provided by a centralized service repository. To construct a more robust system, we implemented this service repository using the Resource Management Framework (RMF) [14].

The RMF is a P2P system that collects a number of nodes to logically provide a single distributed hash table called the *Information Space* of the RMF. This information space allows to publish and retrieve data elements that are called *resources*. Leasing and replication are used to ensure persistence of the published information even under conditions of node failure. The RMF provides mechanisms to modify and search for resources in the information space and to subscribe to resource changes on elements already published or published in the future. Resources in the RMF are XML elements that have the following child elements:

- The mandatory ID of a resource that is used to uniquely identify the element. This can either be a globally unique UUID or some fully qualified hierarchical name, guaranteeing uniqueness of the ID.
- An optional name of the resource to be used as a user friendly name for application independent presentation of the resource.
- An optional list of keywords to be associated with the resource.
- Any number of application specific XML elements.

Developers are free to determine the values of the root element as well as its namespace specification.

When a resource is published in the RMF information space, an internal mapping to peer addresses in the system is calculated to get a list of nodes that are ultimately used to store the resource. The ID and keywords associated with a resource are used to calculate this mapping. The search operation works in two phases. It is directed towards a set of peers that is determined by the same mapping calculation based on a set of given keywords or resource IDs. Afterwards, a query is directed towards this set of peers in order to find the desired information among all resources stored at the specified peers. The XPath query language [15] can be used to formulate queries for resources.

The web service description language is an XML format used to describe web services as a set of endpoints, operations and message formats used in the communication with the service. We have defined a resource format to publish WSDL descriptions of web services in the RMF information space. This mapping from WSDL descriptions to RMF resources is tailored towards answering the query stated by the REL endpoint mapper. A WSDLResource contains the WSDL document as a child element, a generic UUID for identification purposes and the names of the port type, operations and service elements as well as the endpoint address associated with the port definitions of the WSDL document as keywords for the resource.

We use the WSDL4Java [16] API to deserialize WSDL documents into in memory object representations that are then traversed to collect the needed keywords. The REL implementation provides the `WSDL2RMF` class that exposes a set of static `createResource` methods when a WSDL description is either passed as String, Stream or URL reference. The WSDLResource returned by this implementation can then directly be published using the RMF API. The WSDL to RMF mapping is also needed by service providers that wish to publish their services in the information space. Implementing a P2P client that connects to the RMF information space and publishes WSDLResources for a given set of WSDL descriptions is straightforward and requires only a few lines of Java code.

A RMF based implementation of the EndpointMapper interface is provided by the RMFEndpointMapper class. It uses the search method of the RMF API in order to locate the WSDLResource associated with the endpoint address specified in the service invocation that was received by the REL proxy. After retrieval of the WSDLResource from the information space, the endpoint mapper can determine the port type implemented by the target service and issue a second query to the information space that is now based on the port type name. This second query yields a list of registered services that implement the desired port type and are then returned as a list of alternative invocation targets. If the lookup based on the target endpoint address fails (i.e. the service has been unavailable for a long time and the WSDL resource has been pruned from the information space by leasing), the process repository locator is used to determine the port type of the target service.

3.2 Process Repository Connector

The BPWS4J engine uses a set of java server pages for the deployment and removal of processes. Our implementation of the process repository connector is an extension of this management application. It extends the deployment and undeployment functionality by taking a snapshot of the BPEL process specification to be used by the REL. In addition to the process description, the WSDL descriptions of the partner services involved in the business process are captured by the process repository connector.

The BPEL specification respectively the WSDL descriptions are parsed to collect a set of port type to service endpoint mappings that can later on be used if the port type of a service can not be resolved by a query to the RMF. For this purpose, the repository connector exposes the method getServiceDescription that takes a target endpoint specification as input. Our prototypical implementation of the process instance manager uses the process repository connector's functionality to gain knowledge about the process descriptions to enable process instance distinction based on the messages used to invoke partner services.

3.3 Process Instance Manager

The basic functionality of the REL implementation has been tested using a single process instance in the BPWS4J engine. In this limited setting, no explicit distinction of the process instance is needed. A first prototypical implementation of the process instance manager has been created to experiment with the usage of instance tokens emitted as SOAP headers by the process execution engine.

Additionally, a first implementation of a process instance manager has been developed that uses the process specification returned by the process repository connector in conjunction with the definition of outbound correlation sets. In this case, the process instance manager parses the SOAP messages to identify the message properties included in the correlation set definitions.

4 Usage Scenario

Using the REL has a potential impact on the business conversation governed by a business process description both for the initiator and for the external service providers. We will discuss motivations for using the self-healing behavior of the REL for both parties in the setting of a travel planning scenario. We selected this scenario because it is easy to understand, and often referred to in the literature [17][1].

Assume that a number of individual service providers offer web services that enable customers to search for hotel rooms, flight and car rental offers and book them. A travel agency may describe a business process (referred to as travel process) that composes these services into a new service that is capable of offering full travel packages including airline tickets, hotel accommodation and a rental car.

If the hotel booking service fails during the lifetime of an instance of this travel process, no offer for a travel package can be made to the customer, assuming a standard modeling of this process in BPEL. This is true even if another hotel booking service provider offers the same service and a solution would exist in principle. Using the REL this other service provider would be contacted allowing the travel agency to provide the travel offer. This way, we can reduce the risk of process failure and thus enhance customer satisfaction. While the benefit for the user of the services is obvious, the service providers might be reluctant to participate in the system since it might enable their customers to dynamically switch to another provider on system failure. We believe that service providers will nevertheless accept this, since they effectively participate in a marketplace where robustness against service failure can be a competitive feature. In order to make its web services resilient against failure, one provider may install a high availability or load-leveling system. This is basically a provider side proxy that uses a number of backend service providers to relay client requests to. Instead of using such an expensive and hard to maintain solution, the service provider may also directly publish the services available at the backend layer into the P2P repository where the REL can find the set of backend servers and use them accordingly. The two approaches are illustrated in Fig. 8. The REL approach has been implemented for this sample use case, and basic functionality could be shown.

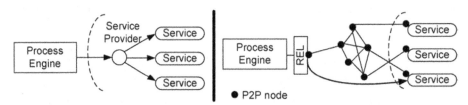

Fig. 8. Service Provider using dedicated load balancing and high availability component on the left side and direct service publishing in the P2P infrastructure on the right side.

5   Related Work

The P2P based lookup mechanism for web services is a key component for the REL. In [18] an approach to web service discovery in P2P indices based on space filling curves is presented that allows for range queries about keywords. Currently only literal keyword queries are needed to support the REL, additionally range queries over keywords are currently being implemented in the RMF – our underlying P2P information infrastructure. Other approaches for decentralized web service discovery focus on

---

[1] In the ATHENA project, we are applying the REL in a more complex automotive supply chain application.

the use of ontologies and service semantics to organize web service registries into collections [19] or perform web service discovery on the semantic web [20], this is not the focus of our work.

In [21] a framework for autonomic modeling and simulation of business processes is proposed, this work focuses on supporting the design and development of business processes, not on autonomic process execution.

General requirements for self-healing system architectures are analysed in [22]. Robustness against external or internal failure is one of the relevant requirements to achieve a self-healing architecture style, it is also a feature our REL introduces to the process execution environment. In [23] the authors quantify the effectiveness of self-healing strategies used within service discovery systems, our work focuses on the architectural extension of the business process execution environment to achieve self-healing capabilities. The self-healing service discovery mechanism is only a part of that work that we assume to be addressed in the underlying P2P system. The work in [24] proposes a path to a more autonomic behavior of web services, a general extension of the service oriented archictecture is proposed that does not address the requirements of business process execution. The author of [25] evaluates different message passing strategies for optimization of message flow in process based EAI systems, he does not show an architecture that generally offers self-healing capabilities for different process execution engines.

6 Conclusions

The research described in this paper is motivated by the idea of introducing self-healing mechanisms to business process execution by integrating state-of-the-art service-based business process execution languages and infrastructures (exemplified by BPEL) on the one hand, and of P2P architectures on the other. The main contribution of this paper is twofold: Firstly, we presented an analysis of the shortcomings of existing business process execution frameworks concerning flexible failure handling; secondly, we presented the design and implementation of a middleware framework called Robust Execution Layer that acts as a transparent, configurable add-on to any BPEL execution engine to support the self-healing execution of business processes that are managed by the engine. The combination of BPEL with Siemens' P2P Resource Management Framework enables service-level resilience without the explicit need of additional dedicated hardware or communication redundancy, and transparently supports different underlying software architectures.

We will further investigate the problem of process instance identification at the service level in a loosely coupled infrastructure setting in the future. We believe that P2P computing offers an interesting architectural approach to leverage the functionality of today's client-server business process engines to the case of cross-organizational business processes that are characterized by heterogeneity, constant change, autonomy of partners, and limited information/service access due to organizational boundaries and competition. This paper investigated the application of P2P resource management to the *service* level. Thus, an important aspect for our future research is to extend the scope of this work by investigating the applicability of P2P concepts to other facets of distributed business resource management, including *business objects* (e.g. the secure seamless access to business documents such as a request for quotation in a sourcing application, or a technical specification in a collaborative product design scenario) and *processes* (e.g. bottom-up organization of a cross-organizational business process through the P2P interaction of multiple business process engines). Furthermore, it would be interesting to investigate the potential of applying the REL in service oriented grid computing environments [26] when modeling grid applications as process oriented service compositions.

Acknowledgements

Part of the work reported in this paper is funded by the E.C. within the ATHENA IP under the European grant FP6-IST-507849. The paper does not represent the view of the E.C. nor that of other consortium members, and the authors are responsible for the paper's content.

References

1. W3C Recommendation: "WSDL 1.1", http://www.w3.org/TR/wsdl, 2001.
2. "Universal Description, Discovery and Integration", Technical White Paper, 2000.
3. IBM (2003) "BPEL4WS: Business Process Execution Language for Web Services", http://www-106.ibm.com/developerworks/webservices/library/ws-bpel/
4. ATHENA. Advanced Technologies for Interoperability of Heterogeneous Enterprise Networks and their Applications. European IP FP6-IST-507849. http://www.athena-ip.org.
5. Müller, J. P., Bauer, B., Friese, T.: "Programming Software Agents as Designing Executable Business Processes: A Model-Driven Perspective". In Proceedings of the 1st Int. Workshop on Programming Multi-Agent Systems, Melbourne, Australia, Vol. 3067 of Lecture Notes in AI, Springer-Verlag, 2004.
6. W3C Recommendation: "SOAP Version 1.2", http://www.w3.org/TR/SOAP, 2003.
7. Microsoft (2001): "XLANG – Web Services for Business Process Design".
8. IBM (2001):"Web Services Flow Language".
9. Khalaf, R., Mukhi, N., Weerawarana, S.: "Service-Oriented Composition in BPEL4WS". In: Proceedings of The Twelfth International World Wide Web Conference, 2003.
10. W3C Recommendation, "XML Schema", 2001.
11. Oram, A.: "P2P: Harnessing the Power of Disruptive Technologies", O'Reilly, 2001.
12. IBM Business Process Execution Language for Web Services Java Run Time. http://www.alphaworks.ibm.com/tech/bpws4j
13. Apache Software Foundation: "Apache Jakarta Tomcat 5.x".
14. Friese T., Freisleben B., Rusitschka S., Southall A.: "A Framework for Resource Management in Peer-to-Peer Networks", In Proceedings of NetObjectDays 2002, Volume 2591 of Lecture Notes in Computer Science, pp. 4—21, Springer-Verlag.
15. W3C Recommendation "XML Path Language (XPath), Version 1.0", 1999.
16. IBM (2003), "The Web Services Description Language for Java Toolkit" JSR110 reference implementation, http://www-124.ibm.com/developerworks/projects/wsdl4j/
17. Ingham, D., Caughey, S., Watson, P., Halsey, S.: "The Informed Traveller: A Case Study in Building Internet Brokering Services", Proceedings of the IEEE Workshop on Internet Applications, 1999, p. 44.
18. Schmidt, C., Parashar, M.: "A Peer-to-Peer Approach to Web Service Discovery", World Wide Web Journal, Volume 7, Issue 2, June 2004, pp. 211 – 229.
19. Sivashanmugam, K., Verma, K., Mulye, R., Zhong, Z., Sheth, A.: "Speed-R: Semantic P2P Environment for diverse Web Service Registries".

20. Schlosser, M., Sintek, M., Decker, S., Nejdl, W.: „A Scalable and Ontology-Based P2P Infrastructure for Semantic Web Services". Second International Conference on Peer-to-Peer Computing (P2P'02), 2002.

21. Yu, X., Zhang, L., Li, Y., Chen, Y.: „WSCE: A Flexible Web Service Composition Environment", Proceedings of the International Conference on Web Services, San Diego, California, 2004, p. 428.

22. Mikic-Rakic, M., Mehta, N., Medvidovic, N.: "Architectural Style Requirements for Self-Healing Systems", In Proceedings of the First Workshop on Self-healing Systems, Charleston, South Carolina, 2002, pp. 49 – 54.

23. Dabrowski, C., Mills, K.: "Understanding Self-healing in Service-Discovery Systems", In Proceedings of the First Workshop on Self-healing Systems, Charleston, South Carolina, 2002, pp. 15-20.

24. Birman, K., Renesse, R. van, Vogels, W.: "Adding High Availability and Autonomic Behavior to Web Services", In Proceedings of The 26th International Conference on Software Engineering, Edinburgh, Scotland, United Kingdom, 2004, pp. 17 – 26.

25. Caseau, Y.: "Self-Adaptive and Self-Healing Message Passing Strategies for Process-Oriented Integration Infrastructures", In Proceedings of the 11th Int. Conference on the Engineering of Computer-Based Systems, Brno, Czech Republic, 2004, pp. 506 – 512.

26. Smith, M., Friese, T., Freisleben, B.: "Towards a Service-Oriented Ad Hoc Grid", Proceedings of the 3rd International Symposium on Parallel and Distributed Computing, Cork, Ireland, 2004.

Runtime Adaptation of Applications Through Dynamic Recomposition of Components*

Arun Mukhija and Martin Glinz

Institut für Informatik,
University of Zurich, CH-8057, Switzerland
{mukhija,glinz}@ifi.unizh.ch

Abstract. Software applications executing in highly dynamic environments are faced with the challenge of frequent and usually unpredictable changes in their execution environment. In order to cope with this challenge effectively, the applications need to adapt to these changes dynamically. CASA (Contract-based Adaptive Software Architecture) provides a framework for enabling dynamic adaptation of applications, in response to changes in their execution environment. One of the principle adaptation mechanisms employed in the CASA framework is dynamic recomposition of application components. In this paper, we discuss implementation issues related to the approach for dynamic recomposition of application components in CASA.

1   Introduction

A major challenge for software applications executing in highly dynamic environments (such as those in pervasive and ubiquitous computing scenarios) is the consistently changing execution environment of these applications. The changes in execution environment can be in the form of (i) changes in *contextual information* (user's location, identity of nearby objects or persons etc.), or (ii) changes in *resource availability* (bandwidth, battery power, connectivity etc.).

Contextual information refers to (purely) the *information* about the context of an application that may influence the service provided by the application (such as locational information, temporal information, atmospherical information etc.), in contrast to resources that form the *physical infrastructure* available to the application for providing this service (such as communication resources, data resources, computing resources etc.). A change in contextual information may present an opportunity for an application to adapt its behavior, in order to provide a more relevant service with respect to the changed contextual information. Similarly, a change in resource availability may require an application to change its resource consumption accordingly, necessitating an adaptation of the application's behavior.

---

* The work presented in this paper was supported (in part) by the National Center of Competence in Research on Mobile Information and Communication Systems (NCCR-MICS), a center supported by the Swiss National Science Foundation.

M. Beigl and P. Lukowicz (Eds.): ARCS 2005, LNCS 3432, pp. 124–138, 2005.
© Springer-Verlag Berlin Heidelberg 2005

The existing approaches for dynamic adaptation of applications have focused mainly on runtime changes in resource availability. Most of these approaches try to adapt the lower-level services used by applications at the middleware level, and thereby influence the resource consumption due to these applications. Examples of adaptation of the lower-level services include modifying the quality or compression level of the data being transmitted over a communication channel in response to a change in the available bandwidth, changing the caching policy in response to a change in the available memory etc.

However, we argue that a dynamic change in application code should be provided as a means of application adaptation, *in addition* to the adaptation of the lower-level services at the middleware level, in order to effectively deal with the changes in execution environment.

This is because: (1) In response to a change in contextual information, a corresponding change in the functionality of an application is usually required, which typically requires a change in the application code. For example, if the contextual information related to a *Tourist Guide* application changes from *shopping mall* to *open-air cinema*, the application needs to provide relevant information about the weather conditions and show-timings, in place of the information about the availability of the items in the user's shopping list in the shopping mall. This kind of change in functionality requires a change in application code. (2) Even if small variations in resource availability can be handled by adapting the lower-level services, for large variations a change in application code is usually required. For example, consider a *Disaster Control* application transmitting the live video stream of an erupting volcano from a mobile node to a coordination center. For a small drop in the available bandwidth, an adaptive middleware may try to reduce the quality of the video transmitted, in order to save bandwidth. But for a significant drop in the bandwidth, it may be more apt for the application to send a textual description of the volcano (along with frequent images, if possible), rather than reducing the quality of the video beyond a threshold level. This kind of adaptation again requires a change in application code.

A runtime change in application code can be most primitively achieved by hardwiring the adaptation mechanism within an application (e.g. using programming constructs like if-else or switch-case etc.). However, this is a very tedious and limited solution to the problem. It makes the process of application development more complex, because the adaptation code is intertwined with the application code. Moreover, with this approach the adaptation policy cannot be changed during runtime, because of the hardwiring of the adaptation mechanism, posing a limitation to its usefulness for dynamic environments.

Recent approaches for dynamic weaving and unweaving of aspects, influencing the crosscutting functionality of an application such as security or persistence management, are a step in the right direction (the term *aspect* used in the sense of the aspect-oriented programming [6]). But, as the name indicates, these approaches are restricted to adapting the crosscutting functionality of an application. Whereas in practice, an adaptation of the core functionality of an application may be required *as well*, like in the examples of *Tourist Guide* and *Disaster Control* applications above.

Modern software applications are composed of components, where each component implements a subtask of the application (we will use the term *component* to refer to *application component* in this paper). In a component-based application development, the components encapsulate their implementation details, interact with each other only through their well-defined interfaces (using method calls), and generally follow the principle of *separation of concerns*. This makes it possible and convenient to alter the application code dynamically by recomposing the components at runtime.

CASA (Contract-based Adaptive Software Architecture) [1, 10] provides a framework for enabling dynamic adaptation of applications executing in dynamic environments. The CASA Runtime System monitors the changes in the execution environment of applications, and in case of significant changes carries out dynamic adaptation of applications. The adaptation policy of every application is defined in a so-called application contract. In order to meet adaptation needs of a broad and diverse set of applications, CASA supports the following adaptation mechanisms: dynamic change in lower-level services, dynamic weaving and unweaving of aspects, dynamic change in application attributes, and dynamic recomposition of components. The adaptation concerns are separated from the application, thereby reducing the complexity involved in developing adaptive applications. In this paper, we discuss implementation issues related to the approach for dynamic recomposition of components in CASA.

The rest of the paper is organized as follows. In Section 2, we give a brief overview of the CASA framework. In Section 3, we identify the key requirements for dynamic recomposition of components. In Section 4, we discuss implementation issues related to dynamic recomposition of components in CASA. In Section 5, we give an overview of related work. And in Section 6, we conclude the paper and indicate future direction of our work.

2   Overview of the CASA Framework

Figure 1 shows the conceptual working of the CASA framework. Every computing node hosting adaptive applications is required to run an instance of the CASA Runtime System (CRS). The CRS is responsible for monitoring the changes in execution environment on behalf of these applications, and to adapt these applications as and when necessitated by a change in execution environment. The adaptation policy of every application is defined in a so-called application contract.

A three-step adaptation process is illustrated in Figure 1. Every time the CRS detects a change in the execution environment (step 1), it evaluates the application contracts of the running applications with respect to the changed state of the execution environment (step 2). If the CRS discovers a need for adapting certain applications, it carries out the adaptation of the affected applications, in accordance with the adaptation policies specified in the respective application contracts (step 3).

Application adaptation can be realized using one or more of the following adaptation mechanisms supported by CASA, depending on the adaptation needs of a specific application:

- *Dynamic Change in Lower-Level Services:* For a dynamic change in lower-level services used by applications, CASA can be integrated with any adaptive middleware for this purpose that supports external regulation of its adaptation strategy. Several reflection-based adaptive middleware fit in this category, such as Odyssey [11], QuO [15] etc.
- *Dynamic Weaving and Unweaving of Aspects:* For dynamic weaving and unweaving of aspects, CASA relies on a flexible and efficient system for this purpose called PROSE [13].
- *Dynamic Change in Application Attributes:* For a dynamic change in application attributes, the application needs to provide appropriate callback methods that can be called by the CRS at runtime.
- *Dynamic Recomposition of Components:* For dynamic recomposition of components, CASA follows an indigenous approach described in Section 4.

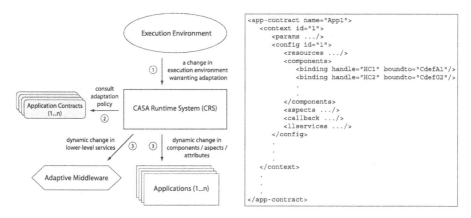

Fig. 1. Working of CASA.   **Fig. 2.** Application contract.

An excerpt of an application contract is shown in Figure 2. The application contract is external to the application, and is specified using an XML-based language. This enables easy modification, extension, and customization of the adaptation policy at runtime. Moreover, it facilitates separating the adaptation concerns from the application.

The application contract is divided into <context> elements, where each <context> element represents a state of contextual information of interest to the application (the parameters characterizing this state are specified within <params> element). Each <context> element in turn contains a list of alternative configurations of the application, suited to the particular state of contextual information. These configurations are listed in a special ordering that reflects their user-perceived preference. Each <config> element, representing a configuration, specifies the resource requirements of the configuration, the components and aspects constituting the configuration, the callback methods to be called for the configuration, and the lower-level services corresponding to the configuration. The detailed specification of an application contract is not described in this paper as it is not relevant to our discussion of the approach for dynamic recomposition of components, except the specification of <components> element which is discussed partially in Section 4.

Depending on the current state of the execution environment (contextual information and resources), the appropriate configuration from the application contract is selected and activated by the CRS. More details on the CASA framework can be found in [1, 10].

3   Requirements for Dynamic Recomposition of Components

A *component composition*, or just *composition*, is a collection of components qualified to do the required application task under a specific state of the execution environment.

A primary and obvious requirement for application adaptation through dynamic recomposition of components is:

Requirement 0: An adaptive application needs to provide a number of alternative compositions for different states of the execution environment.

We can now define *dynamic recomposition of components* as changing between alternative compositions of an application at runtime.

Any two alternative compositions may vary in just a few components, while many other components remain the same across both compositions. When changing from one alternative composition to another, there may be some new components to be added and some old components to be removed.

Dynamic replacement of components is a special case of a dynamic removal of a component A followed by a dynamic addition of a component A', such that A' is able to serve all those components that could be served by A, in an alike manner as A itself.

If a component A can be dynamically replaced by a component A', then both A and A' must subscribe to the same component *contract* (the term *contract* used in the sense of the Design by Contract approach [9]). That is, the following two requirements need to be satisfied by A and A' (in CASA, dynamic replacements are bidirectional, i.e. if A can be dynamically replaced by A', then it automatically implies that A' can also be dynamically replaced by A):

Requirement 1: Both A and A' must conform to the same interface, i.e. the method signatures of the publicly-accessible methods of A and A' must be the same.

Requirement 2: The pre and post conditions of the publicly-accessible methods of A and A', which must be satisfied for the interaction of these methods with their clients, must be the same. The pre and post conditions may also include certain non-functional assertions or constraints.

Next, we state a requirement for mapping the state of A to the state of A'. For this purpose, we define the *persistent* state of a component as the state that needs to remain persistent in between its executions.

Requirement 3: A valid *persistent* state of A when mapped to A', using an appropriate state mapping function, must become a valid *persistent* state of A'.

The following two requirements pertain to the dynamic removal and dynamic addition of components.

Requirement 4: If a component A is removed during dynamic recomposition, then it must be replaced dynamically by a component A' or else all the components depending on A must also be removed along with A.

Requirement 5: If a component A' is added during dynamic recomposition, then the components on which A' depends either must already be present or they must be added along with A'.

Requirements 4 and 5 are related to ensuring the *completeness* of alternative compositions.

Both *completeness* and *correctness* of every alternative composition, in terms of its ability to do the required application task under its corresponding state of the execution environment, need to be ensured by the application developer at the time of composing the alternative compositions.

The following two requirements are related to ensuring the *consistency* of the application.

Requirement 6: If a component A is replaced dynamically by a component A', then A' must be able to continue the execution from where A left.

Requirement 7: The integrity of the interactions among components must not be compromised due to dynamic recomposition.

Requirements 6 and 7 above help to protect the application from being in an inconsistent state as a result of the dynamic recomposition.

4   Implementation of Dynamic Recomposition of Components in CASA

In this section, we discuss the implementation issues related to dynamic recomposition of components for the applications developed using object-oriented programming languages. In particular, we consider Java as a target language, because of its widespread use and popularity. However, we will try to keep our discussion as language-neutral as possible, so that the results are applicable for a wide range of object-oriented programming languages.

A dynamic recomposition implies adding/removing/replacing components dynamically. Dynamic replacement of components is of particular interest here, as it is more critical than simple addition or removal of components which is relatively straightforward to carry out. Hence we will focus on dynamic replacement of components in the following.

In principle, there are two possible strategies for dynamic replacement: Lazy replacement and Eager replacement. Below we briefly discuss the two.

Lazy Replacement: In this strategy, once the decision for dynamic recomposition is taken, an already running component is allowed to complete its current execution before being replaced.

Eager Replacement: In contrast to the lazy replacement strategy, here the execution of a running component is suspended once the decision for dynamic recomposition is taken, and the execution resumes again from the point where it was suspended, after the component is replaced.

Figure 3 illustrates lazy replacement (Figure 3a) and eager replacement (Figure 3b). In Figure 3, the horizontal axis represents the time line, and the vertical dashed line represents the time T when the decision for dynamic recomposition is taken. In this example, the components A, B, C and D are to be replaced by the components A', B', C' and D' respectively as a result of dynamic recomposition (dark bars denote the execution of old components, and light bars denote the execution of new components). Only the components A and C are under execution at time T. In Figure 3a (representing lazy replacement) A and C are allowed to complete their execution before being replaced by A' and C' respectively. Whereas in Figure 3b (representing eager replacement), the execution of A and C is suspended at time T, they are replaced by A' and C' respectively, and the execution resumes again with A' and C'.

Since the eager replacement strategy is able to give a faster response to a change in execution environment than the lazy one, we decide in favor of eager replacement for CASA. However, as discussed later, it may not always be possible to use eager replacement, and thus sometimes lazy replacement may be the only option.

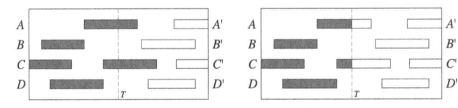

Fig. 3a. Lazy replacement strategy.   **Fig. 3b.** Eager replacement strategy.

4.1 Dynamic Replacement Process

In terms of object-oriented programming, a component is essentially an instance of a class (with a restriction that, unlike normal class instances, components cannot have any externally-visible state). Thus, from an implementation point of view, replacing a component involves replacing the corresponding class definition of the instance. We will use the terms "component" and "class instance" interchangeably throughout the rest of this paper.

We now define an *adaptable class* as the one whose instances are dynamically replaceable (i.e. can replace, or be replaced by, instances of other classes dynamically). Additionally, we define a *set of alternative classes* as a collection of adaptable classes whose instances can dynamically replace each other. That is, all the adaptable classes that are members of the same set of alternative classes, and by implication the instances of these adaptable classes, conform to the requirements 1–3 identified in Section 3.

To ease our implementation process, we impose the following additional conditions:

(i) An instance A of a class C can be dynamically replaced by an instance A' of a class C' only if C and C' are members of the same set of alternative classes.

(ii) Any given composition may contain instances of only one of the adaptable classes from any given set of alternative classes. That is, no two instances in a given composition may be of different classes from the same set of alternative classes.

We use a variant of the Bridge pattern [2] for hiding the complexities of dynamic replacement from the application code. In particular, every set of alternative classes is associated with a unique *Handle* class. The *Handle* class conforms to the same interface as the adaptable classes in its associated set.

The *Handle* class acts as an *abstraction* that can be bound to any of the adaptable class *implementations* from its associated set of alternative classes at runtime (the terms *abstraction* and *implementation* used in the sense of the Bridge pattern [2]).

We know that (i) any given composition may contain instances of only one of the adaptable classes from any given set of alternative classes, and (ii) every set of alternative classes has a unique *Handle* class associated to it. Therefore, we can conclude that: for any given composition there is a unique adaptable class bound to any given *Handle* class.

The binding between a *Handle* class and its corresponding adaptable class for a given composition is represented as a part of the composition specification in the application contract (refer <binding> element within <components> element in Figure 2).

In order to provide a layer of transparency between the application code and the dynamic replacement process, wherever there is a need for creating an instance of an adaptable class in the application code, an instance of the corresponding *Handle* class is created instead. This *Handle* class instance is then linked to an instance of the adaptable class that is currently bound to the *Handle* class, at runtime (as explained below).

Let a set of alternative classes S consist of the adaptable classes CdefA, CdefB and CdefC, and the associated *Handle* class for the set S be HC. At any given time, HC will be bound to a unique adaptable class from the set S, depending on the currently active composition. However, this binding may change dynamically as a result of dynamic recomposition.

In the application code, when a new instance objHC of the *Handle* class HC is created, the constructor of objHC invokes the CRS (CASA Runtime System). The CRS gets the information about the adaptable class currently bound to HC, say CdefA, from the specification of the currently active composition, and returns the namespace location of the class CdefA back to the constructor of objHC (the

CRS also registers `objHC` for future recompositions). The constructor of `objHC` then creates an instance of `CdefA`, say `objA`, and stores it internally as *active* adaptable class instance.

Although a *Handle* class conforms to the same interface as the classes in its associated set of alternative classes, it does not provide a *real* implementation for any of the methods in this interface. The methods of a *Handle* class instance simply forward the method calls invoked on them to the corresponding methods of the *active* adaptable class instance, and return the results as received from the latter. For example, if a method `foo()` is invoked on `objHC`, then `objHC.foo()` simply invokes the method `objA.foo()`, and returns the result as received from `objA.foo()`.

If there is a change in the binding between the *Handle* class `HC` and its corresponding adaptable class, due to dynamic recomposition, then the CRS passes the namespace location of the newly bound adaptable class, say `CdefB`, to all the instances of `HC` (including `objHC`). The instances of `HC` replace the old adaptable class instances with the instances of `CdefB` as *active* adaptable class instances (the details of this replacement are discussed next). The calls to an instance of `HC` will now be forwarded automatically to the new adaptable class instance in place of the old one. This way, the *Handle* class instances help to hide the details of dynamic replacement from the application.

Figure 4 illustrates the above example of dynamic replacement. In Figure 4a the *Handle* class instance `objHC` is linked to the old adaptable class instance `objA`, just before the dynamic replacement is carried out. And in Figure 4b, `objHC` is linked to the new adaptable class instance, say `objB`, just after the dynamic replacement is over. The external components (`extObj1`, `extObj2` and `extObj3`) are largely unaffected by this dynamic replacement, as their links to `objHC` remain undisturbed by the change.

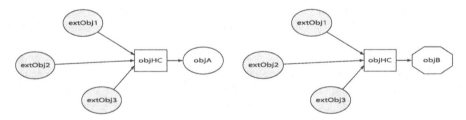

Fig. 4a. Before dynamic replacement.   **Fig. 4b.** After dynamic replacement.

Below we discuss the sequence of steps to be carried out by `objHC` when replacing `objA` with `objB` (as per the eager replacement strategy).

Sequence of Steps

1. Deactivate `objA`
2. Suspend the execution of `objA`
3. Create `objB`
4. Transfer the state of `objA` to `objB`
5. Activate `objB`

If objA is not running at the time of replacement then step 2 is not required. Below we discuss the implementation of the above-mentioned steps.

Step 1: Deactivate objA: First, on receiving an indication from the the CRS about dynamic replacement, objHC *deactivates* the reference to objA. This ensures that the calls made to objHC during the dynamic replacement process are not forwarded to objA, and rather wait within objHC.

Step 2: Suspend the Execution of objA: Suspending the execution of objA implies suspending all the calls currently executing on objA. But before actually suspending a call executing on objA, it needs to be ensured that the execution of the call has reached a *safe* point where it can be resumed *correctly* by objB, at the end of dynamic replacement. And for this, the *safe* points need to be explicitly defined in the body of objA (more discussion on this follows later).

After deactivating the reference to objA (step 1), objHC sets a signal for the suspension of objA. At every *safe* point, each call executing on objA checks if a signal for the suspension of objA has been set. If such a signal is set, then an exception is thrown on this call, to be eventually caught by objHC. The information about the *safe* point where the call is suspended is also passed to objHC along with the exception. After catching the exception, objHC needs to take necessary actions like reinvoking the call on objB after the completion of the dynamic replacement process. This time the information about the *safe* point where the call was previously suspended is passed as an argument while reinvoking the call, to enable objB to resume the execution correctly. For this, the methods of objB should be able to accept an additional argument of the type SafePoint (during normal forwarding of calls by objHC, the value of this argument will be null).

This step is over when all the calls executing on objA have returned (either normally or after being suspended) to objHC.

Step 3: Create objB: After setting the signal for the suspension of objA, objHC creates an instance of the new adaptable class (passed by the CRS), i.e. objB (the creation of objB may take place while step 2 is still on, i.e. during the time all the calls executing on objA return to objHC).

Step 4: Transfer the State of objA *to* objB: Once all the calls executing on objA have returned to objHC (at the end of step 2), the state of objA is transferred to objB at the initiation of objHC.

For transferring the state, i.e. storing the state and loading the state, every dynamically replaceable component needs to provide appropriate storeState and loadState methods. This is because state parameters (names and types) may vary across the old and new components, which means that the semantic information necessary for state transfer can be provided by the respective components only. The storeState method of objA may need to convert its own component-specific representation of the state into a standard representation (standard for the corresponding set of alternative classes), which the loadState method of objB understands and may again convert into its own component-specific representation.

Step 5: Activate objHC*:* Finally, objHC sets objB as *active* adaptable class instance (objA can now be garbage collected).

Now the execution can continue on objB.

Discussion: The description above assumes that the new component requires the state of the old component to be transferred to it, and also requires the information about the *safe* points where the calls were suspended, in order to continue the execution from where the old component left. However, in practice, either or both of these requirements can be relaxed, depending on the properties of the concerned components (on the other hand, it ultimately rests on the capability of the new component itself to continue the execution correctly, even if both these requirements are satisfied).

That is, in some cases, there may not be a need for passing the information about the *safe* points to the new component, e.g. if the state transferred to the new component provides enough information to resume the execution correctly. And in rather extreme cases, there may not be a need for transferring the state of the old component to the new component, e.g. if the new component is specifically designed to recover from a state loss, though it will most likely result in a degraded performance.

There can be some components that can be suspended abruptly, e.g. if the new component provides an entirely different functionality and is going to begin its execution from its initial point of execution (as typically in response to a change in contextual information). This means that every point of execution in the old component is in effect a *safe* point. From the implementation perspective, this implies that there is no need for explicitly defining *safe* points in such components, and the already executing calls can be simply suspended by throwing exceptions abruptly in step 2 above.

Queuing the new calls made during the dynamic replacement process within the *Handle* class instance, as well as the calls that were suspended and returned to the *Handle* class instance, and invoking these calls at the end of dynamic replacement, help maintain the integrity of the interactions among components.

Next we show that eager replacement may not be viable for some components, leaving lazy replacement as the only option.

Consider an eager replacement where the state of the old component needs to be transferred to the new component, and the old component is running at the time of replacement. One of the necessary conditions for ensuring the validity of this replacement is that the state transferred gets transformed into a reachable state of the new component. This will most likely not be possible at any random point of execution of the old component, but probably at some specific points. Such points of execution of the old component that ensure that the state transferred gets transformed into a reachable state of the new component are referred as *valid-change* points. If the state transferred at any random point of execution is ensured to get transformed into a reachable state of the new component, then it implies that every point of execution of the old component is a *valid-change* point.

We know that in the eager replacement strategy the state is transferred at the *safe* point where the last of the calls executing on the old component is suspended. Now to ensure a valid replacement, this *safe* point has to be a *valid-change* point. And since we cannot predict in advance at which *safe* point the last call will be suspended, we can say that every *safe* point has to be a *valid-change* point.

However, we argue that there is no guarantee that a *valid-change* point exists in an arbitrary component to be replaced (not counting the control points just before the initial point and just after the last point of execution, as they are not practically very helpful).

To support our argument, we refer to the results provided by Gupta et. al. [3] in the context of a runtime change in software version. They define a valid change as the one in which the state of the old software version gets transformed into a reachable state of the new software version. They also show that locating the points of execution where a valid change may be guaranteed is in general *undecidable*, and approximate techniques based on data-flow analysis and knowledge of application developer are required. This effectively implies that there may not exist any point of execution in the old software version that may guarantee a valid change.

This result can be directly extended to the case of dynamic replacement of components, to support our argument that there is no guarantee that a *valid-change* point exists in an arbitrary component to be replaced.

If a component does not contain any *valid-change* point, then the possibility of defining *safe* points in the component is automatically ruled out. This, in turn, renders eager replacement unachievable for such components, leaving lazy replacement as the only option.

With lazy replacement, the component to be replaced is certainly not running at the time of replacement, and thus the state to be transferred refers to the *persistent* state of the component, in contrast to the *transient* state for a component that is running at the time of replacement. From requirement 3 (Section 3), we know that the *persistent* state of the old component when transferred to the new component is automatically a reachable state of the new component.

For lazy replacement, the replacement process discussed before can be suitably modified in a straightforward manner. In any case, the implementation of either of the two strategies is localized within a *Handle* class instance and the corresponding dynamically replaceable components.

4.2   Performance Evaluation

A prototype, based on the CASA framework, has been implemented in Java, and the results have been encouraging. We have been able to demonstrate the dynamic adaptation features of the CASA framework, at a minimal performance cost. A detailed overview of performance evaluation of the prototype is given in [4]. Below we present some of the indicative results.

During normal operation of an application, the only performance overheads are due to using an additional level of indirection when accessing a dynamically replaceable component through a *Handle* class instance, and for checking a signal for component suspension at every *safe* point within the component code. Both these overheads were found to be quite insignificant – in the order of a few micro seconds.

The performance overhead during dynamic replacement of components varied widely depending on the number of components to be replaced – for the test results, the values were 2–7 ms for a single component and 25–100 ms for twenty components, depending on the processor speed (assuming no delay for the calls executing on the old components to reach their respective *safe* points).

The overhead for the state transfer between components was found to be very small (in the order of a few micro seconds), while the size of the state to be transferred did not have much influence on the results.

The frequency of *safe* points in a component code has an obvious positive impact on the swiftness of dynamic replacement. Since the overhead due to each *safe* point during normal operation is negligible (a couple of micro seconds), it is recommended to define *safe* points quite frequently in every dynamically replaceable component, if possible.

5 Related Work

Over the last few years, some approaches have been proposed for software adaptation using dynamic change in application components. Rasche and Polze [14] present an approach for dynamic reconfiguration of component-based applications for the Microsoft .NET platform. This approach uses a transaction-based component model to decide the appropriate timing and order for reconfiguration. However, dynamic reconfiguration here implies adding new components, removing old components, changing the connections among components, or changing the component attributes, while it does not provide means for dynamic replacement of components involving state transfer etc.

The Accord framework [7] enables a dynamic change in application behavior according to the rules associated with every application component. However, with this approach, the interactions between application components need to be defined in terms of rules associated with the corresponding components, in order for these interactions to be changeable at runtime by changing the corresponding rules. Since the number of potential interactions between application components can be quite large, the number of possible rules can be exponential, making the rule management quite complex and inducing performance overhead due to execution of all these rules at runtime.

Some more work has been done on runtime software evolution, which has a close bearing with the software adaptation using dynamic change in application components. Oreizy et. al. [12] provide a software architecture-based approach for runtime software evolution, and discuss dynamic recomposition of application components at the architecture level. In this approach, the components interact with each other only through the connectors that mediate all component communications. This makes it possible to alter a component composition by changing the component bindings of the connectors at runtime. The role of connectors here is similar to the role of *Handle* components in CASA, though in CASA only the dynamically replaceable components need to be accessed through *Handle* components.

Dynamic Java classes [8] provide a generic approach to support evolution of Java programs by changing their classes at runtime. This approach shares the same goals as our implementation approach. A drawback of this approach, however, is that it takes a much harder way of modifying the JVM to implement dynamic replacement of classes. Using a customized JVM may result in reduced portability, and may eventually restrict the usage of this approach. Similarly, the approach of dynamic C++ classes [5] allows a version change of a running C++ class. However, with this approach, once the version of a class has been changed, only the new instances created after the version change belong to the newer version. The already created instances belonging to the older version are either allowed to continue till they expire normally or they are destroyed abruptly, while no attempt is made to replace these instances with ones belonging to the newer version. Clearly, such an approach is not suitable for our purpose.

6   Conclusion and Future Work

The CASA framework enables dynamic adaptation of applications in response to changes in their execution environment. With a view to meet adaptation needs of a broad and diverse set of applications, the CASA framework supports dynamic adaptation at various levels of an application – from lower-level services to application code. In this paper, we discussed the implementation issues related to the adaptation of an application by recomposing its components dynamically, as supported in the CASA framework.

An underlying presumption in realizing application adaptation through dynamic recomposition of components is that the application provides alternative component compositions for different states of the execution environment. The cost of developing these alternative component compositions would be mitigated by the amount of reuse of the components constituting these compositions. We have also presumed that the correctness and completeness of alternative component compositions is ensured by the application developer at the time of composing these compositions. We envisage that appropriate tools to help ensure this would be available to the application developer.

In the near future, we intend to identify dynamic adaptation needs of different kinds of applications executing in dynamic environments. Based on this information, we will verify which of these adaptation needs are met effectively by our current approach and where modifications or extensions will be required.

References

1. The CASA Project. http://www.ifi.unizh.ch/req/casa/
2. E. Gamma, R. Helm, R. Johnson and J. Vlissides. *Design Patterns: Elements of Reusable Object-Oriented Software.* Addison-Wesley, 1995.
3. D. Gupta, P. Jalote and G. Barua. A Formal Framework for On-line Software Version Change. *IEEE Transactions on Software Engineering*, 22(2), 1996.

4. A. Gygax. *Studying the Effect of Size and Complexity of Components on the Performance of CASA*. Internship Report, IFI, University of Zurich, 2004. http://www.ifi.unizh.ch/req/ftp/papers/casa-perf.pdf

5. G. Hjalmtysson and R. Gray. Dynamic C++ Classes: A lightweight mechanism to update code in a running program. *Proc. of USENIX Annual Technical Conference*, 1998.

6. G. Kiczales, J. Lamping, A. Mendhekar, C. Maeda, C.V. Lopes, J.M. Loingtier and J. Irwin. Aspect-Oriented Programming. *Proc. of 11th European Conference on Object-Oriented Programming*, 1997.

7. H. Liu, M. Parashar and S. Hariri. A Component Based Programming Framework for Autonomic Applications. *Proc. of 1st International Conference on Autonomic Computing*, 2004.

8. S. Malabarba, R. Pandey, J. Gragg, E. Barr and J.F. Barnes. Runtime Support for Type-Safe Dynamic Java Classes. *Proc. of 14th European Conference on Object-Oriented Programming*, 2000.

9. B. Meyer. Applying "Design by Contract". *IEEE Computer*, 25(10), 1992.

10. A. Mukhija and M. Glinz. A Framework for Dynamically Adaptive Applications in a Self-organized Mobile Network Environment. *Proc. of ICDCS 2004 Workshop on Distributed Auto-adaptive and Reconfigurable Systems*, 2004.

11. B.D. Noble, M. Satyanarayanan, D. Narayanan, J.E. Tilton, J. Flinn and K.R. Walker. Agile Application-Aware Adaptation for Mobility. *Proc. of 16th ACM Symposium on Operating Systems Principles*, 1997.

12. P. Oreizy, N. Medvidovic and R.N. Taylor. Architecture-Based Runtime Software Evolution. *Proc. of 20th International Conference on Software Engineering*, 1998.

13. A. Popovici, T. Gross and G. Alonso. Dynamic Weaving for Aspect-Oriented Programming. *Proc. of 1st International Conference on Aspect-Oriented Software Development*, 2002.

14. A. Rasche and A. Polze. Configuration and Dynamic Reconfiguration of Component-based Applications with Microsoft .NET. *Proc. of 6th IEEE International Symposium on Object-Oriented Real-Time Distributed Computing*, 2003.

15. J.A. Zinky, D.E. Bakken and R.E. Schantz. Architectural Support for Quality of Service for CORBA Objects. *Theory and Practice of Object Systems*, 3(1), 1997.

An Observer/Controller Architecture for Adaptive Reconfigurable Stacks

Thorsten Schöler and Christian Müller-Schloer

Institute of Systems Engineering – System and Computer Architecture,
University of Hannover, Appelstraße 4, 30167 Hannover
{schoeler,cms}@sra.uni-hannover.de

Abstract. In this paper, we discuss the necessity of new observation and control structures for organic computing systems starting from the basic contradiction between bottom-up behaviour and top-down design. An Observer/Controller architecture serves the purpose to keep emergent behaviour within predefined limits. As an illustration, a framework for reconfigurable protocol stacks is introduced, which contains an agent-based monitoring framework as well as a reconfiguration manager. After describing a TCP/IP protocol stack implementation, based on the framework, similarities between the introduced framework and the Observer/Controller architectural pattern will be pointed out.

1 Introduction and Outline

1.1 Organic Computing

Due to the increasing complexity of today's software systems, new ideas for the design and management of those systems have to be found. Most software architects still design their systems following the top-down approach, trying to master this increasing challenge. While a good part of software complexity stems from once well-meant ideas to tackle the complexity like reuse of object oriented components, a considerable part of the complexity is caused by the general attitude of engineers to keep control of all details of the system under design.

To ease this potentially dangerous situation, organic computing tries to mimic key phenomena observed in nature for computer systems, such as self-organisation, selfconfiguration, self-healing, self-protection, self-explanation, and context awareness. Thus, an organic computer is a technical system, which adapts dynamically to the current conditions of its environment [1] without being exactly programmed to certain environment changes.

An exciting example of an organic system is disclosed by a look into the human brain. Low-level structures (brain stem), which react on sensory inputs thus, implementing a subconscious stimulus-response pattern, can be considered as an execution function.

Higher-level structures (e.g. the limbic system), observe and manipulate this execution function in several ways (especially emotions and regulation of visceral motor activities) [2]. Initial discussions on organic computing systems [1, 3] suggest that a two-level architecture with a low level execution and a higher-level control layer represents a general pattern present in natural as well as artificial organic systems. We call

M. Beigl and P. Lukowicz (Eds.): ARCS 2005, LNCS 3432, pp. 139–153, 2005.

this architectural pattern Observer/Controller architecture. It will be described in this paper and illustrated with an example from telecommunication research.

1.2 Software Defined Radio, Mobile Adaptive Terminals

This paper will introduce a software framework for organic protocol stacks of mobile terminals, so-called software defined radio (SDR) devices. Therefore, a short introduction to SDR will be given in this section.

A software-defined radio is a system, which uses software for the modulation and demodulation of radio signals [4]. This normally includes the RF front end, the analogue/digital as well as the digital/analogue converters, and the base band processing (BB). In our research, we understand SDR in a much broader sense. An adaptive mobile terminal contains not only a reconfigurable radio system but also a reconfigurable operating system, reconfigurable protocol stacks, middleware, services and applications.

The idea of reconfiguration on software levels yields higher flexibility by better resource utilisation. For example, an adaptable mobile terminal is able to choose from different implementations of a multimedia CODEC, depending on the current resource situation. Such a terminal will favour a less energy consuming hardware CODEC when the battery power is getting low, whereas a CODEC implemented in software is preferred, when the availability of processing power in dedicated hardware (DSPs, FPGAs, etc.) is crucial and when there is plenty of CPU power at hand. In this paper, we will focus on the protocol stack software as a reconfigurable software system, which will benefit from organic computing ideas. Such a protocol stack can be used in SDR devices and other mobile terminals as well.

1.3 Outline

First, we want to introduce the Observer/Controller architectural pattern. We will begin with a short characterisation of the phenomenon of emergence and will point out the arising basic contradiction of top-down design vs. bottom-up development, which we will run into if we try to exploit emergence in technical systems. Then we will show how we can escape this contradiction, basically by combining creative bottom-up mechanisms with a mechanism which enforces top-down constraints.

An example for a complex software system – a reconfigurable protocol stack – will be used to explore analogies to organic feedback systems. We will describe the introduced protocol stack framework, its fundamental components, and exemplary protocol stack implementations.

Having described the theoretical background and the system implementation, we will review the implementation of the Observer/Controller structure. We will end up with implementation results, conclusions and an outlook on future work.

2 How Can We Control Emergence?

2.1 Self-organisation

Properties of complex systems have been investigated predominantly with the help of natural systems like dissipative structures [5], autocatalytic cycles [6] or ant hives. Lansing and Kremer [7] have analysed the organisation patterns of rice growing on the island of Bali. Their assumption of a locality-based co-adaptation coordination algorithm ("Do as your best neighbour does!") leads to a simulated distribution of cropping patterns very similar to the one observed in reality. Ilya Prigogine [5] has investigated dissipative structures – chemical autocatalytic reactions far from thermal equilibrium –, which show self-organisation effects of high aesthetic appeal. Even technical systems like the Internet have been shown to reveal self-organisation patterns. A visualisation of communication patterns reveals a surprising degree of order although the Internet has developed without an explicit master plan. It has been shown that these traffic patterns are subject to the so-called small world effect [6, 8, and 9] which seems to be characteristic for complex communication systems like the brain.

Another experiment, which has been carried out with miniature robots as well as in simulations is that of the "candle movers". A robot is able to move one or two tea candles. If it encounters more than two it stops, turns in an arbitrary direction and moves straightly until it finds the next candles and so on. Intuitively, a random distribution of candles on a floor subject to a collection of randomly moving robots should result in a random distribution of candles. The experiments, however, show consistently that under these conditions the candles are assembled into a very small number of heaps. This is a nice example of very simple local rules leading – in cooperation with many autonomous components – to a global pattern exhibiting higher degrees of order.

Systems capable of self-organisation seem to have the following properties: They consist of *autonomous* processes, which use *local* information (context) for local behaviour. They develop by *evolutionary* mechanisms (recombination, selection, and mutation), using *trial and error*. This implies *large populations* of elements. The stability of such systems seems to increase with an increasing *interconnectedness* [10].

2.2   Emergence

A central notion of self-organising systems is the concept of emergence. Emergence is a property of our world. The development from chaotic starting conditions towards systems exhibiting higher degrees of order can be described as an effect of emergent behaviour. Emergence is defined as a property of a total system, which cannot be derived from the simple summation of properties of its constituent subsystems. Emergent phenomena are characterised by (i) the interaction of mostly large numbers of individuals (ii) without central control with the result of (iii) a system behaviour, which has not been "programmed" explicitly into the individuals (www.beart.org.uk/Emergent/).

An example of an emergent system property is the resonance frequency of a resonant circuit. It is a system property, which cannot be explained in terms of the properties of a single constituent. It develops from the dynamic cooperation of the capacitor and the inductivity.

Emergent behaviour in a complex technical system is an ambivalent property, especially if this system has safety-critical tasks. We must develop strategies, which leave sufficient degrees of freedom for self-organisation while keeping control over the emergent system to avoid unwanted results. This requirement leads to the problem of *controlled emergence* as discussed below. But how can we build emergent systems in the first place? There are quite a few "toy" systems showing creative behaviour in computer simulations. Examples are Tom Ray's Tierra system [11], Karl Sims' "Virtual Creatures" [12], Lindenmayer Systems [13], or "Woods"-like environments [14]. Characteristic for these algorithms is the evolutionary or genetic paradigm: It works with large populations of individuals (representing solutions), random mutations, recombination and a selection mechanism based on an objective function. Due to their low speed, genetic algorithms [15] and similar approaches like simulated annealing or fuzzy classifier systems [16] have been used so far predominantly for off-line optimisation. It is a topic of future research to enable such algorithms to run under real time conditions and with restricted resources.

2.3 Top-Down vs. Bottom-Up

The classical top-down design process is based on the assumption that the developer is in principle able to predict all possible system states. In order to achieve this goal, the design process is organised strictly hierarchically. It consists of a sequence of modelling steps starting with a high level specification leading through a number of refinements finally to a model, which can serve directly to control a manufacturing machine or generate executable code. Today's technical systems, however, begin to show complexities to such an extent that a complete prediction becomes impossible.

Emergent behaviour reflects bottom-up constraint propagation. In the candle mover example, it is not possible to predict the exact positions of the robots or the candles but we get some similar kind of order every time we run the experiment. From the technical perspective it would be highly desirable to be able to predict more exactly the final outcome, in other words: We would like to be able to describe the relationship between local and global behaviour.

The top-down procedure is at the very heart of the engineering paradigm: We (the designers) set the goals, which have to be reached by the technical system. It is not very realistic to expect a collection of metal parts to assemble into a Mercedes car! This means that the exploitation of emergence within technical systems leads to a basic contradiction, namely the requirement of "controlled emergence". It is not clear today how controlled emergence can be realised but the Observer/Controller structure is a possibility.

2.4 Observer/Controller Architectures

The solution seems to be in the middle between pure top-down and pure bottom-up. In future, we expect a gradual increase of the degrees of freedom, which a technical system has during run time. The behaviour of a complex system will then be a combination of preset objectives and constraints, as defined by the system developer and adaptive "islands" where the system is allowed to make its own decisions. In order to develop such adaptive systems, we must introduce new system architectures, which allow the replacement of hard coding by goal setting (or motivation). This means, however, that our system now runs under the assumption of best effort and it can deliver sub-optimal results or even make mistakes. Hence we must take provisions to guide the system towards the optimum and guarantee that certain error conditions can never occur.

A basic structure supporting such a pattern is the Observer/Controller architecture. It borrows from a very simplified analogy to the human brain [17], where we find low level "circuits" (the brain stem) with the task to immediately react to sensory input (especially to pain in order to escape dangerous situations). These reactions occur subconsciously. Conscious decisions, generated by the neocortex, are filtered by certain areas of the interbrain – with the limbic system adding the emotional colouring –, before they are transformed into motion or other reactions by the brain stem. This filtering constitutes the influence of emotions on our actions. In case of a blocking decision by the limbic system the instruction from the neocortex is not executed.

In a technical system the Observer/Controller plays the role of the limbic system: It observes the external environment via the sensory input as well as the internal behaviour of the low level execution unit and manipulates it in several ways, as we will discuss below. The usage of Observer/Controller structures can be regarded as the introduction of emotions into technical systems. A computer might then decide (by means of its "limbic system") that it will not act as commanded by the user! Here, a word of caution seems appropriate: In a technical system we expect the goals to be set by the user (i.e. top – down) even if the exact procedure of execution is left to a creative lower level mechanism. In the brain it is not at all clear if the neocortex, the seat of consciousness, is the (single) origin of the commands. There seems to exist evidence that the brain stem could be the active part while the neocortex is asked for a second opinion from time to time [17].

The basic Observer/Controller structure is shown in Figure 1. In addition to the low level execution unit responsible for the working level stimulus/response mechanism, we have now a higher level Observer/Controller. The observer part receives input from the environment as well as from the execution unit (e.g. data about the present load conditions). The controller compares the situation reported by the observer to the goals set by the user and reacts by reconfiguring the execution unit.

In order to discuss this mechanism in more detail, we have to introduce a few terms:

- iStructure and iBehaviour mean the internal relationship of the components of a system and their procedural behaviour in time. An example is the composition of a CMOS inverter from an n-channel and a pchannel transistor (iStructure) and their cooperation in terms of electrical voltages and currents (iBehaviour).

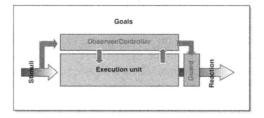

Fig. 1. Basic Observer/Controller structure. The controller intervenes by changing the behaviour of the execution unit and/or by setting filter functions in the guard to prevent erroneous outputs.

- eBehaviour (external behaviour) means the abstracted view from the outside on this system. In the above example of the inverter circuit the eBehaviour could be a logical view with one input, one output and the two states 0 and 1.[1]

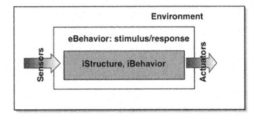

Fig. 2. Fixed system: The embedded system reacts to external stimuli. No modification of its external behaviour (eBehaviour) is possible at runtime. Internal structure and behaviour are fixed.

A conventional embedded system (such as an ABS[2] controller) shows a fixed external behaviour (eBehaviour in Figure 2) based on a fixed internal structure and specified internal behaviour (iBehaviour, iStructure): The ABS controller receives sensory input, processes it and reacts through actuators.

In a first step towards adaptivity we allow an external controller (possibly the human designer) to modify the eBehaviour by changing internal parameters of the system (Figure 3).

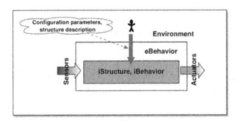

Fig. 3. Adjustable system: External (human) controller sets internal parameters such that the desired eBehaviour is reached.

Instead of modifying a large number of those parameters, it would be more desirable for the (human) external controller to declare or specify the eBehaviour on an higher abstraction level and leave it to an internal controller to translate those high level goals to low level parameter changes (Figure 4). These goals are comparable to motivations if we regard our technical system as an autonomous "animal". Now it is the task of the internal controller to permanently check the consistency of the current goals, the state of the environment and the internal state of the embedded system (like error or over-

---

[1] There is also an external structure (eStructure), which we will neglect for simplicity.
[2] Anti Lock Braking system.

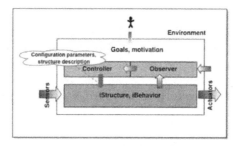

Fig. 4. Constant goals (homeostasis) are maintained by the Observer/Controller.

load conditions). In analogy to living systems we can speak of homeostasis[3]. This adds an additional higher level feedback loop to the system, in addition to the lower level productive feedback loop responsible for the actual function (e.g. the ABS system).

It remains largely open at his point in time how we can formulate the high level goals and how they are transformed into low level structural and behavioural changes. A promising approach to this problem is based on the software technology of design-bycontract and assertions (as introduced by [18]). Assertions are if-then rules inserted into code. The if-part can contain logical (a $\leq$ 5) or timing (event2 @ 5 ms after event1) conditions. The violation of an assertion leads to a reaction as specified in the then-part. The reaction could simply be a call to the observer, which takes appropriate action. The assertion mechanism has been shown to be very useful especially in combination with system simulations [19] since in a simulated virtual prototype, we can instrument not only the software with assertions, but also the modelled hardware.

A second solution to the control of emergent mechanisms is the introduction of a guard. A guard receives the output from the adaptive control mechanism and filters it according to rules set by the Controller. An example for such a filtering action would be the detection of the creative attempt of a learning traffic light controller to set all traffic lights to "green". A reinforcement learning mechanism will probably punish this attempt but in a real world situation we must guarantee that such dangerous outputs are not realised.

The system behaviour – when following the Observer/Controller architectural pattern – will be a combination of preset objectives and constraints as well as adaptive "islands" where the system is allowed to make its own decisions (and errors!).

To implement an organic system, hard coded behaviour must be replaced by fuzzier goal settings, which describe the overall systems motivation leading to additional degrees of freedom. This should lead to a satisfactory behaviour even under unprecedented conditions but it may also yield suboptimal results or even allow the system to make errors. For the research of organic computer systems, an observable system described

---

[3] Homeostasis is one of the most remarkable and most typical properties of highly complex open systems. A homeostatic system (an industrial firm, a large organization, a cell) is an open system that maintains its structure and functions by means of a multiplicity of dynamic equilibriums rigorously controlled by interdependent regulation mechanisms. Such a system reacts to every change in the environment, or to every random disturbance, through a series of modifications of equal size and opposite direction to those that created the disturbance. The goal of these modifications is to maintain the internal balances (http://pespmc1.vub.ac.be/HOMEOSTA.html).

by internal structure and behaviour must be found and extended with observer and controller components. The following sections will introduce a reconfigurable protocol stack architecture as exemplary execution unit of an organic computer system. Subsequently it will be shown, that an agent-based monitoring system is capable of observing the protocol stack structure and behaviour. Furthermore, the described reconfiguration component implements the controller entity as projected in the Observer/Controller architectural pattern.

3   Reconfigurable Protocol Stack Architecture

The following section describes a reconfigurable protocol stack architecture similar to architectures like [20], but specially tailored for mobile terminals [22] and enhanced with ideas from organic computing. After a general overview, basic framework components will be described, enabling the design and implementation of actual protocol stack instances, which in turn are supervised by an agent-based monitoring framework.

3.1   Overview

Modern mobile terminals are supporting a huge number of various communication standards such as GSM, GPRS, EDGE, WLAN, Bluetooth, and so on. To manage the increasing software complexity, new approaches for designing such complex software systems and for managing such systems during run-time have to be found.

Supported by the depicted framework approach, the software designer has an extensive library of components and modules at his hands to choose from whilst implementing actual protocol stack software. The experience gained so far shows that building protocol stacks from a component library specially tailored for protocol stack design, eases the complex implementation task because the implementer can concentrate on protocol stack specific parts or components. Furthermore, a protocol stack library of generic components shortens implementation time as well as debugging time.

During run-time, the framework offers the ability to exchange protocol stack modules on the fly without loosing network connection. Protocol stack modules in the portrayed framework are much more fine granular than e.g. kernel modules of the Linux kernel. This offers a much higher degree of reconfiguration options of the protocol stack structure. For example, in the proposed TCP/IP implementation, there are only four layers. Assumed that there are three different implementations to choose from, this leads to $3^4 = 81$ possible configurations. In future, reconfiguration will be supported on class level, yielding a barely limited number of possible configurations. In addition, to fix errors or just to update to a newer version, protocol stack modules even can be downloaded from a device management server situated somewhere in the network.

3.2   Protocol Stack Framework

The protocol stack framework, as shown in Figure 5, consists of three major components. The framework itself, providing management and supervision functionalities, the component library, providing the protocol stack modules and the protocol stack instances itself, executing in the framework.

The following paragraphs describe the major framework components in detail.

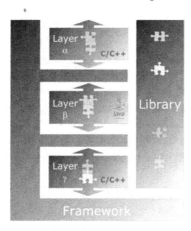

Fig. 5. Software architecture of protocol stack framework.

3.2.1   Framework Component

The protocol stack framework bundles all of its management and supervision function-ality in the framework component. The main framework component is the configuration and control manager. The configuration manager parses XML descriptions of protocol stacks. A protocol stack description is a graph consisting of nodes (modules, layers) and edges (connectors). Layers have to implement defined data and control interfaces to become exchangeable. Furthermore, the configuration manager decides which pro-tocol stack will be constructed from the textual descriptions to satisfy the applications request for a certain network connection. The matching protocol stack for the requested network connection is matched by using QoS[4] parameters that an application requests by opening a network socket.

Applications running on top of the protocol stack use a socket interface (similar to the BSD socket interface [21]) to communicate with the network. For protocol stack internal message passing, the framework offers data message passing functionality as well as a mailbox system for control message passing between protocol stack layers. Because the framework uses the thread-per-message model for internal data message passing [22], thread management is another major functionality implemented by the protocol stack framework.

Another special component of the framework is the monitoring component, which will be described in detail in Section 3.4.

3.2.2   Library

The framework library provides generic classes for basic tasks, which are carried out in every protocol stack, implemented for the framework. Provided classes range from simple byte arithmetic/manipulation, checksum, fragmentation classes up to data and control message passing classes. Further to the generic classes already provided in the library, specific protocol stack classes can be stored in the library or downloaded over the air from a configuration management server as well and can be subsequently used in protocol stack configurations as well.

---

[4] Quality of Service.

3.2.3   Protocol Stack Instances

Protocol stack instances, as created by the configuration manager, may contain any combination of modules interconnected by defined connectors. Due to the fact, that traditional protocol stacks are implemented in native programming languages such as C and C++, native protocol stack modules are supported by implementing a module wrapper. Such a wrapper is a Java class implementing the necessary data and control interfaces, connecting the native implementation to the stack framework by JNI[5]. A number of protocol stack configurations, some of them contain only Java modules, some of them contain Java modules and wrapped native modules, have validated the described mechanism.

3.3   Protocol Stack Examples

As mentioned before, protocol stack instances are built from generic components found in the frameworks library as well as protocol stack specific components. The protocol stack architecture has been validated with a number of TCP/IP protocol stack configurations. Figure 6 shows an example TCP/IP protocol stack configuration.

The example TCP/IP protocol stack consists of four layers derived from generic library components (Layer class). The partitioning is more or less carried out according to the ISO OSI seven-layer model [23]. There is a dedicated layer for each of the TCP/IP protocol suite protocols. The application communicates with the protocol stack using a BSD socket interface. The framework "fingers", between adjacent layers, provide monitoring and supervision capabilities, which help in detecting degradation in network performance or rogue terminal[6] behaviour as achieved by the agent-based monitoring component.

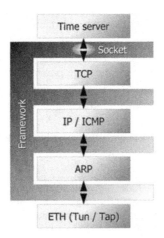

Fig. 6. TCP/IP protocol stack as configured by the protocol stack framework.

---

[5] Java Native Interface.

[6] The term rogue terminal stems from computer terminals or ID card terminals becoming rogues. They try to steal resources (i.e. network capacity, bandwidth), confidential information (i.e. passwords, encryption keys), or try to harm the network, user or equipment.

Various TCP/IP stack configurations have been validated by prototype implementations. The reconfiguration of protocol stack instances has been exemplarily validated by exchanging the ARP[7] layer during run-time. The ARP layer exists in two implementations: A pure Java implementation and an ARP implementation in C (wrapped in Java), which have been exchanged during run-time without loosing the applications open socket connection.

The reconfiguration process has been triggered by the agent-based monitoring framework, which will be described in the following section.

3.4 Agent-Based Monitoring

The main characteristic of an organic computer is its ability to adapt dynamically to current conditions or its environment [1]. For that, a technical system has to contain a component, which monitors the systems current internal structure and behaviour. For the protocol stack framework, this task is carried out by the agent-based monitoring component as seen in Figure 7.

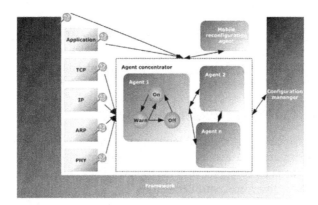

Fig. 7. Agent-based monitoring software architecture.

The main component inside the agent-based monitoring framework is the so-called agent concentrator. As shown by Tarkoma and Laukkanen in [24], agents do not have to be heavy-weight, they can be suitable for resource-constraint mobile devices as well. By dynamically concentrating one or more light-weight agents in a networked manner, the characteristic features of agents, such as autonomy, adaptiveness, collaborative behaviour, and mobility [25] can be utilised for processing observed structure and behaviour information, gained from the currently installed or executing protocol stack instances. In the depicted protocol stack framework, the agents observe communication and thread status information (internal behaviour) such as sent and received packets/bytes and number of send/receive threads currently executing in the framework. Furthermore, the agents can request the current protocol stack configurations from the configuration manager (internal structure) to decide how they have to be reconfigured.

---

[7] Internet Address Resolution Protocol as described in RFC 826 (Request For Comments 826, Internet Standards).

Observable internal protocol stack structure or behaviour information is produced by socalled software probes, provided by the framework, and inserted into executing protocol stack instances. The agents in turn evaluate the information they have subscribed for by the observer pattern (see Section 4.1 for details).

For implementation of the internal behaviour, we recommend a finite state machine model. For that, the monitoring agent framework provides generic agent, state and transition classes, as well as classes, which can host rule-based decision-making algorithms. This approach is lightweight enough to allow multiple agents to execute on mobile terminal platforms.

The intelligence of the reasoning system is currently captured in rules that contain conditions and actions. Because rule-based systems are limited in their level of intelligence, smarter reasoning algorithms like classifier systems [26] can be easily integrated into the connected agent's finite state machine approach. Even external agents (provided by third parties) can be integrated by over-the-air download/synchronisation from a device management server.

The protocol stack framework configuration manager component provides a reconfiguration interface for reconfiguration actions, issued by the agent-based monitoring system. Currently executing protocol stack instances can be tuned (e.g. change parameters, etc.) or even structurally reconfigured (e.g. exchange of protocol stack layer implementations) during run-time. Completely new protocol stack configurations can be requested as well, in order to optimise network communication performance or to accomplish the user preferences better.

4   Observer/Controller Implementation

As mentioned in Section 1.2, a closed loop control pattern, consisting of a controlled process, sensors, an observer and a controller, can be typically found in organic computing systems. The main components of the protocol stack architecture can be mapped quite naturally onto Observer/Controller entities.

An executing protocol stack instance can be regarded as observed process. The analysis of protocol stack structure and run-time information, such as parameters, stack status, statistics, configuration, etc., will be carried out be the agent concentrator component and its intelligent agents. Whenever the multi agent system concludes, that the protocol stack's current structure or behaviour is not optimal, it informs the protocol stack framework configuration manager (controller component). The configuration manager in turn can then change configuration, parameters, and structural description of the executing protocol stack instance.

Although the user is still in control of the protocol stack framework by issuing abstract goals, motivations, or preferences, such as QoS requirements like bandwidth, accepted costs, etc., the organic computing system has taken over the fine-tuning of concrete protocol stack configurations and their settings from the designer or user of the system.

4.1   Observation: Implementation for Monitoring Agents

As seen in the last section, the agent concentrator component of the protocol stack framework implements the observer component of the earlier introduced Observer/Controller architectural pattern.

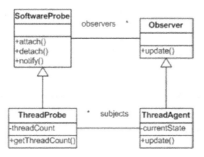

Fig. 8. Observer pattern as implemented by ThreadProbe and Thread-Agent.

The concrete monitoring agents, accommodated in the agent concentrator, are part of the observer pattern [27] for getting system status information from software probes. As seen in Figure 8, the observable object ThreadProbe is inherited from the abstract SoftwareProbe class. Observers like the ThreadAgent (inherited from the abstract Observer class) can subscribe to SoftwareProbe objects by calling the SoftwareProbe.attach() method. If the information stored in a SoftwareProbe e.g. ThreadProbe changes, all attached Observers will be informed by calling their update() method.

The use of the observer pattern eases the attachment and detachment of monitoring agents to software probes and reduces the information distribution complexity. Furthermore, monitoring agents again can become observable objects, allowing other agents to subscribe to their processed information. This mechanism is the foundation for building complex multi agent networks inside the agent concentrator component for monitoring the protocol stack instances.

4.2   Control: Implementation of a Configuration Manager

The controller component of the Observer/Controller architectural pattern is responsible for actually changing the processes internal behaviour and structure by issuing new parameters or process configurations. In the depicted protocol stack architecture, the reconfiguration manager component is responsible for tuning and configuring protocol stack instances. In the current approach, the actual decision that a reconfiguration is necessary is currently completely taken by the monitoring agents (observer). This leaves only the execution of a reconfiguration to the reconfiguration manager (controller). The reconfiguration manager consequently only implements the generation of protocol stack instances from given protocol graphs, stored in the XML protocol stack descriptions. Furthermore, the reconfiguration manager implements additional methods, which provide information about possible protocol stack configurations, and their properties to assist the monitoring agents in their reconfiguration decision.

The Observer/Controller architecture pattern also allows splitting the decision-making in a different way. The decision-making can be carried out completely in the controller entity; mixed approaches are feasible as well.

5   Conclusion and Outlook

The concept of observers and controllers has been introduced in this paper. A framework for reconfigurable protocol stacks and its agent-based monitoring framework have been portrayed. It has been shown, that the Observer/Controller architectural pattern is a natural way of implementing an organic, self-monitoring, self-organising and selfconfiguring software system. Each major component of the protocol stack framework has a matching counterpart in the Observer/Controller architectural pattern.

The current implementation status of the protocol stack framework shows, that the framework approach is feasible and furthermore speeds up implementation for future protocol stacks. Due to similarities in protocol stack design, the generic components from the library are a welcome simplification of the implementation process. Specific protocol stack functionalities were easily implemented based on the framework. The prototype TCP/IP implementation has served as a good validation platform for the portrayed ideas and will serve in future as a valuable platform for further research.

The described agent-based monitoring implementation has demonstrated, that intelligently controlled reconfiguration of a protocol stack is possible and will yield performance advantages. It also decreases the user's effort for performance corrections.

It has also become clear that the degree of freedom, which the "creative" part of the reconfigurable stack architecture is given, should be increased. We are considering to using a rule-based approach like fuzzy classifier systems for this purpose. But it must also be clear that there exists a delicate balance between increased freedom and security concerns. Future work in the protocol stack framework will comprise the integration of more intelligent reasoning technologies into the agent-based monitoring. Accompanying the work on the organic capabilities, the framework will be extended to support more networking standards and protocols (Bluetooth, WLAN, etc.).

References

1. Müller-Schloer, C.: Organic Computing – On the Feasibility of Controlled Emergence. Proceedings of CODES+ISSS 2004. ACM. Stockholm. September 2004.
2. Brainexplorer. Available at http://www.brainexplorer.org. September 2004.
3. Herkersdorf, A., et. al.: Towards a Framework and a Design Methodology for Autonomic Integrated Systems. In Dadam P., Reichert, M., editors, Proceedings of the Workshop on Organic Computing, Informatik 2004, Ulm, September 2004.
4. Software-defined radio (SDR). Available at http://en.wikipedia.org/wiki/Softwaredefined_radio. September 2004.
5. Prigogine, I. and Kondepudi, K.: Modern Thermodynamics: From Heat Engines to Dissipative Structures. John Wiley & Sons, Chichester, 1998.
6. Albert, R. and Barab'asi, A.: Statistical mechanics of complex networks. Review of Modern Physics, 74:47, 2002.
7. Lansing, J. and Kremer, J.: Emergent properties of balinese water temple networks: Coadaptation on a rugged fitness landscape. In C. Langton, editor, Proceedings of the Workshop on Artificial Life (ALIFE '92), (Santa Fe, NM, USA, June 1992), Reading, MA, 1994. Addison-Wesley.
8. Cohen, D.: All the world's a net. New Scientist, 174(2338):24, April 2003.
9. Mendes, J. and Dorogovtsev, S.: Evolution of networks: from biological nets to the internet and WWW. Oxford University Press, 2003.
10. Prigogine, I. and Stengers, I.: Dialog mit der Natur, page 181. Piper, 1990.
11. Ray, T. S.: An approach to the synthesis of life. In C. Langton, C. Taylor, J. Farmer, and S. Rasmussen, editors, Artificial Life II, volume X of SFI Studies in the Sciences of Complexity. Addison-Wesley, Redwood City, 1991.

12. Sims, K.: Evolving virtual creatures. In Computer Graphics (Siggraph '94 Proceedings), New York, July 1994. ACM Press.
13. Prusinkiewicz, P. and Lindenmayer, A.: The algorithmic beauty of plants. Springer Verlag, New York, 1990.
14. S. Wilson. Classifier fitness based on accuracy. Evolutionary Computation, 3(2):149–176, 1995. (Section 4.3).
15. Goldberg, D.: Genetic Algorithms in Search, Optimization, and Machine Learning. Addison-Wesley, Reading, Massachusetts, 1989.
16. Koblitz, D. and Müller-Schloer, C.: Extension of fuzzy classifier-mechanisms for adaptive embedded systems through a-priori-knowledge and constraints. In D. Polani, J. Kim, and T. Martinetz, editors, Fifth German Workshop on Artificial Life – GWAL-5, Berlin, 2002. Akademische Verlagsgesellschaft Aka.
17. Roth, G.: Aus Sicht des Gehirns. Suhrkamp, 2003.
18. Meyer, B.: Object-Oriented Software Construction. Prentice Hall, 2nd edition, 2000.
19. Oodes T., Krisp, H., and Müller-Schloer, C.: On the combination of assertions and virtual prototyping for the design of safety-critical systems. In ARCS 2002/Trends in Network and Pervasive Computing (Karlsruhe). Springer, 2002.
20. Schmidt, D. C. et al.: ADAPTIVE: A dynamically assembled protocol transformation, integration, and evaluation environment. Journal of Concurrency: Practice and Experience 5 (4), 269–286. June 1993.
21. Stevens, W. R.: Unix Network Programming. 1990. Prentice-Hall.
22. Schöler, Th., et. al.: Design, Implementation and Validation of a Generic and Reconfigurable Protocol Stack Framework for Mobile Terminals. Workshop on Dynamic and Reconfigurable Architectures DARES 2004. Hachioji. 2004.
23. Zimmerman, H.: OSI Reference Model – The ISO Model of Architecture for Open Systems Interconnection. IEEE Transactions on Communications COM-28, No. 4: April 1980.
24. S. Tarkoma and M. Laukkanen. Supporting software agents on small devices. In AAMAS '02: Proceedings of the first international joint conference on Autonomous agents and multiagent systems, pages 565–566. ACM Press, 2002.
25. Feldman, S. and Yu, E.: Intelligent agents: A primer. Available at http://www.infotoday.com/searcher/oct99/feldman+yu.htm. October 1999.
26. Richards, R. A.: Zeroth-order shape optimization utilizing a learning classifier system. Section 3.1 3.1 Introducing the Classifier System. Available at http://www.stanford.edu/ buc/SPHINcsX/. 1995.
27. Gamma, E., et. al.: Design Patterns: Elements of Reusable Object Oriented Software. Addison Wesley Longman, Inc. October 1994.

The Organic Features
of the AMIDAR Class of Processors

Stephan Gatzka and Christian Hochberger

TU Dresden, 01062 Dresden, Germany
{Stephan.Gatzka,Christian.Hochberger}@inf.tu-dresden.de

Abstract. In this contribution we present a novel general model for adaptive processors with organic features. We describe its basic principle of operation. The adaptive operations that are possible with this model are thoroughly discussed with respect to organic computing. The model allows runtime variations of the type and number of functional units as well as variations of the communication structure. Experimental results show that a processor implementing this model can self-optimize its architecture for several diverse applications.

1 Introduction

Configurable Systems on a Chip (CSoC) are becoming more and more important in the embedded systems market. The main reasons for their growing popularity can be found in their cost effectiveness and flexibility. Mask costs will be very high in the future due to the required high resolution [16]. CSoCs will be cost effective under these circumstances since they offer the possibility to implement multi protocol/multi standard systems with a single chip and thus can be produced in much larger quantities. They will be flexible since the reconfigurable part can be used to adapt the hardware to future requirements that are unknown at the time of the initial development.

With CSoCs it will be possible to implement new IO functionality and peripherals in an existing system. It will also be possible to have peripherals to increase the performance (e.g. crypto accelerators), but the processor core itself cannot be changed or enhanced. To overcome this problem, we introduce the AMIDAR class of processor (*Adaptive Mi*croinstruction *D*riven *A*rchitecture). It is a novel model and architecture of processors that can be adapted during runtime to the requirements an application and exhibits several organic features. The main purpose of this contribution is to discuss these organic features.

Although C as a programming language still dominates the development of embedded software, the growing tendency to use Java as a programming language for embedded systems makes this language an attractive object of study. Due to the code shipping abilities of Java [10], it is most likely, that especially systems programmed in Java will experience a shift in the requirements during their lifetime. Also, Java is used in many computing systems with adaptive and organic features. One example is the Caruso framework for Low-Power autonomic systems [2]. The most prominent reason for choosing a Java bytecode processor to evaluate our model, is that Java bytecode can be analyzed during runtime much easier than most other assembly languages and thus it is the ideal basis for a dynamic hardware/software partitioning.

M. Beigl and P. Lukowicz (Eds.): ARCS 2005, LNCS 3432, pp. 154–166, 2005.

1.1 Related Work

Hardware implementations of Java bytecode processors are available in a large number. Yet, to our knowledge only the JEM-II processor can be customized for the application requirements [1]. But in this case only new bytecodes can be introduced as microcode sequences.

Also, recently some work has been conducted to build customized accelerators to speed up the execution of Java bytecode [11]. In this case only a small part of the bytecode execution is implemented in hardware and the main execution is done on a conventional processor.

Other researchers have addressed (re)configurable processors in general. Some are just parameterized RISC cores [3], while others are truly reconfigurable. They typically depend on compile time analysis and generate a single datapath configuration for an application beforehand [4, 5, 12]. Very few processors are really reconfigured at run-time [15]. But even in this case, the configurations and the time of reconfiguration are defined at compile time.

To the best of our knowledge, there is no general model for an adaptive processor.

1.2 Paper Outline

In the following section we will shortly discuss organic computing and its implications on hardware design. In section 3 we will describe the general model of an adaptive processor in detail. In section 4 we will then present the various adaptive operations that are possible with this model. Section 5 introduces some simple heuristics that can be used to adapt a specific architecture to applications. Experimental results for a Java bytecode processor are shown in section 7. Finally, a conclusion and an outlook onto future work are given.

2 Organic Computing

Organic computing [17] has recently been introduced as a means to structure computing systems in a biologically inspired way. The key idea is to use mechanisms of natural systems to enhance the robustness and ease the deployment of computing systems.

Organic computing shares several ideas with autonomic computing, an initiative started by IBM in 2001 [13, 14]. Autonomic computing focuses on the self-X properties of computing systems: self-monitoring, self-optimizing, self-protecting, self-healing, self-configuring, ...

Many of these properties will be required in future embedded systems, since we will not be able to individually configure, monitor, repair and optimize the exploding number of such devices in the future. We will not address all of those self-X properties in this paper, since they have very different complexity. Self-monitoring, self-optimizing and partly self-configuring are already part of the work presented here. We will also discuss how other self-X properties can be incorporated in the AMIDAR processor model.

But organic computing is more than autonomic computing, since an inherent feature of organic computing systems is the emergence of structure which was not plainly put into the algorithms and structures of the system, but comes from unforeseen interactions and mutual influences of components of the system.

The biological model which inspired the work presented here is that of a bone. A bone is reinforced in places where it is heavily loaded and is weakened in places where the load is reduced. The emergent structure of a bone is optimized to the sustained static load which is applied to the bone. If this load changes, the bone will adapt its internal structure to the new load. In an evolutionary sense this can even mean to grow some extra bones for new tasks.

3 Model

In this section we will describe how our model of an adaptive processor works in general and we will also give a formal description of it.

It is useful to have a general model of an adaptive processor to identify and categorize the elements of the architecture which are subject to adaptivity. This model should achieve the following goals: The model must be general enough to express different architectures, it should expose as much parallelism as possible, it should be applicable for a simulation and it must be close to a hardware implementation.

3.1 Overview

Figure 1 shows the basic structure of an AMIDAR processor.

It consists of four main types of components: a token generator, functional units (FU), a token distribution network and a communication structure. The token generator is a specialized functional unit, which is always required. It controls the other components of the processor by means of tokens. These tokens are sent to the FUs over the token distribution network. The tokens tell the FUs what to do with input data and where to send the results. Functional units can have a very wide range of meanings: ALUs, register files, program and/or data memory, specialized address calculation units, etc.

Data is passed between the FUs over the communication structure. This data can have various meanings: program information (instructions), address information or application data.

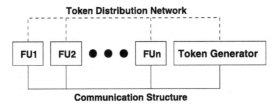

Fig. 1. General model.

3.2 Definitions

A functional unit is a piece of hardware that executes a specific task in the processor. Each FU has at most one output port[1] and an arbitrary number of input ports. A functional unit can be characterized by the values latency L, interval I and area A. The

---

[1] In fact, the token generator seems to be the only FU that potentially doesn't need an output port.

latency specifies the time needed by the FU to complete a single operation, whereas the interval specifies the time required between the start of two consecutive operations. The area specifies the required amount of chip resources for this unit. There can be different variations of FUs for the same task (latency optimized with minimal L, throughput optimized with minimal I or area optimized). Typically, latency optimal versions will not be throughput optimal and vice versa. Also, we assume that the consumed area is a monotonic function with respect to the values L and I. This means that a decrease of L or I always leads to an increased area. Other characterizations may be of interest like energy consumption or energy efficiency.

A token is a 5-tuple: $T = \{UID, OP, TAG, DP, INC\}$. UID identifies the functional unit to which this token belongs. OP specifies, which operation this FU has to carry out on the tagged data. The TAG is used to distinguish different data that is sent to the same FU. DP is the destination address, where the result of the operation is to be sent. It consists of a UID and a port number, since functional units can have more than one input port. INC is a boolean value, that controls the creation of the tag that is sent out with the result data. If it is *false*, the tag is passed unchanged. Otherwise the tag value is incremented. The meaning of this increment field is described in [6] and [9] in more detail. $UID(T_i)$ denotes the functional unit to which the token T_i is to be sent. $OP(T_i)$ denotes the operation that has to be carried out by token T_i. The meaning of $TAG(T_i)$, $DP(T_I)$ and $INC(T_i)$ is analogous.

An instruction is a composition of an arbitrary number of tokens: $Ins = \{T_1, T_2, \ldots, T_N\}$. The model itself doesn't require an order of the tokens, but specific implementations may impose restrictions on the order in which tokens are distributed to the functional units.

The communication structure consists of an arbitrary number of buses. A bus is a pair of sets of ports $B = (S, D)$ where S is the set of source ports driving the bus and D is the set of destination ports which read data from the bus. $S(B)$ denotes the set of source ports driving bus B and $D(B)$ denotes the set of destination ports of bus B. Since input ports and output port of FUs are always disjoint, buses are unidirectional.

3.3 Principle of Operation

Program information (i.e. the instructions) is sent to the token generator. Now, the token generator creates a set of tokens for this instruction and distributes them concurrently to the functional units. A functional unit begins the execution of a specific token as soon as the data ports have the data with the corresponding tag. Upon completion of an operation $OP(T_i)$ the result is sent to the destination $DP(T_i)$. The tag that is sent together with the result depends on $INC(T_i)$. $TAG(T_i)$ is used if it is false, otherwise $TAG(T_i) + 1$ is used. An instruction is completed, when all the corresponding tokens are executed. To keep the processor executing instructions, one of the tokens must be responsible for sending a new instruction to the token generator.

This data driven approach has a number of advantages:

- It implies a maximum of parallelism, which is only limited by data dependencies between consecutive instructions. It should be noted, that these dependencies can only originate from application data (like user register values or stack data).

- It does not rely on a particular timing of the FUs. Execution of an instruction will work, no matter how long a single FU needs to complete its token. Also, it is not necessary to know the structure of the communication network beforehand. Thus, it can be changed during runtime without the need to reconfigure the token generator. This is an ideal basis for the implementation of self-healing since it allows us to use redundant communication structures.
- It allows overlapping execution of instructions, since the token generator can start distributing tokens for more than one instruction. It only has to increment the tag field of the token for each instruction to separate data belonging to different instructions.
- It allows the introduction of new FUs and instructions using these FUs. For this purpose a small part of the token generator must be reconfigurable, to store the token set for new instructions and to attach new FUs to the token generator (which are not addressed by normal instructions). This allows us to implement a dynamic hardware/software partitioning according to the current requirements. Thus, the processor can be self-optimizing.

3.4   Special Precautions for Dynamically Synthesized FUs

It may be necessary to establish a synchronization mechanism between the FU and the token generator for dynamically synthesized FUs, like very data intensive FUs. Such functional units often are deeply pipelined to achieve a high throughput, but the latency on the other hand is also high. Other functional units waiting for the results may be blocked resulting in critical deadlock states. For this reason it is desirable to block the token generator from delivering new tokens until the FUs completed their calculations. For this task we introduce a SYN token which will be sent to the specialized functional unit. The token generator will not send further tokens until it receives the appropriate data from the FU. The functional unit receiving the SYN token must send a corresponding (to the tag inside the SYN token) data packet to the token generator. Now the token generator will continue to issue tokens. The data sent to the token generator may be used only to inform the token generator to continue its work, but may also be used to signal special states of the functional unit, for instance an exception. The token generator now can react on this special situation. It should be noted, that the usage of SYN tokens eliminates the parallelism inside the processor. The synchronization mechanism is certainly only required for dynamically synthesized FUs. The performance gain provided by such FUs should always be high enough to neglect the effects of the synchronization tokens.

Until now single data transfers between different FUs were introduced. Dynamically synthesized FUs often require high data volumes for high utilization. Single data transfer will not provide the required data bandwidth for such FUs. To overcome this problem AMIDAR-class processors may include support for burst and bulk transfers. Obviously, the token generator could distribute a single token for each of the required data transfers, but this seems to be very inefficient. In order to better support this situation we propose two specialized memory access tokens:

- Burst Data Transfer. In this case the memory needs two words of information to commence the operation: the starting address and the number of words to transfer. In case of a read request the memory starts to deliver data from consecutive addresses to the targeted FU upon reception of this information. In case of a write request the memory waits for the data to arrive and writes each incoming word to consecutive addresses.

- Bulk Data Transfer. It may occur that the synthesized FU needs to access the memory in irregular address patterns. In this case the FU needs to supply an address word for each transfer. The addresses are transfered to the memory over existing bus connections. This type of access is not as fast as a burst transfer, but is still much more efficient than distributing a set of tokens for each transfer (at least one for the address and one for the data).

3.5 Applicability

In general, the presented model can be applied to any kind of instruction processing, where a single instruction is composed of microinstructions. Obviously, the model doesn't produce good results, if there is a strict order of those microinstructions, since in this case no parallel execution of microinstructions can occur.

As previously mentioned, intermediate virtual assembly languages like Java bytecode or the .NET code seem to be good candidates for instruction sets. The range of FU implementations and communication structures is especially wide, if the instruction set has a very high abstraction level and basic operations are sufficiently complex.

The great advantage of this model is that the execution of an instruction is not dependent on the exact timing of FUs. Thus, FUs can be replaced at runtime with other versions of different characterizations. The same holds for the communication structure, which can be adapted to the requirements of the running applications. Thus, this model allows us to optimize global goals like performance or energy consumption.

4   Adaptive Operations

Adaptivity in this model can be seen on two hierarchical levels. On the top level the available chipsize is partitioned into an area for communication infrastructure and an area for functional units. Most of the currently available reconfigurable devices will not fully support this type of adaptivity, since resources for communication may not be suitable for functional units and vice versa. Yet, the model should be general enough to capture these possibilities. On the lower hierarchical level we have adaptive operations that reconfigure each of the two main areas. Figure 2 illustrates the different adaptive operations of our model.

Within the communication area several adaptive operations are possible:

- **Adding and Removing Connections.** If a functional unit has to send a data packet to another FU but is not connected to it, it is necessary to create a new connection.
- **Folding Buses.** Two buses may be merged to a new bus, if there are only few collisions on both buses.
- **Splitting Buses.** Buses with a high utilization and many delays can be split into two buses. The decision, which bus has connections to which FU is done by the heuristics as described in section 5.
- **Removing Buses.** Although this operation is already implied by folding of buses, it is useful as a separate operation, because folding of buses has a higher complexity than a simple remove.

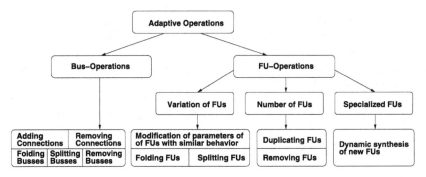

Fig. 2. Adaptive operations.

Several self-X features play a role regarding the adaptation of the communication network. Of course, the network is self-optimizing. The optimization process must be based on statistical data, which will be collected inside the AMIDAR processor, so an AMIDAR processor is necessarily self-monitoring. The monitoring aspects will be discussed in section 5.1 in more detail. Depending on the structure of the communication there may exist redundant communication paths, so AMIDAR processors may implement self-healing but until now we did not develop strategies to assist this process.

The emerging communication structure will arise only due to the requirements of a running application. No external trigger influences this process.

Within the functional unit area three different categories of adaptive operations can be applied:

– **Variation of FUs.** In this case variations of a certain FU may be available. From these variations the heuristics (see section 5) choose the most appropriate. This operation is fairly simple because it does not affect the token generator.
  Moreover, it is possible to split an FU into more specialized ones. For example, an ALU may be used for address calculations. This ALU may be split into an address calculation unit and a normal ALU. Folding of FUs into one FU is the complementary operation to FU splitting. Just like the variation of the communication structure this is an self-optimizing process based on self-monitoring.
– **Increase and Decrease the Number of Instances of an FU.** If the interval I of an FU cannot be decreased by a more specialized version, it is possible to duplicate this FU. Moreover, this concept may be used to introduce self-healing for AMIDAR processors. Vital FUs may be duplicated to continue program execution in erroneous conditions.
  Token distribution must be adapted to this new situation which must also care about an equal utilization of the new FUs. Therefore, this adaptive operation is not as easy to implement as a simple FU exchange.
– **Addition of Newly Synthesized FUs.** It is also possible to identify heavily used instruction sequences and synthesize a new FU for such sequences. The instruction sequence is replaced by a new instruction and the token generator is updated with a token sequence for this new instruction. It may be applicable to synthesize complete methods or functions. The calling function can easily replace the calling code

to access the new hardware. This is the most complicated adaptive operation, but promises the highest performance gain. The synthesis of new FUs is a combination of self-optimizing and self-configuring. A more detailed discussion about the effect of newly synthesized FUs for AMIDAR processors can be found in [8].

It should also be noted that the adaptive operations for functional units are inherently emergent. The synthesis of new FUs only emerges from code sequences that are very often in use. This new FU is only useful in the special context of the running application. This is also true for the variation of existing functional units. The combination of FUs evolves during the running application.

The general goal of all the adaptive operations is: the weakest bone will be strengthened.

5   Heuristics

According to the adaptive operations described in section 4 we need heuristics to decide which adaptive operations lead to the best results regarding the requirements of the running application. The configuration manager (section 6) is responsible for the implementation of the heuristics regarding a predefined policy. The heuristics have to decide, how the available chip area should be divided. There must be global heuristics that calculates the ratio between chipsize for FUs and chipsize for buses. Furthermore, we need local heuristics to assign the resources within the different areas of adaptivity (communication and FUs). Figure 3 shows the interaction between global and local heuristics.

5.1   Statistical Data

To achieve the self-optimizing and selfconfiguring features as described in section 4 the AMIDAR processor must be self-monitoring. Self-monitoring means, that the processor has to collect statistical data. This is possible on two architectural levels. On the one hand the processor should be able to identify code fragments, methods etc. as candidates for a specialized hardware unit. Some preliminary results about this topic will be presented in [7].

On the other hand statistical data is required to identify the bottlenecks of the current communication structure and the general purpose functional units. This data is the input to several heuristics which decide how to achieve the optimization goals best.

Up to now all heuristics focus on performance optimization and are based on stalls and utilization of functional units and buses. The stalls are divided into *input stalls* and *wait stalls*, so every component requires two counters to store them. An input stall occurs, if a component (FU or bus) could not accept data because it is currently working. Input stalls can occur in buses and functional units. This is an indicator, that a component is apparently not efficient enough to handle incoming data. More precisely, an input stall in an FU indicates that the interval I of the FU is not low enough.

Wait stalls occur if a component is ready to work, but has to wait for input data. Wait stalls are saved in the sending component, because the sending component is not efficient enough to deliver data in time, i.e., the latency L is to high.

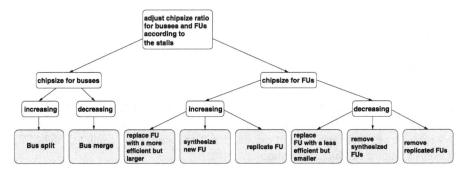

Fig. 3. Interaction between global and local heuristics.

5.2   Global and Local Heuristics

The collected statistical data is the input for the heuristics. The global heuristics are very straightforward. The main idea of the global heuristics is a slider, which divides the overall chipsize into chipsize for communication and chipsize for functional units. The criterion for shifting the ratio of chip size for communication and chip size for FUs is based on monitoring stalls inside the communication structure and the FUs. An attenuation factor ensures that only long-termed requirements cause a reconfiguration. Thus, after a large number of execution steps the global heuristics can shift one cost point between the communication structure and the FUs.

The local heuristics decide autonomously how to deal with the globally assigned chip area. There are local heuristics for the communication structure and for the functional units.

If the local heuristics for buses can use more chipsize, the heuristics try to split the bus with most stalls. The source and destination information for delayed data packages are used to make new connections between functional units. If the local heuristics for communication structures have to save chip area, it will first try to merge two buses. If no buses can be merged, connections of buses that were very seldom in use would be removed.

The heuristics for functional units have more different operations. If the heuristics can use more chipsize, it is possible to replace an FU by a more efficient one, duplicate an FU and synthesize a new FU. First of all, the heuristics try to exchange the FU with most stalls by a more efficient one. The different types of stalls control, which variation of an FU is used to replace the current FU.

If an FU has many input stalls, it cannot accept data because it is currently working. The FU is replaced by a throughput optimized one. If the FU has many wait stalls, this indicates, that another FU was waiting for data. So we need a latency optimized version of the FU. If a functional unit could not be improved anymore, the heuristics may consider to duplicate this FU.

If the heuristics for functional units have to save chipsize, it first removes duplicate FUs. If the heuristics have to save more chipsize, FUs with the fewest stalls and lowest utilization are replaced by slower but smaller versions.

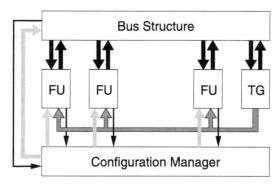

Fig. 4. Model with configuration manager.

Heuristics that trigger a direct synthesis of a specialized FU cannot only be based on stalls inside an FU. The code memory has to track which opcode sequences or methods/functions are often used. If these sequences are often slowed down by stalls in the FUs, it may be feasible to trigger a synthesis process for this opcode sequence.

6   Configuration Management

Up to now, the presented model does not include any component to manage the replacement of FUs or reconfiguration of the bus structure. Fig. 4 shows an extension of the model in order to manage the configuration of the processor.

The configuration manager gathers statistical data from the functional units and the bus structure. Typically, most of this data is collected with simple counters in the functional units and the buses. Also, the code memory can record how often selected parts of the code are executed. Based on this information the configuration manager can now act according to its policy: replacement of FUs, reconfiguration of the bus structure, synthesis of specialized FUs or deactivation of malfunctioning elements. Obviously, part of the configuration manager must be implemented in hardware, but the major part should be implemented in software. This software is then responsible for the implementation of the self-X properties like self-optimizing, self-healing and self-configuration.

7   Experimental Results

To test the organic features of our model we derived the architecture of a Java bytecode processor from it. A simulator implements this model to verify it and to prove that adaptivity leads to a measurable gain. Figure 5 shows the architecture of the Java bytecode processor.

Currently, the simulator adapts the communication structure to the requirements of the application (adding and removing of connections to buses, splitting and merging buses) and is able to exchange functional units. So the simulator can test the self-monitoring and self-optimizing (regarding performance optimization) features of the AMIDAR bytecode processor. Self-healing and self-configuring (dynamic synthesis of FUs) is currently not implemented. The heuristics and cost model are the same as described in section 5.

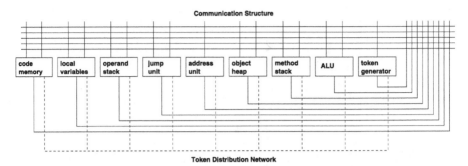

Fig. 5. Architecture of a Java bytecode processor.

7.1 Test Applications

To prove the effectiveness of adaptivity in the Java bytecode processor, two test applications with different characteristics had to be selected that are expected to lead to different structures. Therefore, a data dominated application and a control dominated application were chosen.

A Java program that calculates the Integer Discrete Cosine Transformation (IDCT) of an 8x8 byte array was used as the data dominated application. The control dominated application is a finite state machine (FSM). We expected that the resulting structures look different because of the very different usage of some functional units in the test applications. The IDCT heavily uses the object heap (for array accesses) and the ALU, whereas the state machine will use the jump unit especially. Operand stack and local variable memory will be used in both applications in the same manner. The different characteristics are reflected in the appearance of different bytecodes. The IDCT consists basically of array and ALU operations. In contrast, the state machine uses if-bytecodes, goto's and only few ALU operations.

7.2 Results

To evaluate the speedup of the dynamic bus adaption and FU exchange in comparison to a static architecture both test programs were executed in the simulator in different modes. Firstly, we measured the minimal cost (worst case performance), which results in one single bus for all components and slowest FUs. Then we measured the best case performance. Faster FUs were used if they lead to a performance improvement. The results are shown in table 1. It turns out, that the maximum speedup is 16% for the FSM and 27% for the IDCT. The small speedup for the FSM especially comes from the amount of jump instructions in the program. That's why the program code can't be parallelized very well.

Secondly, we ran the applications in adaptivity mode with a cost limit. According to table 1 the adaptive circuit for the IDCT program performs only 1% slower than the best case architecture, and the circuit for the state machine program is 5% slower than the best case circuit. The cost limit in both cases is set to 82% of the best case circuit. Figure 6 shows more clearly, that the adaptive circuit is nearly equally fast as the best case but only requires half the cost increase compared to the cost increase of the best

Table 1. Measurements for the IDCT and FSM application.

	circuit	costs	clocks	used FUs		
				stack	loc. vars	ALU
IDCT	best	113	69802	piped	piped	piped
	worst	69	95952	normal	normal	slow
	adaptive	93	70578	piped	piped	piped
FSM	best	113	78327	piped	piped	piped
	worst	69	93416	normal	normal	slow
	adaptive	93	81580	piped	normal	normal

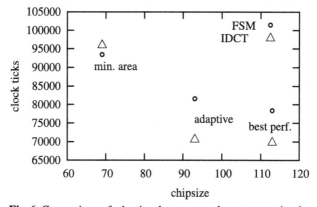

Fig. 6. Comparison of adaptive, best case and worst case circuits.

case. Table 1 also shows, which functional units were replaced during the simulation. In the best case circuit, of course, all memory components (stacks, local variables) and the ALU are throughput optimized variants. It can be seen, that in the adaptive case the different applications cause the usage of different FUs.

8   Conclusion

We presented a novel model of an adaptive processor with organic computing properties. The execution model allows any component of the processor to be replaced at runtime as well as redundancy. We simulated the implementation of a Java bytecode processor using this model. Although, we do not exploit all the self-X properties in this simulation, it already shows the benefits of this approach.

9   Future Work

Some of the self-X features are implemented in a rudimentary way. We need to improve the self-monitoring in order to support self-healing and other goals for self-optimizations. Also, we need to find feasible algorithms that allow us to synthesize FUs inside the system.

Other work will be required to improve non organic features of AMIDAR processors: the inclusion of peripheral components into the processor, the usage of other intermediate assembly languages or a better parallelizing of bytecode through the separation of bytecode traces.

References

1. ajile Systems. aj-100 Datasheet, 2000. http://www.ajile.com/.
2. U. Brinkschulte, J. Becker, K. Dorfmüller-Ulhaas, R. König, S. Uhrig, and T. Ungerer. Caruso – project goals and principal approach. In P. Dadam and M. Reichert, editors, *GI Jahrestagung (2)*, volume 51 of *LNI*, pages 616–620. GI, 2004.
3. F. Campi, R. Canegallo, and R. Guerrieri. IP-Reusable 32-bit VLIW Risc Core. In *European Solid State Circuits Conference (ESSCIRC)*, pages 456–459, September 2001.
4. Y. Chou, P. Pillai, H. Schmit, and H. P. Shen. Piperench Implementation of the Instruction Path Coprocessor. In *Proceedings of the 33th Annual International Symposium on Microarchitecture*, pages 147–158, Monterey, December 2000.
5. C. Ebeling, D. C. Cronquist, and P. Franklin. Rapid – Reconfigurable Pipelined Datapath. In R. W. Hartenstein and M. Glesner, editors, *Field-Programmable Logic, Smart Applications, New Paradigms and Compilers*, pages 126–135, Berlin, 1996. Springer Verlag.
6. S. Gatzka and C. Hochberger. A new General Model for Adaptive Processors. In T. P. Plaks, editor, *Proceedings of the 2004 International Conference on Engineering of Reconfigurable Systems and Algorithms (ERSA'04)*, 2004.
7. S. Gatzka and C. Hochberger. Hardware Based Online Profiling in AMIDAR Processors. In *to appear in Proceedings of RAW 2005*, 2005.
8. S. Gatzka and C. Hochberger. On the Scope of Hardware Acceleration of Reconfigurable Processors in Mobile Devices. In *to appear in Proceedings of HICSS 38*, 2005.
9. S. Gatzka and C. Hochberger. The AMIDAR Class of Reconfigurable Processors. *Journal of Supercomputing*, to appear 2005.
10. S. Gatzka, C. Hochberger, and H. Kopp. Deployment of Middleware in Resource Constrained Embedded Systems. In *Tagungsband der GI/OCG-Jahrestagung 'Informatik 2001'*, pages 223–231, Wien (Österreich), September 2001. Österreichische Computer Gesellschaft.
11. Y. Ha, R. Hipik, S. Vernalde, V. Diederik, M. Engels, R. Lauwereins, and H. De Man. Adding Hardware Support to the HotSpot Virtual Machine for Domain Specific Applications. In M. Glesner, P. Zipf, and R. Michel, editors, *Field-Programmable Logic and Applications. Reconfigurable Computing Is Going Mainstream (LNCS 2438)*, pages 1135–1138, Berlin, Heidelberg, 2002. Springer.
12. R. Hartenstein, M. Herz, T. Hoffmann, and U. Nageldinger. Using the KressArray for Reconfigurable Computing. In J. Schewel, editor, *Configurable Computing: Technology and Applications, Proc. SPIE 3526*, pages 150–161, Bellingham, WA, 1998. SPIE – The International Society for Optical Engineering.
13. P. Horn. Autonomic Computing: IBM's Perspective on the State of Information Technology, 2001. http://www.research.ibm.com/autonomic/.
14. J. Kephart and D. Chess. The vision of autonomic computing. *IEEE Computer Magazine*, 36(1):41–50, Jan. 2003.
15. K. V. Palem, S. Talla, and P. W. Devaney. Adaptive Explicitly Parallel Instruction Computing. In J. Morris, editor, *Proceedings of the 4th Australasian Computer Architecture Conference*, Singapore, 1999. Springer Verlag.
16. SIA – Semiconductor Industry Association. The international technology roadmap for semiconductors. http://www.itrs.net/, 2001.
17. VDE/ITG/GI. Organic Computing: Computer- und Systemarchitektur im Jahr 2010. http://www.gi-ev.de/download/VDE-ITG-GI-Positionspapier Organic Computing.pdf.

Reusable Design of Inter-chip Communication Interfaces for Next Generation of Adaptive Computing Systems

Vincent Kotzsch[1], Jörg Schneider[2], and Günther Döring[1]

[1] Fraunhofer IIS, Branch Lab Design Automation, Zeunerstr. 38, D-01069 Dresden
{vincent.kotzsch,guenther.doering}@eas.iis.fhg.de
[2] Dresden University of Technology, Department for VLSI-Design,
Diagnostics and Architecture, D-01062 Dresden
jsch@ite.inf.tu-dresden.de

Abstract. The SoC *(System-on-Chip)* technology is used in small and flexible consumer electronic devices. SoCs include one or more microcontroller, memory, programmable logic, and the input/output logic control. Additionally, sophisticated SoCs support partial dynamic reconfiguration. Those are preconditions to build the next generation of adaptive computing systems which make it possible to implement selforganizing systems that are self-configuring and self-optimizing. The design of applications and the development of tools for system design are a great challenge. In this paper we describe an approach that is used to support the design of applications by generator tools. This approach allows the re-use and the generation of communication interfaces between the components in partial run-time reconfiguration (pRTR) systems. The generator tool approach based on a methodology which enables a formal representation of adaptive systems and its timing schedule control. We prove our methodology and generator approach by applications from the field of signal processing.

1 Introduction

The development of small, fast, low-cost, and flexible systems is still a challenge for SoC designers. The complex structured reconfigurable SoCs with special features like partial dynamic reconfiguration makes it more difficult to design such systems. Thereby, the usage of both reconfigurable SoCs and SoC prototyping platforms requires efficient design methods like re-use and generation support of HW and SW modules for several applications. Up to now SoC design tools did not support the design of pRTR applications suf- ficiently. Our solution for the domain of FEC *(Forward Error Correction)* applications is to expand the design flow for reconfigurable SoCs by generator tools to provide optimized system modules for several prototyping environments.

This paper is structured as follows: Section 2 explains the advanced re-use based design flow. Furthermore, the assignments of our generator approach are illustrated. In section 3 we present of our inter-chip communication interface. In Section 4 we discuss the implementation results. Several RS *(Reed-Solomon)* codec implementations for different prototyping environments are explained. Section 5 concludes this paper and provides an outlook to further work.

M. Beigl and P. Lukowicz (Eds.): ARCS 2005, LNCS 3432, pp. 167–177, 2005.

2 SoC Design Flow

In order to fit demands of shorter development time *(time-to-market)* within the embedded systems, we provide a SoC design flow based on a generator tool developed by us [10],[11]. This generator tool is located on the top of the design flow and appear as an addon feature to different design flows for reconfigurable SoCs (see figure 1).

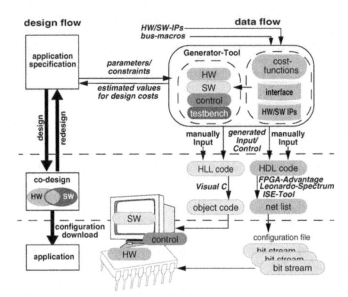

Fig. 1. Advanced SoC Design Flow

Generator tools provide parametrizable cores, which can easily be implemented into a complex design *(design-by-reuse)*. For the design of portable applications we developed HW and SW libraries [12, 1]. The outputs of the generator tool are cores described in HDL *(hardware description language)* and HLL *(high level language)*. Thereby, they are suitable for different design flows and can be processed from several design tools. As a synthesis result the generated bitstream files are usable for our prototyping platforms e.g. Atmel FPSLIC, AVR-Butterfly [18], Alpha-Data ADM-XRC XCV-1000 [20], Ashling EVBA7 ARM7 [21], etc.

2.1 Hierarchy Level Model

For a formalizing abstraction of the generator tool approach we developed a hierarchy level model with two abstraction levels [11]. This hierarchy level model is shown in figure 2 and gives an abstraction of HW/SW systems into two dimensions. The horizontal direction specifies the functional layers which defines the system borders. The layers are divided into the "board layer", "application layer", and "operating layer". The "operating layer" is divided into the "operating layer – static" and "operating layer – dynamic" whereby the dynamic part of this layer is used to model partial dynamic reconfigurable systems. The vertical direction specifies the physical levels and they are used for the development of HW and SW interface libraries.We divided the physical levels into the "functional level" on the top, the "processing level" in the middle, and the "interface level" at the bottom. The different layers and levels are independent. Furthermore, the horizontal layers use special interfaces for data exchange. It is possible to map all kind of HW and SW systems into this model.

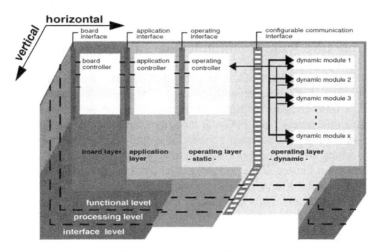

Fig. 2. Hierarchy Level Model

2.2 System Architecture of the Generator Tool

Established to the hierarchy level model described in section 2.1 we build the system architecture of our generator tool (see figure 3).

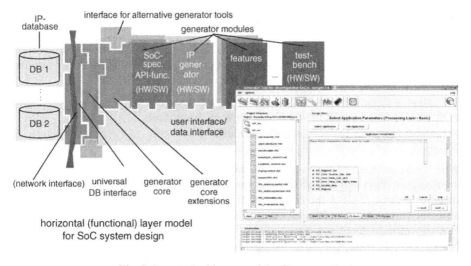

Fig. 3. System Architecture of the Generator Tool

The generator tool uses a re-use database, which contains all design modules consisting of both HW/SW and interface modules [12],[1]. Additionally the generator tool allows the selection of different design parameters which are used for the generation of parametrizable design modules. Generator modules are responsible for the generation of design modules whereby every generator module is applied to a special design task.

3 Reusable Inter-chip Communication Interfaces

SRAM based reconfigurable SoCs such as the Xilinx Virtex architecture [16] support features like partial run-time reconfigurability. The sequential execution of pRTR modules in a time-division multiplex manner enables the implementation of large designs into a moderately sized FPGA at the same chip location. For our reconfiguration flow we assume that a design consists of a static part located at the operating layer static which will not be modi- fied during system run-time, and a dynamically reconfigurable part located at the operating layer dynamic in form of a pRTR module [3]. In the case of the Xilinx Virtex architecture the smallest configuration unit is a CLB *(Configurable Logic Block)* column. The physical size of the pRTR module must always be a multiple of a CLB column. The modules are placed in the same location range and separated by CCI *(Configurable Communication Interface)*.

3.1 Concept of CCI

For an universal concept of chip-intern interfaces it is necessary to analyze the two parts of system abstraction [Section 2.1]. With regard to the "interface level", the physical structure of the interface components and their HW-specific properties have to be analyzed. When using Xilinx Virtex FPGAs, the "interface level" is based on the special Xilinx Bus Macros *(BMs)* [8], which realize the communication between different modules over the strict boundaries. The physical structure is shown in figure 4a. With regard to the "functional level", the abstracted functional structure of the dynamic reconfigurable application has to be analyzed. This functional structure is shown in figure 5b. The choice of the implemented interface blocks depends on the structure of static and dynamic parts. It can be varied by the:

- number of the implemented dynamic and static modules,
- number of communication interfaces between the modules,
- realization of data memory management and
- integration of the controller for data- and control flow.

With the knowledge of these characteristics it is possible to build a communication interface, which consists of different communication modules realized with the HW-specific features [7]. For the communication between dynamic and static parts, four different communication blocks are specified. The connection to a central memory block located in the static part will be realized with two special memory access blocks. On one hand, access to the RAM-module is integrated as a communication block, which is implemented for saving the data flow of the different dynamic modules *(Modular Memory Block - MMB)*. On the other hand, access to several FFregisters, which can be used for saving control signals, is provided (*Signal Memory Block - SMB*). Furthermore, the interface provides separate data channels (*Inter Communication Block - ICB*) for the inter system communication e.g. with special i/o components. For checking the dynamic module status, several signals are integrated in the "Module Header" (*MH*). This block based interface design allows the generative design of the CCI. For the configurability of the CCI the designer can select a number of these reusable interface blocks, which will be integrated in a CCI module. The physical data transmission of the block-specific signals is realized with the special Xilinx Bus Macros. The CCI module can be used in the further design process for building a dynamic reconfigurable application. It is also possible to generate an CCI module, which integrates several dynamic and static parts with different block based communication interfaces. The block based functional structure of the CCI is shown in figure 4b.

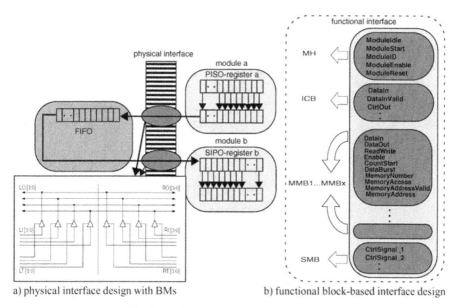

a) physical interface design with BMs   b) functional block-based interface design

Fig. 4. Configurable Communication Interface

The advantage of generator-based design of CCI is that the HW-designer can develop a dynamic reconfigurable application without knowledge about the physical specifics of the used FPGA [7], [14]. So he designs the functional structure of the application and a generator tool provides the dedicated interface for the communication between the modules. Figure 5a shows the concept of the generator based design. The adaptation of CCI to any application is possible by choosing the required number of interface blocks. For the determination of the block properties, it is necessary to make a pre-design-analysis. Thereby, the entity signals of the several dynamic modules must be merged and in order to provide the required data each time, the module-implement-time-data dependency between the modules is important to check. After this analysis the generator tool can build the CCI-module, based on specified parameters.

3.2 Design of CCI

The design process is based on the hierarchy-level model introduced in section 2.1. As shown in figure 5b the CCI is integrated in "operating layer". For the abstraction from the physical HW it is necessary to design several vertical hierarchy levels in separate modules. So it is possible to build functional application modules which are independent from the target architecture [11]. An adaptation layer connects the functional modules to the HW specific level. With this design method an application can be mapped to various architectures without any change in the structure of modules. For the different target architectures special components, which realize the physical HW binding must be provided. By using Xilinx Virtex FPGAs for building dynamic reconfigurable applications, the special features of the Xilinx Modular Design Flow (*XMDF*) [8], [2] must be applied.

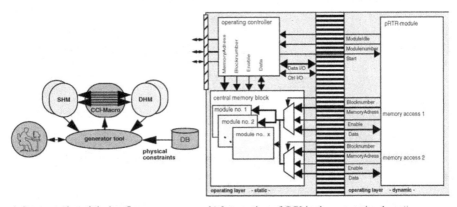

a) Generator based design flow   b) Integration of CCI in the „operating layer"

Fig. 5. CCI integration

The integration of CCI in the vertical hierarchy level model is shown in figure 6b. This picture shows the data flow over the boundaries between dynamic and static modules. A special CCI wrapper, located in "processing level", binds several functional operation modules to the CCI. The signal processing of module communication is realized on the "interface level" by integrated BMs. Because one BM only provides communication of four signals, the CCI must contain as many BMs as needed for all required signals. Considering that a BM realizes a tristate binding on special global routing resources, it is important to specify the direction of the signal flow. Figure 6a shows a BM binding. By using the developed VHDL code generator for the creation of the CCI, this tool realizes the correct binding of BMs. The CCI wrapper has two main tasks. On one hand, it converts the module signals for the communication over the CCI; on the other hand it controls the states of module processing. There are three states: fetching the required data from memory, running the module and resave data into memory. Due to this structure it is possible to re-use many parts of the CCI wrapper for the different operation modules. Based on this level implementations the further design process with the XMDF is possible. The output of this design flow are special bitfiles from the static and dynamic modules for programming the Xilinx

FPGA. The developed VHDL code generator for the creation of the CCI is realized by an ANSI-C imlementation. Based on specific information of CCI, deposed in an ini-file, the generatortool builds a CCI macro module with error-free and XMDF-synthezable VHDL-code for integration in further design process. This approach of the level-based model for building dynamic reconfigurable applications can also be used for other architectures than Xilinx Virtex FPGAs, e.g. for the Xilinx Virtex II/II PRO architecture. Only the code generator has to be modified with the target specific properties for communication in pRTR environments. For efficient storage of the data during the reconfiguration of FPGA a memory model has been developed. This model allows the flexible access to several independent memory blocks based on using the Xilinx specific BlockRAMs. With the combination of the CCI and the memory model a universal and flexible approach for using dynamic recon- figuration in Xilinx FPGAs has been developed.

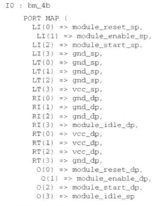

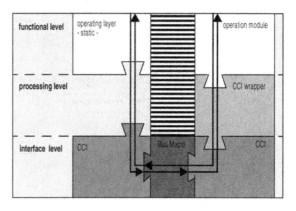

a) BM binding   b) Data flow through the vertical hierarchy level

Fig. 6. Classification of the CCI

4 Experiments

We examined our design methodology within a DVB-T (*Digital Video Broadcasting Terrestrial*) utilizing FEC applications [9].

4.1 FEC-Applications

In order to explain our methodology and its objectives we select the RS codec appli-cation. RS codes are block-based channel codes which are used in a wide range of applications for digital communication systems e.g. for data transmission, data storage and data retrieval systems (CD, DVD) [9]. Utilization of RS code allows detection and correction of errors within a data stream without further retransmissions.

The most expensive part within the RS decoding is the error correction process shown in figure 7. The error correction process of the received code includes the five single steps "syndrome calculation *(SYN)*", "calculation of the error locator polynomial *(LOC)*", "find the error locations *(POS)*", "calculation of the error magnitudes *(VAL)*" and error correction. To optimize the detection and correction of up to two errors we implement additionally a detection module *(DECI)*, a one error correction module *(oneErr)*, and a two error correction module *(twoErr)* shown in figure 7a [6]. The range of variation of the implemented RS codec modules allows different capabilities for execution and design configuration. At the right side of figure 7b (as an example) the RS codec modules *DECI, oneErr* and *twoErr* are configured and executed on the SoC. If the number of errors increases then the error correction flow according to the left side of figure 7b is executed.

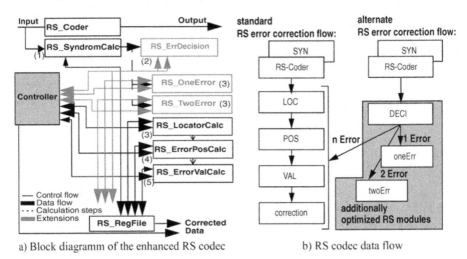

a) Block diagramm of the enhanced RS codec   b) RS codec data flow

Fig. 7. Reed-Solomon codec

4.2 Implementation results for Configurable Communication Interfaces

The complex structure of CCI and the consideration of many design flow parameters makes it necessary to implement an efficient VHDL code generator, which creates a CCImacro for communication between parts of dynamic reconfigurable application. For each communication block in the CCI a determined LoC *(Lines of Code)* will be generated in the VHDL macro file. By increasing of the bit-width of data vectors or the number of integrated CCI blocks, the CCI will be more complex and the generated LoCs rises. Furthermore, for an estimation of complexity of CCI with regard to the used BMs, it is important to know how many of these BMs are implemented. The reason for this is the maximum number of possible BMs in the FPGA. Table 1 lists the LoC and BM values in dependence of the bit-width and the number of integrated CCI blocks. Based on this table it is possible to create a cost function for any CCI in the pre-design-analysis. This table also shows the flexibility of the block based CCI. The different blocks can be combined with each other, can be varied in different parameters and the code generator tool creates a proper VHDL macro for each application. The efficiency of such code generators rise with the number of generated LoCs and thus with frequency of use.

Table 1. Generated LoCs and used BMs of CCI blocks

Block	n	1-Bit		4-Bit		6-Bit		8-Bit	
		LoC	BMs	LoC	BMs	LoC	BMs	LoC	BMs
MMB	1	-	-	192	5	216	6	240	7
	2	-	-	384	10	432	12	479	14
	3	-	-	576	15	648	18	720	21
	4	-	-	768	20	864	24	960	28
ICB	1	43	0,5	67	1,25	67	1,75	91	2,25
	2	58	1	107	2,5	131	3,5	155	4,5
	3	99	1,5	147	3,75	195	5,25	219	6,75
	4	114	2	186	5	234	7	282	9
SMB	1	54	0,75	102	2,25	126	3,25	155	4,25
	2	100	1,5	172	4,5	220	6,5	268	8,5
	3	146	2,25	242	6,75	314	9,75	385	12,75
	4	167	3	311	9	407	13	503	17

4.3   Utilization of the CCI Inside the FEC Application

For testing CCI, the RS codec application has been transferred from a static implementation to a dynamic reconfigurable implementation. The integration of RS codec in the CCI concept is shown in figure 8b. All steps of design flow must be run. Firstly, all error correction modules are specified as pRTR modules. Based on the pre-design-analysis data of the RS codec modules it is possible to generate a CCI by the generator tool. After generating the interface different CCI wrappers have to be designed. Thereby, the reuse-factor is very high because the basic structure of every Wrapper is equal. With the designed components it is possible to run the XMDF for creating the special bitfiles of the static and dynamic modules. This flow is shown in figure 8a. Based on the partial bitfiles it is possible to integrate the RS codec application into a schedule algorithm. The scheduler monitors the run of each module and reconfigures it as soon as the module has completed its work.

The advanced sequence flow of RS codec application is shown in figure 7b. The result of the implementation is shown in figure 9. There is a picture of FPGA implementation of the static and dynamic part (SYN module) with an integrated CCI.

5   Conclusions

The configurable communication interface design approach presented in this paper suggest a new design methodology for the design of the next generation adaptive computing systems. Our work has a particular importance for reusability, flexibility, and for the support of the generator based design methodology. Basing on the presented interface approach we build a plug-in for our generator tool to generate communication interfaces automatically. A generated communication interface fits exactly with a specific application for reconfigurable SoCs. The feasibility of the proposed method has been demonstrated by an implementation of a RS codec design on a *Xilinx Virtex XV1000* device. Future work will address the design of configurable communication interfaces for other reconfigurable SoCs and the utilization of the interfaces in a wide range of applications.

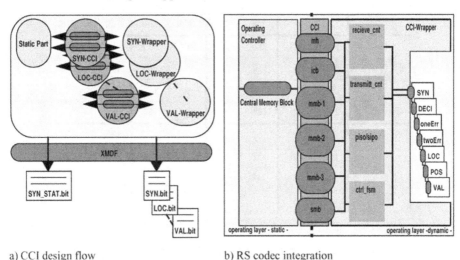

a) CCI design flow   b) RS codec integration

Fig. 8. Classification of the RS codec Application into CCI concept

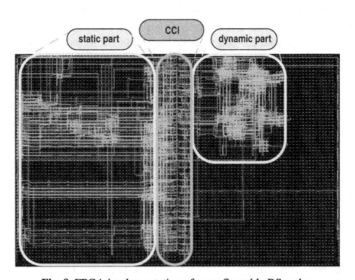

Fig. 9. FPGA implementation of reconfigurable RS codec

References

1. M. Boden, J. Schneider, K. Feske and St. Rülke: "Enhanced Reusability for SoC-based HW/SW Co-Design", Euromicro Symposium on Digital System Design, September 4 - 6, 2002, Dortmund, Germany
2. A. Erni, S. Reichmuth: "Inter-Task-Communication in Reconfigurable Operating Systems" Masters Thesis, ETH Zürich, 2003
3. Haase, J. Schneider u.a.: "Design of a Reed Solomon decoder using partial dynamic reconfi- guration of Xilinx Virtex FPGAs-a case study", DATE'02, Paris, France, 4-8 March, 2002
4. E. Horta and J.W. Lockwood, "PARBIT: a tool to transform bitfiles to implement partial recon- figuration of field programmable gate arrays (FPGAs)", Tech. Rep. WUCS-01-13, Washington University in Saint Louis, Department of Computer Science, July 6, 2001
5. N.Kasprzyk, A. Koch: "Verbesserte Hardware-Software-Partitionierung für Adaptive Computer", 17th International Conference on Architecture of Computing Systems, ARCS'04, March 23-26, 2004, Augsburg, Germany
6. M. Koegst, St. Rülke: "Conditions for the Number of Errors in a Reed-Solomon Codec", 3th int. symposium on mobile multimedia systems and applications, MMSA'02, December, 2002, Delft, Netherlands
7. V. Kotzsch: "Entwurfsautomatisierung von internen Kommunikationsschnittstellen in dynamisch rekonfigurierbaren Systems on Chips (SoCs) ", Diploma Thesis, Hochschule für Technik und Wirtschaft Dresden (FH), September, 2004
8. D. Lim, M. Peattie: "Two Flows for Partial Reconfiguration: Module Based or Small Bit Manipulation", Application Note XAPP 290, Xilinx Inc., November, 2003
9. W. W. Peterson: "Error-correcting codes", MIT Press, 1994
10. J. Schneider, V. Kotzsch: "Wiederverwendungsgerechte Codegenerierung von FEC-Applikationen für dynamisch rekonfigurierbare Systeme", 17th International Conference on Architecture of Computing Systems, ARCS'04, Workshop - Dynamisch Rekonfigurierbare Systeme -, March 26, 2004, Augsburg, Germany
11. J. Schneider, V. Kotzsch, S. Rülke: "Demonstrator: Reuse Automation for Reconfigurable System-on-Chip Design within a DVB Environment", International Conference on Parallel Computing in Electrical Engineering, PARELEC'04, September 7-10, 2004, Dresden, Germany
12. J. Schneider, M. Boden, St. Rülke: "Eine wiederverwendungsgerechte Entwurfsmethodik für rekonfigurierbare SoC-Architekturen", GI/ITG/GMM Workshop: "Methoden und Beschreibungssprachen zur Modellierung und Verifikation von Schaltungen und Systemen", February 25-27, 2002, Tübingen, Germany
13. U. Tangen: "Selbstorganisation und Evolution elektronischer Hardware", GMD Spiegel, May, 2000
14. J. Thorvinger: "Dynamic Partial Reconfiguration of an FPGA for Computational Hardware Support", Diploma Thesis, Lund Institute of Technology, June 2004
15. "Virtex FPGA Series Configuration and Readback", Application Note XAPP 137, Xilinx Inc., July 11, 2002
16. "Virtex 2.5V Field Programmable Gate Arrays", Product Specification, DS003-1, Xilinx Inc., April 2, 2001
17. Herbert Walder, Simon Steinegger, Marco Platzner, "Implementation of a Runtime Environment for Reconfigurable Hardware Operating Systems", Swiss Federal Institute of Technology Zurich (ETH) Computer Engineering and Networks Laboratory, TIK Report Nr. 195, Zurich, Switzerland, June 2004
18. Atmel: "http://www.atmel.com"
19. Xilinx: "http://www.xilinx.com"
20. Alpha Data: "http://www.alpha-data.com"
21. Ashling: "http://www.ashling.com"

DESCOMP: A New Design Space Exploration Approach

Mario Schölzel and Peter Bachmann

Brandenburg University of Technology, Computer Science Institute,
Postfach 101344, 03013 Cottbus, Germany
{mas,peterbachmann}@informatik.tu-cottbus.de

Abstract. In this paper, we introduce a new approach in Design-Space-Exploration (DSE) for non-clustered VLIW architectures. It differs from existing techniques by using a "bottom-up" strategy. While other approaches start with the design of an architecture, followed by building a possible schedule, we firstly build a schedule and after that an architecture is synthesized, which is suitable to execute this schedule. So, the results can be obtained fully automatically and in very short time. Furthermore, we can explore arbitrary types of functional units without increasing the design space exploration time significantly. We evaluated our method and compared the obtained results to an existing DSE approach for clustered and non-clustered architectures. We almost always obtain better results in the case of non-clustered architectures. In many cases the ports of the register file are decreased, which, in consequence, leads to higher clock rates. Compared to the results for clustered architectures for some examples our non-clustered architecture is better than the best clustered one.

1 Introduction

By Design Space Exploration (DSE) a well suited processor for a given application (or its most frequently executed parts) is figured out. Instruction level parallelism (ILP), well supported by VLIW architectures, is a favored technique to achieve the necessary short run times. The data path of a non-clustered VLIW consists of a single register file and a certain number of functional units (FUs). Each FU supports a certain set of operations (e.g. addition, multiplication, shift, etc.) and can access the full register file. The operation to be executed in each cycle by each FU is coded into a single very long instruction word. All operations coded into an instruction are carried out in parallel. Because of its regular data path, the parameters of a VLIW can be adopted to the applications demand during DSE and easily be mapped into hardware. Most important is the number of functional units (FUs) and their types. By the type of a FU we mean the kinds of operations performed by it. Incrementing the available ILP (i.e. number of FUs) leads, in general, to higher performance. But this increases also the number of ports of the register file, which increases its area, power dissipation and delay. While area and power dissipation grows by n^3, delay grows by $n^{3/2}$ for n FUs [12]. For this reason the register file becomes the bottleneck in the design of a VLIW architecture. To save hardware costs and to reduce the power consumption, the degree of parallelism supported by the processor must be restricted to a minimum and should be the main goal in DSE for VLIWs.

M. Beigl and P. Lukowicz (Eds.): ARCS 2005, LNCS 3432, pp. 178–192, 2005.

Most existing DSE approaches use a top-down strategy. I.e., for a given architecture the required tools (compiler, simulator) are generated and used to evaluate the performance of the application on this architecture. If necessary, the architecture is changed, either by hand or automatically, and the evaluation starts again. Such an approach is the PICO project [4, 13]. Beside the VLIW architecture, also memory architecture and special hardware extensions are explored. The exploration of the non-clustered VLIW architecture is done by a search in the design space (spacewalk). Several search strategies are introduced, one of them is a pareto-optimal search. For each architecture which has the maximal performance among all architectures of the same or higher costs, new architectures are derived by adding new FUs or registers. The implemented operation types in each new FU are determined by static and dynamic estimations of the given application. In [16] a clustered VLIW data path is synthesized. For a given number of clusters and a given number of FUs per cluster a schedule of minimal length is searched. Before scheduling, operations are bound to clusters. A $n + 1$ cluster architecture is derived from a n cluster architecture for which the shortest schedule was found. The configuration of the previous n clusters remains untouched and the configuration of the new cluster is obtained by producing schedules for different FU configurations in the new cluster. FUs for addition and multiplication are considered separately. This leads to a high number of ports in each register file. Taking other operation types into account, would increase the exploration time for the additional cluster dramatically. In [2], an exhaustive DSE for the TriMedia64 CPU is done. The exploration space was limited to a non-clustered architecture with five FUs. The considered operation types for exhaustively DSE were limited to the most frequently used operation types in the used benchmarks. Thus, port sharing is allowed. The allocation of the remaining operation types is done in a second step by extending the best architectures from the first step. In all these approaches the inner structure of the algorithm is not taken into account for optimizing the architecture. Our idea is to use a compiler for DSE, which analyzes the algorithm. It compiles the application without any architectural constraints and optimizes the hardware during compilation. A similar idea is proposed in [6] to determine an architecture for DSPs. However, there, the number of FUs is defined in advance. The same idea is also proposed in [8] for clustered VLIWs and a clustering algorithm is introduced but no further parameters of the architecture are determined so far by a compiler.

Our proposed idea is related to High-Level-Synthesis (HLS). There, a behavioral description (e.g. a data flow graph) must be mapped into hardware, using as less hardware blocks as possible. This can be done by scheduling and binding. The operations in the data flow graph (DFG) must be scheduled in such a manner, that during the binding stage as much hardware blocks as possible (e.g. adders and multipliers) can be reused. In [14] simulated annealing is used to couple scheduling and binding. In [11] and [3] several scheduling techniques are introduced and the binding problem is solved by constructing a conflict (or compatibility) graph. However, the optimization goals in HLS differs from those in DSE for VLIWs. In HLS, mapping the DFG into hardware leads to a data flow architecture. Such an architecture does not require large register files. The outputs of an hardware block are directly used as inputs for the next hardware block, if possible. The major delay and costs in such hardware solutions arises from the hardware blocks, whose number must be minimized, therefore. In opposite to this, a VLIW architecture must match all the basic blocks of the application. Because the centralized register file is the bottleneck, the number of all operations carried out in parallel, and not only the number of operations of each type carried out in parallel, must be minimized. For this reason scheduling and binding algorithms proposed in HLS must be adopted to these optimization goals.

2 DESCOMP

2.1 Overview

A schedule is a sequence of instructions. It determines for each operation its execution cycles. The type of an operation v is denoted by $type(v)$. Each operation type may has an individual latency time and individual hardware costs. Both is to specify before DSE starts. In the schedule, an operation may occupy several consecutive instructions, if its latency time is greater than 1. I.e., executing such an operation by a FU takes several cycles. Full forwarding must be supported by the architecture, this means that the result of an operation is available in the next cycle after finishing the operation in the pipeline. Heterogeneous FUs which carry out operations of different types, for instance addition and multiplication, are allowed. But this is just an aspect of modeling and means that the hardware for several operation types can share the same ports in the register file. Instruction level parallelism is fully controlled by the compiler and the schedule is exactly executed in the given order. Thus, no hidden stall cycles are introduced by the processor, except in the case of cache misses. This guaranties a good static estimation of the execution time of the given kernel, only on the basis of the length of the schedule and the clock rate of the processor.

Starting point for our DSE approach is a basic block, represented as an acyclic data flow graph (DFG). In the scheduling stage, all operations from the DFG are scheduled within a given number of l instructions and the schedule is optimized with subject to:

- a minimal width, in order to use as less FUs as possible and
- a minimal number of operations of the same type within the same instruction, in order to save hardware costs.

Note, after scheduling only the execution time of an operation is fixed. Thus, the scheduling stage determines the required number of FUs and registers. But so far, register usage is not optimized. The required number of registers can be determined by counting the maximal number of simultaneously alive values in the schedule. In the binding stage, the operations are assigned to FUs. This determines the type of each FU. In order to find the best architecture for a piece of software, for each basic block a sequence of schedules with increasing length is calculated. From these schedules the best combination is chosen to meet the time constraints while keeping the hardware as cheap as possible.

2.2 Scheduling Stage

In the scheduling stage the only constraint is to build a schedule of a given length l from a DFG. For every node v in the DFG we compute its mobility $mob(v) = let(v)-eet(v)$ by the so-called time frame, consisting of its earliest (eet) and latest (let) execution time:

$$eet(v) = \max\left\{eet(w) + lat(w) | (w, v) \in E\right\}, \text{ where } \max \varnothing = 0,$$

$$let(v) = \min\left\{let(w) - lat(v) | (v, w) \in E\right\}, \text{ where } \min \varnothing = l - 1.$$

Here, E denotes the set of all edges (data dependencies) of the DFG and $lat(v)$ is the latency time of the operation type of node v. Note, that an increased length of the schedule leads to increased mobility. The scheduling algorithm, similar to force-directed-scheduling [9], has to schedule each operation within its time frame. It works stepwise. In every step one node, selected by a *priority function*, is scheduled. An *objective function* is used to choose the instruction to which the selected node is assigned.

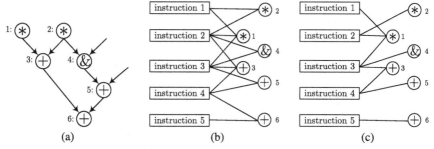

Fig. 1. (a) DFG, (b) Interval graph for the DFG in (a) and a schedule length of $l = 5$, (c) Interval graph for the DFG in (a) after scheduling operation 2 into instruction 2.

Priority function as well as objective function is calculated on the basis of an interval graph. The interval graph has l instruction-nodes and, additionally, all the operation-nodes of the DFG. An edge connects an instruction-node i with an operation-node v if and only if the execution of v may take place at cycle i, i.e. $eet(v) \leq i < let(v) + lat(v)$. The number of operation nodes adjacent to an instruction node v is denoted by $deg(v)$. Figure 1 (b) shows the interval graph for the DFG in Figure 1 (a) and $l=5$. At the beginning of each step the priority function selects an operation node v which has a minimal mobility. If there are several nodes with the same mobility, one of them with the most expensive operation type is chosen. This avoids the execution of several expensive operation types in the same instruction.

Scheduling a node v to an instruction i affects the time frames of its successors and predecessors. For example, scheduling node 2 to instruction 2 affects the time frames of the nodes 3, 4, 5 and 6 and causes the deletion of edges in the interval graph, as shown in Figure 1 (c). By T_i^v we denote the interval graph obtained from interval graph T by scheduling v to instruction i and updating the time frames of all affected nodes. For example, if the interval graph in Figure 1 (b) is T, then the interval graph in (c) is T_2^2.

In principle, node v can be assigned to each of the instructions i with $eet(v) \leq i \leq let(v)$. However, some of the assignments can cause instructions without any operations. This is avoided by testing whether for every empty instruction, starting with the earliest one, an unscheduled node v with minimal $let(v) + lat(v)$, can be assigned. If this is possible then instruction i becomes a candidate for scheduling.

In order to determine an instruction to which the selected operation v is assigned, the objective function is applied to every T_i^v where i is a candidate. For every T_i^v three values are calculated:

- $mF(T_i^v)$, an estimation of the required number of FUs for the final schedule,
- $mT(T_i^v)$, an estimation of the expected hardware costs for the final schedule and
- $id(T_i^v)$, which refines the estimation, done by $mT(T_i^v)$.

$mF(T_i^v)$ estimates the effect of the decision to assign operation v to instruction i on the number of FUs in the final schedule by scheduling the remaining nodes. It uses a list scheduling algorithm which aims to get a slight schedule. The schedule, done by mF, is only to estimate the smallest number of required FUs. In order to distinguish from the proper scheduling, we call it e-schedule (estimation-schedule). The e-scheduler picks a node w with minimal mobility and assigns it to instruction k, if

$$\frac{deg(k)}{tF - \sigma_k} \leq \frac{deg(m)}{tF - \sigma_m}$$

holds for all instructions m within the time frame of w. Here, σ_k is the number of nodes which are already assigned to instruction k and $tF := \max\{\sigma_i \mid 1 \leq i \leq l\}$. This means, e-scheduling assigns w to k, if only a few operations are currently assigned to instruction k and the maximal number of operations possibly assigned to k later on will be low. After scheduling w, the interval graph is updated and the next node is selected. Note, that in each e-schedule step tF, σ and deg depend on the actual interval graph. Thus, if during e-scheduling an operation extends the width of the e-schedule we get more freedom for scheduling the rest of the nodes. A lower bound for tF is given by n/l, where n is the number of nodes of the DFG. The e-scheduling algorithm starts with this lower bound. $mF(T_i^v)$ returns the required number of FUs for the final e-schedule and e-scheduling stops.

If there are several instructions for which $mF(T_i^v)$ is minimal, we use this freedom to minimize the hardware costs. Remember, that the scheduling algorithm runs without resource constraints. This means, we have to care about the number of required operation types in the final architecture. Let a cost function $cost(t)$ be given for each operation type t. The additional load of type t is the maximal number of operations of type t which occur in a common instruction and causes new hardware costs. If a function $load(t)$ gives the additional load of each operation type t then

$$mT(T_i^v) = \sum_{t \in \mathcal{O}} load(t) \cdot cost(t)$$

describes the expected hardware costs if node v is assigned to instruction i. $\mathcal{O}$ is the set of all operation types in the schedule.

For every interval graph T and every operation type t there is a minimal load $ml(t)$ independent in which way the schedule goes on. $ml(t)$ is the maximal number of operations of type t which, must be scheduled in a common instruction in T. If an operation type t occurs in the schedule, then of course $ml(t) \geq 1$. For the calculation of $load(t)$ we consider only the amount which exceeds the minimal load. The probability that an operation v will be assigned to an instruction i is

$$\frac{1}{mob(v) + 1},$$

if v is connected to i in the interval graph, 0 otherwise. As load value $p(t, i)$ of an instruction i we take the sum of the probabilities, that an operation of type t is scheduled to i taking into account the minimal load $ml(t)$. So, we get

$$p(t,i) = \sum_{v \in M(t,i)} \frac{1}{mob(v) + 1}$$

where $M(t, i)$ is the set of all nodes v with $type(v) = t$ and v is adjacent with i except the $ml(t)$ nodes with the smallest mobility. For example, in Figure 1 (b) $ml(+) = 1$ and therefore, for the graph in Figure 1 (c) we get $M(+, 3) = \varnothing$ since node 3 is the only + operation connected with instruction 3 and must be excluded because of $ml(+) = 1$. Therefore $p(+, 3) = 0$. It is $M(+, 4) = \{3\}$ since the two + operations 3 and 5 are connected with instruction 4, but $mob(5) < mob(3)$ and, therefore, 5 is excluded. We get $p(+, 4) = 1 / (mob(3) + 1) = 0{,}5$.

The load value associated with type t is the maximal load value of all the instructions:

$$load(t) := \max\{p(t, i) \mid 1 \leq i \leq l\}.$$

This means we schedule node v into an instruction i, such that the remaining nodes can be arranged in a slight schedule and the load of each operation type is well balanced. This leads in consequence to an architecture which has as less FUs as possible and the hardware costs arising from the provided operation types in each FU are minimized. A detailed definition of $id(T_i^v)$ is given in the next section.

2.3 Binding Stage

After scheduling the operations in each instruction are fixed. It remains to assign operations to functional units in such a way that the number of different operation types in each FU is minimized. We do this by coloring an interference graph.

2.3.1 Constructing the Interference Graph

By the interference graph $I = (V, H \cup S)$ we express dependencies between operation types in the schedule. V is the set of operation nodes in the DFG, H and S are two disjoint sets of edges. For coloring the nodes we have as many colors as FUs. All nodes with the same color are executed by the same FU.

Two nodes u and v are adjacent by an edge $(u, v) \in H$, if both operations *must* be executed by different FUs. This holds, if and only if u and v must be executed in the same cycle. For example, in Figure 2 (a) in instruction 1 the + and * operation are executed in the same cycle. Thus, they are adjacent by an H-dependency in Figure 2 (c).

Analogously, two nodes u and v are adjacent by an edge $(u, v) \in S$, if both operations *should* be executed by different FUs. The S-dependencies stems from some operations of the same type, which are executed in different execution cycles. In case, v is such an operation of type t which occurs in instruction i, u is an operation of a different type occurring in another instruction, say j, where also an operation w of type t must be executed then, an edge $(u, v) \in S$ forces to color nodes v and w with the same color. In Figure 2 (a), operation type + occurs in instructions 1,3 and 4. If there are three colors then by the S-edge (8, 10), for instance, it is forced that node 10 gets either the color of node 6 or of node 7, both of type +, since node 8 can not get the same color as nodes 6 and 7.

In detail, the interference graph is constructed from a given schedule in the following way:

1. For each operation type t we take any instruction with the greatest number of occurrences of that type. We denote this instruction by m_t.
2. For every type t, we fill up instruction m_t with *nop* operations, so that it contains exactly k operations if k is the number of available functional units. These additional *nop* operations ensure the aimed effect of the S-dependencies. All the operations, including *nop*-operations, become nodes of the interference graph.
3. For every instruction i in the schedule and each pair u, v of operations within it, we add an H-dependency (u, v) to H.
4. For every instruction i in the schedule we add an edge (u, v) to S if node v occurs within instruction i and has a type t, but node u has a different type and occurs in instruction m_t with $m_t \neq i$.

In Figure 2 (c) the final interference graph for the schedule in Figure 2 (b) is shown. Here $m_+ = 3$, $m_* = 3$ and $m_\& = 2$.

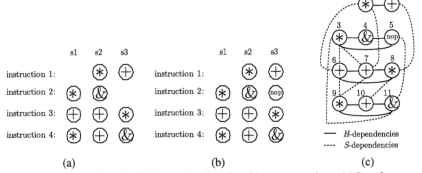

(a)   (b)   (c)

Fig. 2. (a) Example schedule, (b) Example schedule with *nop* operations, (c) Interference graph for the schedule in (b), where $m_+ = 3$, $m_* = 3$ and $m_\& = 2$.

2.3.2 Coloring the Interference Graph

Binding is now performed by coloring. Of course, any coloring algorithm may be used. But, due to the S-dependencies it will not always be possible to obtain a k-coloring as it is shown in Figure 3 (a).

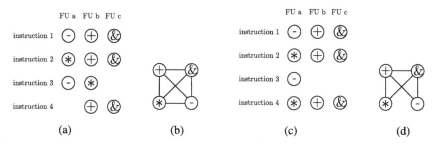

Fig. 3. (a) Schedule, in which each operation type appears at most once in each instruction. Nevertheless, one of *, + or & must be performed by two FUs, (b) Compressed interference graph for the schedule in (a), (c) Schedule in which the dependencies from (a) are resolved, (d) Compressed interference graph for (c).

Here, in the instructions 1 and 2 the operations + and & occur together. To avoid multiple implementations of + and &, the both + operations are executed by FU b and the both & operations by FU c. This enforces the implementation of - and * within FU a. Now, in instruction 3, operations - and * occur together and thus, one of these operation types must be implemented in a second FU. The corresponding interference graph can not be colored with 3 colors because S-dependencies force to use the same color for both operations within instruction 3 which is, of course, forbidden by H-dependencies.

This problem is resolved by another schedule like in figure 3 (c). For this reason, the function id is used during the scheduling stage. Assume, we have the choice to schedule operation * into instruction 3 or instruction 4. In both cases 3 FUs are required and each operation type appears at most once in each instruction. Thus, mF and mT will return equal results in both cases. Nevertheless, scheduling * into instruction 3 will cause the implementation of * in a second FU, whereas scheduling * into instruction 4 will not, which is the better choice. Exactly this kind of dependencies can be found in the compressed interference graph shown in Figure 3. Operation nodes in different instructions but of the same type are mapped onto the same node in the compressed interference graph. Hence, only H-dependencies occur in it. Less dependencies between operation types in different instructions lead to less edges in the compressed interference graph. The objective function $id(T_i^v)$ constructs the compressed interference graph for all scheduled nodes in T_i^v and uses the number of edges in it, to guide the scheduling.

If, however, the schedule of Figure 3 (a) cannot be changed then, to obtain a legal coloring, we must neglect some dependencies. Of course, we can not neglect H-dependencies. But we are allowed to neglect S-dependencies. For this reason, we use a coloring-heuristic which always succeeds, if we neglect all S-dependencies. The worst case, to ignore all the S-dependencies, will not appear in most cases. The used technique is a greedy strategy well-known in graph theory and also used for register allocation [5]. We begin to remove from the interference graph all nodes v and their adjacent edges with less than k neighbors. All such nodes are colorable. Note, that in this process for some nodes the degree is decreased and so, they also can be removed. If all remaining nodes have k adjacent edges or more, then we remove a node, which has less than k adjacent H-edges. It can be shown, that such a node always exists. After that, we continue to remove nodes where again S-dependencies are taken into account. When the last node is removed we insert the nodes and corresponding edges in the reverse order and give them a color, which is not used by an adjacent node. Here we may ignore S-dependencies, but never H-dependencies. In Figure 4 (a) the interference graph from Figure 2 (c) is shown after removing the nodes 2, 1, 4 and 5 in this order.

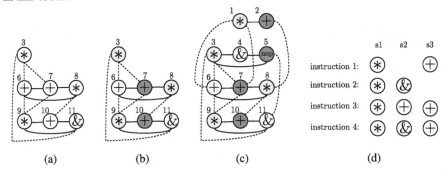

Fig. 4. (a) Interference graph after removing nodes 2, 1, 4 and 5, (b) Colored interference graph after inserting nodes 3, 7, 6, 8, 9, 10 and 11, (c) Colored interference graph after inserting the remaining nodes 5, 4, 1 and 2, (d) Binding result obtained from the colored interference graph.

Now, the graph contains only nodes with 3 or more neighbors. For this reason we remove a node, which is adjacent with less than 3 H-edges and has the lowest hardware costs. In the example this holds for node 11. After removing it, we can proceed with removing the nodes 3, 6, 7, 8, 9 and 10. Inserting these nodes in reverse order and coloring them leads to the colored interference graph in Figure 4 (b). Also node 11 is colorable respecting the S-dependencies, because node 3 and 9 got the same color. Inserting the rest of the nodes leads to the final colored graph in (c). In (d) the final schedule is shown. As we can see, FU a has to implement only the *multiplication*, FU c implements only an *addition* and FU b an *addition* and *logical and*.

2.4 Extension to Several Basic Blocks

So far we have built a VLIW-architecture for a given basic block and given length. In order to build an architecture capable to execute several basic blocks, we assume that in a previous profiling step, the execution frequencies of these basic blocks were determined. Now, the input is a set of program fragments. Each program fragment consists of several basic blocks. For each program fragment p a time constraint $t(p)$ and for each basic block b of p the execution frequency $exe(b)$ is known. Furthermore, a function rpf is given that determines for a given number of register file ports the highest possible clock rate of the VLIW architecture. To figure out an architecture that meets the time constraints for all program fragments the following steps are performed:

1. For each basic block and each possible length the schedules are computed according to our method explained above. So, for each schedule length the number of required FUs and operation types is known.
2. In a second step, the smallest number mfu of FUs is determined, that still allows to execute each program fragment within the required time. We start with $mfu = 1$ and increment it continuously. For the current value of mfu and each basic block b the shortest schedule using no more than mfu many FUs is selected from the schedules of step 1. We denote its length by $mL(b, mfu)$. If for all program fragments p

$$\frac{\sum\limits_{b \in p} mL(b, mfu) \cdot exe(b)}{rpf(2 \cdot mfu)} \leq t(p)$$

holds, we stop, otherwise mfu is incremented again. If mfu becomes larger than the highest number of FUs of any schedule, no architecture can be found to meet all the time constraints.
3. For each basic block and each length a new schedule is generated using mfu as lower bound for tF in the function mF (see 2.2). This relaxes the pressure to minimize the number of FUs and provides more freedom for the function mT to minimize the number of simultaneously executed operations of the same type.
4. For each basic block a schedule is selected which uses at most mfu many FUs and minimizes the number of simultaneously executed operations of the same type. For this reason, the number of each available operation type is decreased stepwise using the following search algorithm:

```
search(a)
  if(not legal(a))
    return a configuration for which confCost is infinite;
  minConfiguration = a;
  foreach OperationType o do
    if(a(o) > 1)
      mc = search(a<o,a(o)-1>)
      if(confCost(mc) < confCost(minConfiguration))
        minConfiguration = mc
  return minConfiguration
```

Here, a configuration a defines for each operation type o the available number of FUs, say n, that are able to execute that particular type (i.e. $a(o) = n$). $a<o,m>$ is the redefined configuration a, where $a<o,m>(o) = m$ and $a<o,m>(x) = a(x)$ for all $x \neq o$. $confCost$ simply sums up the costs of the operation types in the given configuration. In the initial configuration, $a(o)$ is defined as the maximal occurrence of o in all schedules of length $mL(b, mfu)$ for all basic blocks b. For each configuration the shortest schedule of each basic block that can be executed with the available resources (i.e. the available number of each operation type and the available number of FUs) is determined. If the time constraints are met (i.e. the above equation holds) with the selected schedules, the configuration is considered to be legal and further resources will be decreased by the search algorithm. In general, the search has an exponential runtime. However, in practice the runtime is very short because after a few steps the time constraints are exceeded due to the limited number of available resources. The search algorithm results in a minimal configuration m. Therefore, the final architecture must implement each operation type o at least $m(o)$ times to meet the time constraint for all program fragments. For each basic block the shortest schedule that requires each operation type o at most $m(o)$ times is selected and used as input for step 5.

5. The binding algorithm is commonly performed for all schedules selected in 4. A single interference graph is constructed for all selected schedules, simply by treating all schedules together as a single one.

3 Results

The explained DSE approach was implemented in Java using two benchmark configurations. In the first one we applied our approach to single basic blocks (given as DFGs), taken from the PhD thesis of Lapinskii [15]. This enabled us to compare the quality of our approach to the one of Lapinskii. In the second configuration we determined an architecture for a given set of program fragments. Some properties of the used benchmarks are listed in Table 1.

Table 1. Benchmark summary and properties.

Name	number of nodes	critical path length	number of components	number of operations of each type							
				+	-	*	shl	xor	and	or	not
ARF	28	8	1	12	0	16	0	0	0	0	0
DCT-DIT	48	7	1	24	12	12	0	0	0	0	0
EWF	34	14	1	26	0	8	0	0	0	0	0
FFT	38	4	1	9	17	12	0	0	0	0	0
SWIM1	26	4	3	10	8	8	0	0	0	0	0
MD5	24	15	1	12	0	0	4	3	4	3	2

The basic blocks occurred in loop kernels from multimedia and signal processing applications. Nevertheless, our approach can be used for arbitrary application domains. ARF (auto regression filter), DCT-DIT (discrete cosines transformation), EWF (elliptic wave filter) and FFT (fast-fourier-transformation) originally come from [1], SWIM1 (Shallow Water Modelling) from [7]. The MD5 benchmark was taken from [10]. As in [15], we assumed that each operation can be executed within one cycle. Using our implementation we computed for every basic block and for every reasonable schedule length one architecture. In [15], because of the there used top-down-approach, not for each schedule length an architecture could be constructed. In Figure 5 the results are compared for each schedule length for which in [15] a non-clustered architecture was explored. In almost every case our approach leads to better results with respect to register file ports (i.e. FUs). This means, our architecture would be able to run at higher clock rates, if necessary. Especially for short schedules we are able to save up to 40% of the ports.

Only in one case (DCT-DIT, L = 37) our approach leads to a worse result. In general, the heuristic works very stable. That means, to prolong the schedule decreases

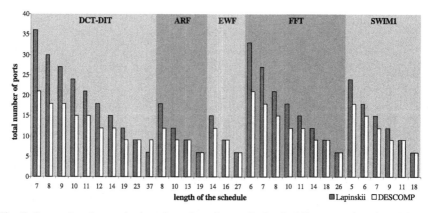

Fig. 5. Comparing the required total number of ports for Lapinskiis approach and DECOMP.

the number of needed FUs. It is difficult to compare the hardware costs in terms of adders and multipliers, because from [15] it is unknown in the non-clustered case, how many of the used FUs are multipliers and how many are adders. In our architectures the number of multipliers and adders may be a little bit higher, due to the higher density of operations in each instruction. On the other hand, the level of ILP is lower, which also has an effect on the width of the instruction words. Furthermore, if in [15] for a given number of FUs a schedule of a certain length was produced, in many cases we found a shorter schedule executable with the same number of FUs as it is shown in the following table:

Table 2. Benchmarks for which in DESCOMP a shorter schedule was found.

benchmark/length	DCT/14	DCT/19	ARF/19	EWF/16	EWF/27	FFT/14	FFT/26	SWIM/18
DESCOMP length	12	16	14	15	19	13	19	13

In Figure 6 our results for a non-clustered architecture are compared to the results in [15] for clustered-architectures. Interesting is, that for some benchmarks our approach is better than any clustered architecture in terms of read/write ports and hardware costs. The reason is, that in [15] a bus capacity of two is assumed for inter-cluster-communication. Thus, two additional read and write ports are required in each cluster. E.g., for the benchmarks ARF and EWF our approach produces non-clustered architectures having the same number of ports as the best clustered architectures. Furthermore, our architecture requires less adders and/or multipliers.

There are many cases where the number of ports is not reduced however, the total number of multipliers, adders and subtractions is. Since each cluster needs its own FUs, in a clustered architecture the total number of FUs is higher than in a non-clustered architecture. In fact, for these cases the non-clustered architecture is not able to reach the performance of the clustered one, but the results indicate, that port sharing by arbitrary FU types should be explored to reduce the number of ports in the register file. This may lead to a cheaper architecture.

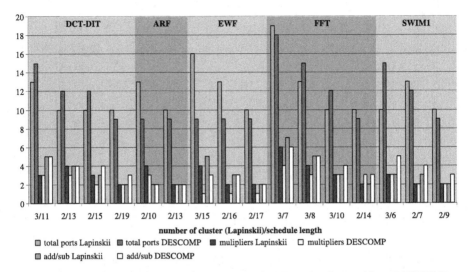

Fig. 6. Comparing clustered architectures from Lapinskii to non-clustered from DESCOMP.

All the results where obtained automatically. The runtime ranges between less than one second and 3 minutes on a PC with 1.5 GHz, depending on the DFG. For longer schedules the runtime grows, due to more flexibility in the scheduling stage.

In a second preliminary test we used our approach to produce an architecture which is tailored to several basic blocks. The used basic blocks were SWIM1, ARF and MD5. Using the MD5 example eight operation types must be performed by the architecture. Each of the benchmarks represents a single program fragment. The execution frequency of each basic block and the time constraints as well as the used *rpf* function are shown in Table 3 and Table 4.

Using an exhaustive search for an appropriate combination of these operation types in FUs (knowing that four FUs are required) more than $4{\cdot}10^9$ architectures must be considered. Using our algorithm 59 schedules were computed. It followed that the final architecture needs four FUs, due to the requirements of the SWIM benchmark. For SWIM a schedule of length 7 was selected. Each longer schedule would fail the timing requirements. This schedule already requires 3 multipliers, 2 adders and 2 subtractions.

Table 3. Assumed constraints of the used benchmarks in the second benchmark configuration.

program fragment	time constraint in ms	execution frequency
MD5	5	500
SWIM1	5	50000
ARF	10	10000

Table 4. rpf-function in the used example.

Ports	2	3	4	5	6	7	8	9	10	11	12	13	14	15	16	17	18
MHz	100	95	90	85	80	75	70	65	60	55	50	42	34	25	16	10	5

For ARF as well as for MD5 the longest schedule would meet the timing constraints. The search for the best architecture starts with the configuration a, where

o:	+	-	*	and	or	not	xor	shl
$a(o)$:	4	3	4	2	1	1	2	1

This configuration was chosen, because the shortest schedule for ARF with 4 FUs would require 4 multipliers and 4 adders. The same holds for the MD5 benchmark respectively. After performing the search algorithm (which stopped after less than 1 second) the required operation types could be reduced as shown in the following configuration b:

o:	+	-	*	and	or	not	xor	shl
$b(o)$:	2	2	3	1	1	1	1	1

Using this configuration, for SWIM1 a schedule of length 7, for ARF a schedule of length 10 and for MD5 a schedule of length 17 was selected. In the final architecture FU 0 implements the operation types {+, *}, FU 1 implements {-, or, shl}, FU 2 implements { and, +, *} and FU 3 implements {+, -, *, xor, not}. Except for addition, this architecture uses no more resources than the schedule of length 7 for SWIM and the longest schedules for ARF and MD5. However, it uses one more adder because of the interdependencies between operation types in different instructions. This problem could be solved by relaxing the length of the schedules within a program fragment (e.g. for ARF and MD5) as long as the performance constraints are met and the complexity of the interference graph (e.g. the number of edges) is reduced. However this is currently not done and remains to solve.

4 Conclusion

We presented an approach for a fully automated Design-Space-Exploration. The strategies to optimize the architecture for a single basic block are similar to the ones in HLS, but the optimization goals differ. Compared to other DSE approaches, we have to compute a schedule only a few times. The complexity, which arises in many DSE approaches from the combinatorial multiplicity of the operation types in FUs is avoided in our approach. Nevertheless, all FU types are fully explored. The good results at the level of basic blocks also leads to good results for optimizing an architecture for more than one basic block. Thus, we believe, that our DSE approach is a good method to explore VLIW architectures in short runtimes. Although we have shown, that in some cases our obtained non-clustered architecture is better than every clustered architecture, in the future we will extend this approach also to explore clustered architectures, with respect to the maximal number of read/write ports in a register file, including the number of ports for inter-cluster communication.

References

1. C.Lee, M.Potkonjak and W.H.Mangione-Smith. MediaBench: A tool for evaluating and synthesizing multimedia and communications systems. Proc. of the 30th Annual International Symposium on Microarchitecture, 330-335. 1997.

2. G.J.Hekstra, G.D.La Hei, P.Bingley and F.W.Sijstermans. TriMedia CPU64 design space exploration. Proc. of the IEEE International Conference on Computer Design, 599-606. IEEE Computer Society, 1999.

3. Giovanni DeMicheli. Sythesis and Optimization of Digital Circuits. 2004.

4. Greg Snider. Spacewalker: Automated Design Space Exploration for Embedded Computer Systems. Technical Report, HP Laboratories Palo Alto. HPL-2001-220. 2001.

5. Gregory J.Chaitin. Register allocation and spilling via graph coloring. SIGPLAN Notices, 17(6), 98-105. 1982.

6. Jie Guo, Michael Hosemann and Gerhard P.Fettweis. Employing Compilers for Determining Architectural Features of Application-Specific DSPs. Proc. of International Conference on Parallel Computing in Electrical Engineering, 39-44. 2004.

7. Kaivalya Dixit. Performance SPECulations-benchmark, friend or foe. 7. International Symposium on High Performance Computer Architecture (Monterrey, Mexico), 2001.

8. Michael L.Chu, Kevin C.Fan, Rajiv A.Ravindran and Scott A.Mahlke. Cost-Sensitive Operation Partitioning for Synthesizing Custom Multicluster Datapath Architectures. Proc. 2nd Workshop on Application Specific Processors, 40-47. 2003.

9. P.G.Paulin and J.P.Knight. Force-directed scheduling in automatic data path synthesis. Procs. of the 24th ACM/IEEE Design Automation Conference, 195-202. 1987.

10. Faraboschi Paolo, Brown Geoffrey, A. F. Joseph, Desoli Giuseppe and Homewood Fred. Lx: a technology platform for customizable VLIW embedded processing. The 27th Annual International Symposium on Computer architecture 2000, 203-213. ACM Press, 2000.

11. R.Camposano. From Behavior to Structure: High-Level Synthesis. IEEE Design & Test of Computers, 7 Number 5, 8-19. IEEE Computer Society, 1990.

12. Scott Rixner, William J.Dally, Brucek Khailany, Peter Mattson, Ujval J.Kapasi and John D.Owens. Register Organization for Media Processing. Procs. of the 6th. High-Performance Computer Architecture, 375-386. 2000.

13. Shail Aditya, B.Ramakrishna Rau, and Richard Jhonson. Automatic Design of VLIW and EPIC Instruction Formats. Technical Report, HP Laboratories. HPL-1999-94. 2000.

14. Srinivas Devadas and Richard Newton. Algorithms for Hardware Allocation in Data Path Synthesis. IEEE Transactions on Computer-Aided Design, 8, 768-781. 1989.

15. Viktor S.Lapinskii. Algorithms for Compiler-Assisted Design-Space-Exploration of Clustered VLIW ASIP Datapaths. Dissertation, University of Texas at Austin. 2001.

16. Viktor S.Lapinskii, Margarida F.Jacome and Gustavo A.de Veciana. Application-Specific Clustered VLIW Datapaths: Early Exploration on a Parameterized Design Space. IEEE TCAD, 21(8), 889-903. 2002.

Design Space Navigation
for Neighboring Power-Performance Efficient
Microprocessor Configurations

Pedro Trancoso

Department of Computer Science, University of Cyprus,
75 Kallipoleos Ave., P.O.Box 20537, 1678 Nicosia, Cyprus
pedro@ucy.ac.cy
http://www.cs.ucy.ac.cy/~pedro

Abstract. Microprocessor design is a considerably complex task. First, microprocessors include many resources that may be configured in different ways. This leads to a time consuming multi-objective optimization problem. Second, currently the designs must take into account not only performance but also power consumption thus making the optimization goal more complex. Third, different types of applications have different demands but producing several different microprocessors would not be cost effective.

This paper proposes an efficient algorithm to explore the design space: *design space navigation*. With this algorithm it is possible to obtain optimal configurations by starting from a baseline and "navigating" on the design space. Different configurations tailored for different applications, but derived from the same baseline, are called *neighboring* configurations. Experimental results show that *navigation* finds designs that achieve better power-performance efficiency for a fraction of the time required by other design space exploration algorithms. Also, the algorithm is used to obtain four neighboring configurations for four types of applications: multimedia, integer and floating-point scientific, and database workloads. The results showed that the navigation configuration achieves a power-performance improvement of 30% to 118% depending on the workload. Using different workloads for navigation and execution may result in a loss of efficiency of as much as 94%.

1 Introduction

Power has recently become an important factor in microprocessor design for both mobile devices as well as high-performance systems [1]. Mobile devices are required to operate consuming as little energy as possible in order to increase the battery life. For high-performance systems, although mobility is not a concern, the energy consumption of a large scale system may be an issue. Furthermore, high frequencies result in increasing average and peak power, which may lead to problems in power dissipation and consequently a reduction in the reliability. Therefore, architects have to find the correct balance between power and performance. The goal is to find system configurations that are efficient in terms of the power consumed for the performance achieved. For high-performance

M. Beigl and P. Lukowicz (Eds.): ARCS 2005, LNCS 3432, pp. 193–206, 2005.
© Springer-Verlag Berlin Heidelberg 2005

systems, such as the one analyzed in this work, the most appropriate power-performance efficiency metric is determined as MIPS^3/WATT as presented by Brooks *et al.* [2], where MIPS represents performance in million instructions per second and WATT represents average power consumption in Watt. Throughout this paper the term *power-performance efficiency* or *efficiency* refers to the MIPS^3/WATT value.

To achieve high efficiency the architect may configure several parameters in the microprocessor such as caches, arithmetic units, and reorder queues, among others. Due to the large number of parameters and the large set of values each parameter may take, a full design space exploration is unfeasible. The main contribution of this paper is a simple algorithm that explores the design space in an efficient and effective way. A second contribution is the use of such an algorithm to tailor a state-of-the-art, high-performance baseline configuration to the needs of each workload.

Several previous works have addressed the issue of optimizing the multi-objective exploration of the design space. Fornaciari *et al.* [3] proposed to efficiently find cache configurations by exploring each parameter independently. This technique reduces significantly the search but it assumes that parameters are independent from each other. Palesi and Givargis [4] proposed the use of genetic algorithms to prune non-optimal subspaces from the complete design space. The authors explored their technique for the design of system-on-chip (SoC) architectures. Palermo *et al.* [5] use a random search tuned to derive an approximation of the Pareto-optimal curves. Agosta *et al.* [6] use Pareto Simulated Annealing in order to derive the efficient configuration. Kin *et al.* [7] use branch-and-bound techniques to reduce the design space exploration for mediaprocessors.

Our proposed technique is simpler, and consequently less time consuming than the previously proposed techniques and at the same time more appropriate to find configurations that derive from a common baseline. We call these configurations "neighboring" configurations. These configurations are relevant in order to reduce manufacturing costs for the "tailored" configurations. A commercial example is the Intel Xeon and the Intel Pentium 4. Both processors share the same platform but the Xeon is tailored for the high-end servers. In addition to the above facts, in this work, a wider range of workloads is used together with the proposed exploration algorithm in order to prove the need to obtain different efficient configurations.

Other studies have proposed power-performance efficient configurations but they usually focus on the optimization of a single parameter. Also, power-aware studies concentrate mostly on scientific workloads [2, 8–17], while only few works focus on other workloads such as multimedia [7, 18, 19] and spatial databases [20]. The work presented in this paper is broader than these works in the sense that a general design methodology is proposed for multi-objective exploration of a large design space.

In order to test the proposed *navigation* algorithm, the different configurations are evaluated using a power-aware architecture simulator. The *navigation* design space exploration is performed for four different workloads: multimedia, integer scientific, floating-point scientific, and database. The results show that the configurations obtained using the navigation algorithm achieve a power-performance efficiency increase of 30% to 118% depending on the workload. This was achieved at a fraction of the time for exhaustive design space exploration. In addition, it is very relevant to use the same configuration for both navigation and execution, otherwise it may result in an efficiency loss of up to 94%

The paper is organized as follows: Section 2 presents different design space exploration algorithms, Section 3 describes the experimental setup, Section 4 discusses the results obtained, and Section 5 presents the summary and the conclusions for this work.

2   Design Space Exploration

This section presents several approaches to the exploration of the microprocessor design space. The goal is to find a design that is optimized for a certain metric.

For the analysis described in the following sections consider that the design space is composed of a set P of modifiable parameters and where each parameter p_i may have one of n_i values. For example, two different parameters are the size of the L1 I-Cache and the number of integer ALUs. The L1 I-Cache may have, for example, seven sizes: 4KB, 8KB, 16KB, 32KB, 64KB, 128KB, and 256KB. The number of ALUs may be one of the four values: 1, 2, 4, or 8. To test the configurations, a set of applications A is used where each application a_i has an execution time of t_i. This is the time required for finding the value for the metric used in evaluating the different configurations. In the case of this work it is the *simulation time*.

2.1   Exhaustive and Restricted Exploration

The first approach is to perform an exhaustive exploration of the design space. Although this approach will result in the configuration that achieves the optimal value for the desired metric, it requires a very long execution time to find it. Unless the design space is small, this technique is not feasible. The execution time for this exploration algorithm to complete may be expressed by the following equation:

$$\sum_{i=1}^{|A|} t_i \times \prod_{i=1}^{|P|} n_i \tag{1}$$

In this equation, the first factor represents the workload execution time while the second factor represents the number of experiments necessary to cover the design space.

Given that the time to find a solution using the previous algorithm is not feasible for most common cases, one solution is to restrict the number of parameters to explore. In this algorithm, the design space is still exhaustively searched but within a smaller set of parameters. The challenge for this algorithm to be successful is the selection of the appropriate set of parameters to explore. One option would be to select the parameters randomly. We call this algorithm the *Random-Restricted Exploration* or *R-Restricted*. Nevertheless, as a single random pick does not guarantee that the solution will be a relevant one, this algorithm may be enhanced by picking s different random sets $(P_1$ to $P_s)$ of m parameters each. In this case the execution time for this exploration algorithm is the following:

$$\sum_{i=1}^{|A|} t_i \times \sum_{i=1}^{s} \left(\prod_{j=1}^{|P_i|} n_j \right) \tag{2}$$

Instead of the random pick, a simple heuristic may be used. The heuristic is based on the fact that intuitively the set of relevant parameters is the set of parameters that independently achieve the largest benefits. In order to determine which are these parameters there is a need to do a *parameter potential analysis* of the different parameters and rank the results. Consequently, it is possible to pick the first m parameters and select them as the subset for the space exploration. This subset is represented as P'. The resulting algorithm is called *Controlled Restricted Exploration* or *C-Restricted*. Depending on the number of parameters selected, the execution time may be reduced significantly. The execution time may be expressed by the following equation:

$$\sum_{i=1}^{|A|} t_i \times \left(1 + \sum_{i=1}^{|P|} (n_i - 1) \right) + \sum_{i=1}^{|A|} t_i \times \prod_{i=1}^{|P'|} n_i \tag{3}$$

In this equation, the first term represents the execution time to complete the parameter potential analysis. Notice that the 1 represents the execution of the baseline configuration and the $(n_i - 1)$ accounts for excluding this same baseline configuration multiple times. The second term represents the execution time for the exploration of design space with set P'.

2.2 Independent Exploration

This algorithm assumes that each parameter is independent from each other. Consequently, each parameter may be studied independently and then the value giving the best result may be selected for the final configuration. The number of experiments required for this technique is small and is the same to the parameter potential analysis above mentioned. The major issue with this algorithm is the fact that in reality parameters are not independent, specially if they are parameters from the same resource (e.g. cache size and associativity). The execution time for this algorithm may be represented by the following equation:

$$\sum_{i=1}^{|A|} t_i \times \left(1 + \sum_{i=1}^{|P|} (n_i - 1) \right) \tag{4}$$

This algorithm may be enhanced with extra experiments in order to guarantee that the change of a new parameter in the configuration is only accepted if it results in an improvement of the desired metric. We call this algorithm the *Controlled Independent Exploration* or *C-Independent*. This algorithm may be performed on a subset P' of the parameter set P. The execution time for this algorithm may be represented as:

$$\sum_{i=1}^{|A|} t_i \times \left(1 + \sum_{i=1}^{|P|}(n_i - 1)\right) + (|P'| - 1) \times \sum_{i=1}^{|A|} t_i \tag{5}$$

2.3 Navigation

Navigation is a proposed algorithm that aims in finding a configuration that achieves an optimization for the desired metric with a small execution time cost. The first step of this algorithm is to try all the possible configurations around the baseline. This way, for each parameter p_i, if x_i is the parameter value for the baseline configuration, we will have the metric results (efficiency) for both values x_{i-1} and x_{i+1}. We call the relative difference between the efficiency for those values and the baseline the *slope*. After testing all parameters it is possible to order the parameters according to the *slope* observed. This ranking is used to "navigate" the configuration from the baseline to the optimized one.

At each step the parameter with the highest *slope*, which has not been analyzed yet, is chosen. New configurations are tested along the direction of the highest *slope*. "Traveling" along that parameter finishes when the configuration results in a smaller efficiency value than the previous one. At this point the configuration is updated with the last value of the considered parameter. The *navigation algorithm* continues with the parameter that has the next higher *slope*. This method guarantees that the final configuration achieves a higher efficiency than the baseline and it also ensures that it converges fast to the optimum value. As the efficiency monotonically increases for the different configurations obtained with this algorithm, it is possible to stop its execution at any step which may be satisfactory. Therefore, in practice, the exploration is performed for a subset P' of the original parameter set. Notice that if the design space contains many optima, the value found by this technique is one of those, not necessarily the best one. Nevertheless, the objective was to determine the "neighboring" configurations. The execution time for the proposed *navigation algorithm* may be expressed by the following:

$$(1 + 2 \times |P|) \times \sum_{i=1}^{|A|} t_i + \sum_{i=1}^{|A|} t_i \times \sum_{i=1}^{|P'|} \frac{n_i - 1}{2} \tag{6}$$

The first term represents the experiments to find out the *slope* values for all the parameters. The second represents the *navigation algorithm* experiments. Notice that instead of testing all the values for a certain parameter, the *slope* information is used to determine which "side" should be used for "guiding" to higher efficiency configurations. This way it is expected that in the worst case, only half of the values are tested and hence the $(n_i - 1)/2$.

3 Experimental Setup

In order to evaluate the different configurations we collect the performance and power values for our analysis, using Wattch [9], an execution-driven simulator that is based on the SimpleScalar [21] simulator. In addition to the architecture metrics that are the output of SimpleScalar, Wattch returns, among other information, the *average power*, the *peak power* and the *energy* for the execution of a particular application on a certain architecture configuration. Wattch also presents a breakdown of power into the different microarchitecture components. In all results, the power values collected are Wattch's realistic conditional clocking (*cc3_*) where the power of a certain component is determined as the sum of two values: active and passive. The active value refers to the active portion of the component, which is directly proportional to the use of the component. The passive value accounts for the power leakage of the inactive portion of the component. The power models used in Wattch are based on the models from the CACTI cache optimization tool [22]. A validation of Wattch's power models has been presented by Brooks *et al.* [9]. That work shows that the accuracy obtained by the simulator is within 10% of the real results.

The architecture simulated was a standard MIPS-like architecture (*PISA*). The processor's characteristics are comparable to an Intel Xeon. The configuration parameters are presented in the central column of Table 1. In addition to the baseline configuration we also present the ranges that were used in the experiments for the parameter potential study. These values are shown in the right column of Table 1.

Table 1. Configuration parameters for the processor: baseline and range of parameters for the experiments.

			baseline	*range*
Frequency / Voltage / Technology			3GHz / 1.9V / 0.10-micron	—
L1 I-Cache,	(il1)	(size)	32KB,	4-256KB,
L1 D-Cache	(dl1)	(assoc)	2way,	1-32way,
		(block)	32B,	8-64B
			1 cycle hit	—
L2 Unified	(ul2)	(size)	2MB,	256KB-16MB,
		(assoc)	8way,	1-64way,
		(block)	64B,	32-512B
			12 cycle hit	—
Memory speed / bus width			800MHz 32ns / 8B	—
Int units	(alu)	(ialu)	4alu	1-8alu
		(imult)	2mult	1-8mult
FP units	(alu)	(fpalu)	4alu	1-8alu
		(fpmult)	2mult	1-8mult
Execution / Fetch queue			out-of-order / 16	—
Decode, issue, commit	(ilp)	(issue)	8	1-64
Reg update / Load-Store (ilp)	(ruulsq)		128 / 64	32-512 / 16-256

The parameter potential study is performed by executing several sets of experiments, where each set is characterized by the fact that only the value of a single parameter is modified. This means that a set of experiments is performed by varying a single parameter within a range while maintaining the values of all the remaining parameters constant. Notice that in some cases the range of a component is limited by the baseline configuration. For example, the number of integer units cannot be set larger than 8 as this is the issue width for the baseline configuration. Also, the cache block sizes of a specific cache are dependent on the block sizes of the upper and lower level caches.

The target applications for our power and energy analysis come from three different benchmarks: *MediaBench* [23], *SPEC CPU2000* [24], and *TPC-H* [25].

Seven applications from *MediaBench* were selected to represent a multimedia workload (*media*): *g721encode, gsmdecode, gsmencode, mesamipmap, mesaosdemo, mpeg2decode* and *unepic*. Six applications from *SPEC CPU2000* were selected to represent a scientific workload: *gcc, gzip, parser, art, equake,* and *mesa.* The three first scientific applications represent an integer workload (*specint*) while the three last applications represent a floating-point workload (*specfp*).

For the execution of the *TPC-H* queries we used PostgreSQL version 7.1.2. The data loaded into the database was the benchmark's standard data generated with *dbgen* and scaled down by a factor of 20 to a total of approximately 50MB for the raw data (tables). We created indexes on every key attribute of the data tables. From this benchmark two queries were selected: *Q9* and *Q12*. This workload is represented as *tpch* in the rest of the paper.

The total number of instructions executed ranges from approximately 10 to 500 million for the *MediaBench* applications, 1 billion for the *SPEC* applications, and 1.5 to 3.5 billion for the *TPC-H* applications. Both the *MediaBench* and *TPC-H* applications were simulated for their complete execution, while the simulation of the *SPEC* applications was skipped for the first billion instructions.

Notice that the system setup is done in such a way that the input data for the different applications completely fits in the main memory. This is not a limitation as the current high-performance systems are equipped with large memory allowing the efficient in-core execution even for large applications [26, 27].

4   Experimental Results

4.1   Potential Analysis and Parameter Ranking

One of the first steps in many of the design space exploration algorithms is to identify which parameters are more relevant for optimization in terms of the considered metric. For this work the metric considered is the power-performance efficiency for a high-end system. According to Brooks *et al.* [2], as it was already mentioned in Section 1, the most appropriate metric in this case is $MIPS^3/WATT$.

For this work we perform a potential analysis of the different parameters in terms of the power-performance metric. This analysis is performed by varying the various parameters "around" a baseline configuration. In this work, *Efficiency Potential* of a parameter p is defined as the relative difference between

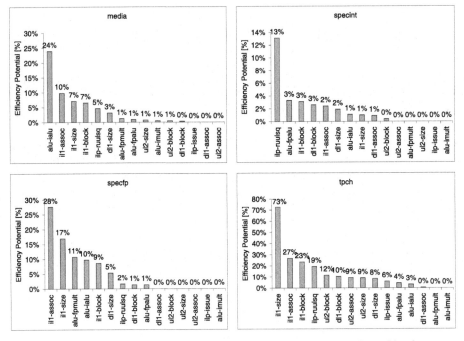

Fig. 1. Parameter ranking for *media*, *specint*, *specfp*, and *tpch* workloads.

the maximum efficiency obtained for a certain value of p and the efficiency for the baseline configuration. According to this definition, a parameter potential of zero represents a case where changes in parameter p result in efficiency values that are smaller or equal to what is achieved for the baseline case. The equation for the *Efficiency Potential* can be expressed as follows:

$$Efficiency\ Potential(p) = \frac{\max Eff(config(p = p_i)) - Eff(baseline)}{Eff(baseline)}$$

The parameter ranking is obtained by ordering the parameter potential results. The ranking for the four different workloads is presented in Figure 1. The x-axis contains the different parameter names while the y-axis presents the potential for each parameter. The parameter names are a concatenation of the parameter category and its resource as presented in Table 1.

The results in Figure 1 show that, considering only the first parameter in the rank, *specint* is the workload that shows the least potential for improvement with a parameter potential of 13% for *ilp-ruulsq*, while *tpch* is the workload with the highest potential with a parameter potential of 73% for *il1-size*. The same conclusion may be taken if instead of considering only the best parameter we consider the aggregate of all parameters that achieve a potential larger than 5%. For *tpch* there are ten parameters that fulfill that criteria with an aggregate of 196%, while *specint* has only one parameter with 13%.

Also important to notice is the fact that the parameters related to the L1 I-Cache occupy the first positions of the ranking of every workload. This is more relevant for both *tpch* and *specfp*, which may be justified by the fact that the miss-per-thousand-instructions is much higher for these two workloads (2x and 13x, respectively). In addition, the ALU parameters dominate for the *media* and *specfp* workloads. For *tpch*, the dominant parameters are mostly the ones related with the three caches L1 I- and D-Cache and L2 Cache. It is interesting to note that, although not apparent from the depicted results, while the trend for the L1 I-Cache is to achieve larger efficiency values for larger configurations, the L1 D-Cache achieves larger efficiency for smaller configurations.

4.2   Design Space Exploration

In order to compare the different algorithms presented in Section 2, Figure 2 presents the relative efficiency increase, compared to the baseline, obtained for the best configuration found with the different exploration algorithms (*config_i*).

$$Efficiency\ Increase = \frac{Eff(config_i) - Eff(baseline)}{Eff(baseline)}$$

The bars in Figure 2-(a) represent the relative efficiency increase for the configurations found with the different exploration algorithms for the *mpeg2decode* application of the *media* benchmark: *Random Restricted* using 3 parameters (*r-restrict3*), *Controlled Restricted* using 3 parameters (*c-restrict3*), *Independent* using 6 parameters (*indep6*), *Controlled Independent* using 6 parameters (*c-indep6*), and *Navigation* using 6 parameters (*nav6*). The line in the same figure represents the relative execution time, compared to *r-restrict3*, for all the different algorithms. From this Figure it is possible to observe that the exhaustive search algorithms have a much larger execution time and still their configurations do not achieve as high efficiency as with the rest of the algorithms. This is mainly due to the fact that the exhaustive algorithms used a more restricted set

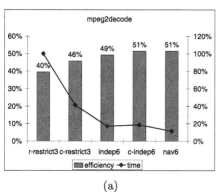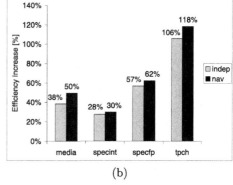

(a)   (b)

Fig. 2. Efficiency increase of the configuration found with: (a) the different exploration algorithms for the *mpeg2decode* application (*media*) and (b) *independent* and *navigation* exploration for all the workloads.

Table 2. Execution time in minutes for the different exploration algorithms running on a Intel Pentium III 1GHz. In parenthesis, next to the algorithm name are shown the number of parameters used in the exploration.

	experimental	model	
Algorithm	mpeg2dec	mpeg2dec	all
Exhaustive	—	4.0×10^{11}	3.1×10^{13}
R-Restricted (3p)	3496	3209	252360
C-Restricted (3p)	1440	1391	109356
Independent (6p)	597	597	46266
C-Independent (6p)	652	642	49771
Navigation (6p)	397	394	30284

of parameters for their configurations. As for the independent and navigation algorithms, their configurations achieve the highest efficiency and it is important to observe that navigation achieves it with slightly more than half of the execution time from *c-indep*. Table 2 contains the detail execution time for the different algorithms.

The results in Table 2 for the *mpeg2decode* application show that the equations presented in Section 2 model accurately the experimental results (error ranging from 0 to 8%). In addition, the table also shows the execution time for determining the configurations for all the applications of all workloads.

Figure 2-(b) presents the efficiency for the different configurations obtained with both the independent and the navigation algorithms for each workload. It is possible to observe that the configurations obtained with navigation always achieve the highest efficiency. Although the difference between the two approaches seems relatively small (7 to 32%) it is important to notice that *navigation* always guarantees a higher efficiency than *independent*. Furthermore, *navigation* finds the configurations faster than *independent* (39% reduction for all workloads.)

It is relevant to observe that using navigation on the same baseline but for different target applications allows to the algorithm to find configurations that achieve large increases in the efficiency, from 30 to 118%, depending on the workload.

Another interesting result is the convergence of the *navigation* algorithm as a function of the number of parameters added to the algorithm. Figure 3 shows the efficiency for each configuration while increasing the number of parameters in the algorithm.

Overall it is possible to conclude that the *navigation* algorithm is the one resulting in the configurations that achieve the same or better efficiency and faster than the time necessary for the other algorithms.

4.3   Designing for Different Applications

As it was previously mentioned, an application for the *navigation* algorithm is the design of "neighboring" configurations for different workloads.

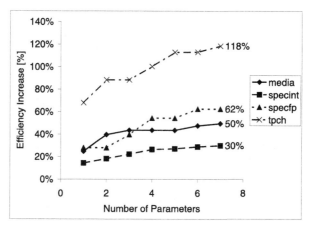

Fig. 3. Efficiency increase of the configuration found with the navigation exploration algorithms for an increasing number of parameters for all four workloads.

Table 3 presents the changes in the baseline configuration in order to obtain the power-performance efficient configurations for the different workloads. These configurations were obtained using the *navigation* algorithm for seven parameters and they all start from the same high-performance baseline configuration described in Section 3.

From Table 3 it is possible to observe that all workloads require changes in the L1 I-Cache with *media* and *tpch* requiring larger cache sizes. For L1 D-Cache the trend is the opposite as it decreases its size to 8-16KB for all workloads except *tpch*. Finally, the efficient configurations for all workloads except *tpch* require a larger number of integer ALUs.

The fact that each workload requires its own tuned configuration in order to achieve high power-performance efficiency is apparent from the results depicted in Figure 4.

Table 3. Power-performance efficient configurations for *media, specint, specfp,* and *tpch.*

parameter	baseline	media	specint	specfp	tpch
L1 I-Cache	32KB	64KB			128KB
	2way	8way	4way	4way	16way
	32B		64B		
L1 D-Cache	32KB	8KB	16KB	8KB	
	2way				
	32B		64B		64B
L2 Unified	2MB				
	8way				16way
	64B				512B
Int units	4alu+2mult	8alu	8alu	8alu	
FP units	4alu+2mult	8mult	1alu	8mult	
RUU/LSQ	128/64		64/64		64/32

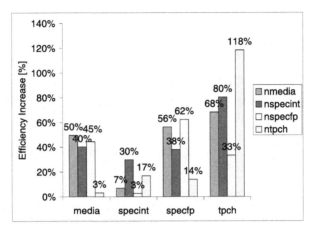

Fig. 4. Efficiency of the configuration found with the navigation exploration algorithm for the different workloads.

This figure presents four bars for each workload. Each of the bars represents the relative efficiency increase for the configuration obtained using *navigation* and tailored for the *media* (*nmedia*), *specint* (*nspecint*), *specfp* (*nspecfp*), and *tpch* (*ntpch*) workloads respectively. From the results in Figure 4 it is interesting to notice that although the configurations for *media* and *specfp* may be used interchangeably for those two workloads with an efficiency loss of at most 10%, the same does not apply to the rest of the workloads. For *media*, if another configuration is used it may result in a loss of at least 94% (using *tpch* configuration for *media* execution.)

Overall it is relevant to notice that each workload requires its own configuration in order to achieve maximum efficiency. The use of a configuration that was tuned to another application may result in large penalties.

5   Conclusions

This work presented a simple technique to explore the microprocessor design space, for multiple parameters, in order to obtain power-performance efficient configurations. Using the *navigation* algorithm it is possible to obtain efficient configurations at a fraction of the time required for other exploration techniques.

Due to its algorithm, with *navigation* design space exploration the configurations obtained are "neighbor" to the original baseline configuration. This makes it easier for manufacturers to adopt these configurations as they reflect small deviations from a common baseline. Using the correct workload for the guiding process seems essential as configurations navigated using workloads other than the executing one may result in penalties up to 94%.

Experimental results have also shown that compared to a high-performance baseline configuration, the configurations obtained with *navigation* design space exploration for the different workloads, differ mostly on the configurations of the L1 I-Cache. Depending on the workload, these configurations achieve an efficiency increase of 30 to 118%.

Acknowledgments

I would like to thank Elena Hadjikyriacou-Trancoso for the valuable reviewing effort and the anonymous reviewers for their input on the work.

References

1. Lefurgy, C., Rajamani, K., Rawson, F., Felter, W., Kristler, M., Keller, T.: Energy Management for Commercial Servers. IEEE Computer **36** (2003) 39–48
2. Brooks, D., Bose, P., Schuster, S., Jacobson, H., Kudva, P., Buyuktosunoglu, A., Wellman, J.D., Zyuban, V., Gupta, M., Cook, P.: Power-Aware Microarchitecture: Design and Modeling Challenges for Next-Generation Microprocessors. IEEE Micro (2000) 26–44
3. Fornaciari, W., Sciuto, D., Silvano, C., Zaccaria, V.: A Design Framework to Efficiently Explore Energy-Delay Tradeoffs. In: Proceedings of the ninth international symposium on Hardware/software codesign, ACM Press (2001) 260–265
4. Palesi, M., Givargis, T.: Multi-Objective Design Space Exploration Using Generic Algorithms. In: Proceedings of the CODES. (2002) 67–72
5. Palermo, G., Silvano, C., Valsecchi, S., Zaccaria, V.: A System-Level Methodology for Fast Multi-Objective Design Space Exploration. In: Proceedings of the GLSVLSI. (2003) 92–95
6. Agosta, G., Palermo, G., Silvano, C.: Multi-Objective Co-Exploration of Source Code Transformations and Design Space Architectures for Low-Power Embedded Systems. In: Proceedings of the SAC. (2004) 891–896
7. Kin, J., Lee, C., Mangione-Smith, W.H., Potkonjak, M.: Power Efficient Mediaprocessors: Design Space Exploration. In: Proceedings of the DAC. (1999) 321–326
8. Bahar, R., Albera, G., Manne, S.: Power and Performance Tradeoffs Using Various Caching Strategies. In: Proceedings of the 1998 ISLPED, ACM Press (1998) 64–69
9. Brooks, D., Tiwari, V., Martonosi, M.: Wattch: a Framework for Architectural-level Power Analysis and Optimizations. In: Proceedings of the 27th ISCA. (2000) 83–94
10. Conte, T., Menezes, K., Sathaye, S., Toburen, M.: System-Level Power Consumption Modeling and Trade-off Analysis Techniques for Superscalar Processor Design. IEEE Transactions on VLSI Systems **8** (2000) 129–137
11. Folegnani, D., González, A.: Energy-Effective Issue Logic. In: Proceedings of the 28th ISCA. (2001) 230–239
12. Gonzalez, R., Horowitz, M.: Energy Dissipation in General Purpose Microprocessors. IEEE Journal of Solid-State Circuits **31** (1996) 1277–1284
13. Hicks, P., Walnock, M., Owens, R.M.: Analysis of Power Consumption in Memory Hierarchies. In: Proceedings of the ISLPED. (1997) 239–242
14. Huang, M., Renau, J., Yoo, S.M., Torrellas, J.: L1 Data Cache Decomposition for Energy Efficiency. In: Proceedings of the ISLPED. (2001) 10–15
15. Miyoshi, A., Lefurgy, C., Hensbergen, E.V., Rajamony, R., Rajkumar, R.: Critical Power Slope: Understanding the Runtime Effects of Frequency Scaling. In: Proceedings of the Int'l Conf. on Supercomputing. (2002) 35–44
16. Su, C.L., Despain, A.: Cache Design Trade-offs for Power and Performance Optimization: a Case Study. In: Proceedings of the 1995 ISLPD, ACM Press (1995) 63–68

17. Zhou, H., Toburen, M., Rotenberg, E., Conte, T.M.: Adaptive Mode Control: A Static-Power Efficient Cache Design. In: Proceedings of the IEEE PACT. (2001) 61–72

18. Hughes, C., Srinivasan, J., Adve, S.: Saving Energy with Architectural and Frequency Adaptations for Multimedia Applications. In: Proceedings of the 34th Annual Int'l Symp. on Microarchitecture (MICRO-34). (2001) 250–261

19. Unsal, O., Ashok, R., Koren, I., Krishna, C., Moritz, C.: Cool-Cache for Hot Multimedia. In: Proceedings of the 34th Annual Int'l Symp. on Microarchitecture (MICRO-34). (2001) 274–283

20. An, N., Sivasubramaniam, A., Vijaykrishnan, N., Kandemir, M.T., Irwin, M.J., Gurumurthi, S.: Analyzing Energy Behavior of Spatial Access Methods for Memory-Resident Data. In: The VLDB Journal. (2001) 411–420

21. Austin, T., Larson, E., Ernst, D.: SimpleScalar: An Infrastructure for Computer System Modeling. IEEE Computer (2002) 59–67

22. Shivakumar, P., Jouppi, N.: CACTI 3.0: An Integrated Cache Timing, Power, and Area Model. Technical report, Compaq Western Research Laboratory (2001)

23. Lee, C., Potkonjak, M., Mangione-Smith, W.: MediaBench: A Tool for Evaluating and Synthesizing Multimedia and Communicatons Systems. In: International Symposium on Microarchitecture. (1997) 330–335

24. Henning, J.L.: SPEC CPU2000: Measuring CPU Performance in the New Millennium. IEEE Computer **33** (2000) 28–35

25. Transaction Processing Performance Council: TPC Benchmark^{TM} H (Decision Support), Standard Specification (1999)

26. Barroso, L., Gharachorloo, K., Bugnion, E.: Memory System Characterization of Commercial Workloads. In: Proceedings of the 25th ISCA. (1998) 3–14

27. Team, T.T.: In-Memory Data Management for Consumer Transactions: The TimesTen Approach. In: Proceedings of the ACM SIGMOD Conference. (1999) 528–529

An Efficient Frequency Scaling Approach
for Energy-Aware Embedded Real-Time Systems

Christian Poellabauer[1], Tao Zhang[2], Santosh Pande[2], and Karsten Schwan[2]

[1] Computer Science and Engineering, University of Notre Dame
cpoellab@cse.nd.edu
[2] College of Computing, Georgia Institute of Technology
{zhangtao,santosh,schwan}@cc.gatech.edu

Abstract. The management of energy consumption in battery-operated embedded and pervasive systems is increasingly important in order to extend battery lifetime or to increase the number of applications that can use the system's resources. Dynamic voltage and frequency scaling (DVFS) has been introduced to trade off system performance with energy consumption. For real-time applications, systems supporting DVFS have to balance the achieved energy savings with the deadline constraints of applications. Previous work has used periodic evaluation of an application's progress (e.g., with periodic *checkpoints* inserted into application code at compile time) to decide *if* and *how much* to adjust the frequency or voltage. Our approach builds on this prior work and addresses the overheads associated with these solutions by replacing periodic checkpoints with iterative checkpoint computations based on predicted best-, average-, and worst-case execution times of real-time applications (e.g., obtained through compile-time analysis or profiling).

1 Introduction

Motivation. Energy management has become a central issue in the embedded systems domain, where an increasing number of devices, including personal digital assistants, cell phones, medical equipment, and solar-powered systems, are supported by rechargeable batteries. If applications have stringent requirements for high performance or real-time guarantees, the energy consumption of these devices has to be carefully balanced with the resource utilization and application needs. Efficient energy management can result in reduced battery specifications (resulting in smaller and lighter devices), maximized battery lifetime, and increased mission duration. Fortunately, embedded applications can take advantage from a multitude of novel energy saving techniques. At the hardware level, consider the StrongARM SA11xx processors, the Intel XScale 80200, or the Transmeta Crusoe with LongRun, all of which support the run-time selection of different frequency or voltage levels [10, 14]. At the network level, wireless cards and disks are built with support for multiple power modes, i.e., these devices can be switched into a power-saving mode when idle [6]. Finally, at the application level, energy-aware transcoding and adaptation techniques [12, 17] reduce the

M. Beigl and P. Lukowicz (Eds.): ARCS 2005, LNCS 3432, pp. 207–221, 2005.

computation or communication needs, and therefore, the energy requirements of these applications. The energy management approach addressed in this paper is the frequency and voltage scaling capabilities of modern mobile processors. Consider a multimedia application in which a mobile device receives one or more video and audio streams that have to be replayed with certain requirements for constant rates and maximum jitter to ensure sufficient quality. This requires that the device allocates sufficient processor and network resources to these applications. However, especially with wireless communications, it is likely that video and audio frames will arrive in bursts, where the receiving device will buffer incoming data until their replay time has arrived. Based on the desired replay rate, a deadline for the replay of each frame can be derived. If the CPU is not fully utilized, frequency or voltage scaling can be used to slow down the execution of the video and audio players, therefore reducing the energy consumption of the device, while still ensuring the timely replay of video and audio.

Problem Statement. Previous work has introduced approaches to dynamically change the speed or voltage at different layers of an embedded system, e.g., as compile-time tool or as operating system extension. These approaches predict application run-time – e.g., from information collected through code analysis – and compute a clock frequency or voltage accordingly. However, variations in the run-time, caused by changes in the application behavior, input variables, or by resource scarcity, can lead to mispredictions, resulting in missed deadlines or inefficient energy management. Therefore, these approaches monitor the progress of a real-time application, e.g., by inserting *checkpoints* [3] or *hints* [1] into the application code or by comparing the progress to statistical application behavior [5]. As a result, speed or voltage are adjusted to compensate for these variations. Our approach builds on this prior work and addresses the overheads associated with these solutions, which stem from two sources: (a) cost of checkpointing and progress evaluation and (b) cost of frequency and voltage adjustments. For example, in the device used in this work, every time the clock frequency is adjusted, all devices fed by it (e.g., LCD controller, DMA controller, serial controllers, OS timer) 'freeze' for a duration of $150\mu s$ and the subsequent synchronization of memory requires up to $20ms$. It is to expect that newer devices will reduce these overheads, however, inefficient energy management approaches can lead to a large number of frequency adjustments, e.g., a process running for 500ms with run-time evaluations every 10ms could potentially experience 50 frequency adjustments during its execution. Instead, the goal should be to minimize the energy and time penalties caused by frequency adjustments, to maximize the number of process deadlines met, and to maximize the energy savings achieved. Simulations or models used in previous research fail to capture these significant overheads of 'real' hardware, therefore, in this paper we perform actual measurements on a handheld device to capture the overheads associated with dynamic frequency scaling. To control the overheads, we replace periodic checkpoints with an approach that *iteratively* computes checkpoints based on the *best-case execution time (BCET)*, *average-case execution time (ACET)*, and *worst-case execution time (WCET)* of a real-time application. These times can be obtained through compile-time code analysis, or through off-line or on-line profiling. For simplicity, we can estimate the average case with $ACET = (WCET+BCET)/2$. At each checkpoint, the application progress is evaluated, a new clock frequency or voltage is calculated and set if required, and a new checkpoint is computed. This reduces the number of checkpoints and potential speed or voltage changes, e.g., our results show that the number of frequency changes is reduced to about a quarter for the experimental scenario used in this paper. This approach assumes an embedded real-time system, where tasks execute until completion (e.g., using an EDF scheduler). The approach introduced in this paper is evaluated with an application from the scientific visualization domain. An embedded device receives visualization data in form of points and lines that are to be displayed. Using profiling we derive a relationship between the number of lines in an image and the application run-time for the best-, average-, and worst-case scenarios.

2   Dynamic Frequency Scaling for Real-Time Applications

Dynamic voltage and frequency scaling (DVFS) has been introduced to trade off system performance (i.e., application execution time) with energy consumption. While this paper focuses on frequency scaling, the approach introduced here is similarly applicable to devices with voltage scaling capabilities. The processor under consideration in this paper is a StrongARM SA1110 processor and the device used in this work is a Compaq iPAQ H3870 handheld with 32MB RAM, 32MB Flash, and an Orinoco Gold 11Mbps wireless card. The processor supports 11 clock frequencies ranging from 59MHz to 206.4MHz in 14.7MHz steps, the default frequency being 206.4MHz. The device runs the *familiar* Linux distribution version 0.7.1 with a 2.4.19 kernel. Figure 1(a) compares the application run-time of a simple test application (i.e., a *for*-loop with 10^7 iterations) at 11 different clock frequencies, showing how the application run-time increases with lower frequencies. In contrast, Figure 1(b) shows the energy consumption

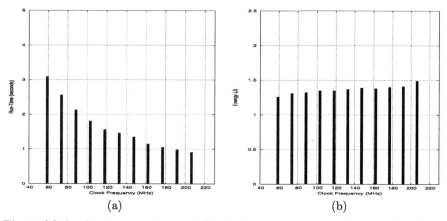

(a)   (b)

Fig. 1. (a) Application run-time and (b) device energy consumption as a function of clock frequency.

$E(Joule) = P_{active} * T_{active} + P_{idle} * T_{idle}$ of the device for the same application, where the shown energy is the sum of the 'active' period of the device (i.e., when an application is executed) and the 'inactive' or 'idle' period of the device over a period of $3.09s$ (the execution time of the application at the lowest clock frequency). For real-time applications it is important to select a clock frequency that allows these applications to meet their deadlines. However, uncertainties in application run-times (e.g., caused by variations in input data, the number of interrupts, etc.) would require that clock frequencies are selected such that all applications can meet their deadlines even for their worst-case execution times. However, this pessimistic approach will not fully exploit the potential energy savings, particularly if average-case and worst-case executions vary greatly. Other approaches, therefore, use dynamic evaluation of an application's progress and adjust the clock frequency if required, e.g., to speed up if the application is at risk of missing its deadline or to slow down to ensure optimal energy savings if an application is 'faster' than expected. Approaches such as profiling and compile-time analysis [1, 3, 16] are used to predict and monitor the run-time of an application. In [1, 3], the authors use checkpoints or hints at certain code locations to estimate the remaining execution time. However, frequent checkpoints can result in significant overheads, caused by the frequent progress evaluation and by the frequency changes. The goal of this paper is therefore to minimize the overheads by delaying progress evaluations and frequency changes until the latest possible times. Figure 2 compares the original periodic approach with the iterative approach introduced this work. In the original approach, checkpoints are placed at regular intervals, where at each checkpoint it is decided if and how to change the clock frequency. In contrast, an iterative approach uses knowledge of best-case and worst-case execution times to determine the latest possible time for progress evaluation. At this point, the clock frequency can be adjusted if required and a new checkpoint, based on the remaining best- and worst-case execution times, is calculated. The idea is that early progress evaluations (i.e., before the location of the checkpoint computed in our approach) are unnecessary and only cause overheads through frequent progress evaluations and frequency adjustments. For example, variations in run-time detected by early checkpoints could result in fre-

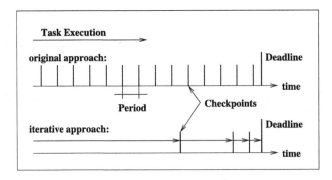

Fig. 2. Progress evaluation with checkpoints.

quency changes that have to be reversed later on because of other variations. Further, the accuracy of progress evaluation and frequency adjustments depend on the accuracy of checkpoint placement, i.e., an error in checkpoint placement could result in erroneous progress evaluations and undesired frequency switches. With the iterative approach, the number of checkpoints are significantly reduced, thereby reducing the negative effects of inaccuracies in progress feedback.

3   Iterative Checkpoint Computation

Assumptions and Definitions. The basis of our approach is the knowledge of the *best-case execution time (BCET)* and the *worst-case execution time (WCET)* of a given real-time application. Approaches to obtain these numbers include compile-time code analysis and profiling; the latter being used in this paper. Further, the *average-case execution time (ACET)* of an application is used to compute an appropriate clock frequency. $ACET$ can be obtained in the same manner BCET and WCET are obtained, however, for simplicity, we assume that $ACET$ is the arithmetic mean, i.e., $ACET = (BCET + WCET)/2$. The maximum deviation from the mean is then $(WCET - BCET)/2$, which we denote as Δt. We assume that an application deadline T_d is either expressed explicitly (e.g., by the application) or derived from the application context, e.g., from the replay rate of a video player. The processor supports multiple clock frequencies in the range from f_{min} to f_{max}; through off-line measurements we can obtain a list of *scaling factors* $k_{n:m}$ to translate application run-times at one clock frequency to application run-times at any other clock frequency. These scaling factors are obtained by executing a sample application at all available clock frequencies and measuring the run-times, i.e., a scaling factor expresses the ratio of the run-times at two different clock frequencies. For example, an application run-time of $2s$ at f_4 and a scaling factor $k_{4:2} = 2$ translates into a run-time of $2*2s = 4s$ at frequency f_2. In the remainder of this document, if not otherwise indicated, all base times are assumed to be calculated for the default clock frequency f_{max}.

Frequency Computation. The goal is to execute a given task P_i with a known deadline T_d at the lowest possible frequency, to allow it to approach the deadline as close as possible without missing it. The basis of our computations is the average case, i.e., we determine the clock frequency to prolong application execution assuming that the application will require the average-case execution time (see Figure 3). Therefore, the frequency f_x is determined such that the following requirements are satisfied: (A) $ACET_{max} * k_{max:x} <= T_d$ and (B) $ACET_{max} * k_{max:x-1} > T_d$. (A) determines that the average execution time multiplied by the scaling factor $k_{max:x}$ (for the transition from f_{max} to f_x) is at most the deadline and (B) ensures that the selected frequency is the lowest possible frequency that would not cause the application to miss its deadline, assuming that the actual run-time will be $ACET$. Since the clock frequency can only be selected at discrete steps, the application run-time $ACET_x$ ($ACET$ at the clock frequency f_x) will result in the application finishing δ time units

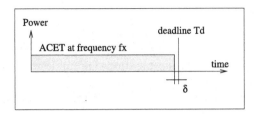

Fig. 3. Frequency selection for ACET.

before the deadline T_d ($\delta >= 0$). Algorithm 1 summarizes the frequency computation, where available clock frequencies and scaling factors are stored in tables
('frequency' and 'factor'). The value of *index* indicates the currently chosen table entries and thereby the clock frequency ($f_{min} <= f_{index} <= f_{max}$). The
algorithm is implemented as a function in a C library, which is linked by the
application. This algorithm is executed at the beginning of application execution, where the application passes the predicted average-case execution time and
the deadline as parameters. The outcome of this algorithm is the selected clock
frequency and the CPU clock is changed accordingly with the *set_clock* system
call, which is caught by a kernel-loadable module that performs the OS-level
clock management tasks.

Checkpoint Computation. Consider Figure 4, which shows the run-times of
process P_i for both the best and the worst case, resulting in the task finishing
$\Delta t + \delta$ time units before the deadline (best case) or $\Delta t - \delta$ time units after the
deadline (worst case). Since these are the both extremes (shortest and longest
paths through the application code), two checkpoints can be computed for these
two scenarios and the earlier one will be the first checkpoint for the evaluation
of the application progress. The remainder of this section shows how the best-
and worst-case execution times are used to determine the first checkpoint.

```
index = maxindex;
while (index > 0) do
    if (ACET * factor[index] <= Td) then
        index − −;
    else
        if (index < maxindex) then
            index + +;
        end
        break;
    end
end
set_clock(frequency[index]);
return frequency[index];
```

Algorithm 1. Frequency computation.

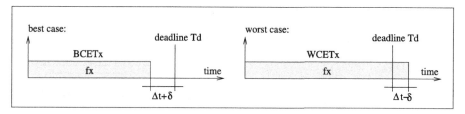

Fig. 4. Best case and worst case task run-times.

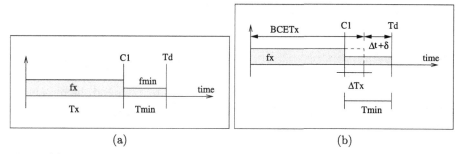

Fig. 5. (a) Desired outcome of frequency selection for best case scenario and (b) checkpoint computation.

(a) Best Case: In the best case scenario, an application will require $BCET_x$ at clock frequency f_x. Figure 5(a) shows the desired approach, i.e., the task is executed as long as possible at frequency f_x (for T_x time units) and at a certain – yet to be determined – checkpoint C_1, the frequency is switched to f_{min}, allowing the application to finish as close as possible to the deadline, i.e., $T_x + T_{min} = T_d$. That means that – in the case the application requires $BCET$ – the first part of the task execution will occur at frequency f_x (based on the assumption the application will require $ACET$) and the remainder will occur at f_{min}, the lowest possible clock frequency. Figure 5(b) shows that scenario, where ΔT_x is an unknown part of the task run-time $BCET_x$, which, if executed at f_{min} will satisfy the following equation:

$$T_{min} = \Delta T_x * k_{x:min} = \Delta t + \delta + \Delta T_x.$$

This leads us further to the following formula:

$$\Delta T_x = (\Delta t + \delta)/(k_{x:min} - 1).$$

Then the first checkpoint (when to evaluate a task's progress for the first time) is computed with:
$$C_1 = BCET_x - \Delta T_x.$$

(b) Worst Case: In the worst case scenario, the task finishes after $WCET_x$; Figure 6(a) shows the desired approach for this case. The task is executed at clock

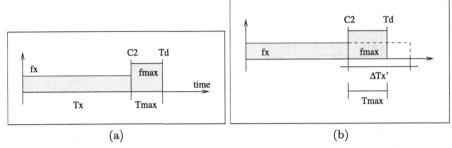

Fig. 6. (a) Desired outcome of frequency selection for the worst case scenario and (b) checkpoint computation.

frequency f_x as long as possible (for T_x time units) and at a certain checkpoint C_2 (yet to be determined), the frequency is switched to f_{max} and the remainder of the task will require T_{max} time units, where $T_x + T_{max} = T_d$. Again, this means that a certain part of the task that would be executed at f_x ($\Delta T_x'$) now has to be executed at f_{max} (see Figure 6(b)). We can establish that

$$T_{max} = \Delta T_x' * k_{x:max} = \Delta T_x' - \Delta t + \delta.$$

Or in words: an unknown time $\Delta T_x'$ of task T_i's execution (measured at clock frequency f_x) will be executed at the highest possible clock frequency f_{max}, such that the deadline will be reached exactly (in the worst-case scenario). This leads us to the following formula:

$$\Delta T_x' = (\delta - \Delta t)/(k_{x:max} - 1).$$

The checkpoint is then computed as follows:

$$C_2 = WCET_x - \Delta T_x'.$$

The earliest of these two checkpoints is now the checkpoint C where the application progress will be evaluated for the first time:

$$C = min(C_1, C_2).$$

Algorithm 2 summarizes the checkpoint computation, which is performed after the clock frequency f_x is determined. This function issues a system call, *set_OS_timer*, which sets an interrupt service routine in the kernel that will be executed once the timer expires. At timer expiration, an upcall into the library is performed, where the application progress is then evaluated.

Progress Counter. Each checkpoint is used to evaluate an application's progress. In addition to checkpoints, a compile-time tool must also insert frequent *progress hints* into application code, to allow checkpoints to make predictions on the remaining run-time. The goal of this paper is to minimize the costly

```
index = maxindex;
while (index > 0) do
    if (ACET * factor[index] <= Td) then
        index − −;
    else
        if (index < maxindex) then
            index + +;
        end
        break;
    end
end
set_clock(frequency[index]);
return frequency[index];
```

Algorithm 2. Checkpoint computation.

checkpoints and frequency adjustments, assuming that the 'hinting' costs are negligible. At compile-time, two different functions are inserted into the application code: (a) a single call to the function *init_progress_counter* at the beginning of the application, initializing a *progress counter* to a pre-determined value and (b) periodic calls to a function called *update_progress*, where each call will decrement the previously initialized value of the progress counter. The initial value of the progress counter and the positions of the function calls are determined such that the progress counter can give sufficient information of the status of the application execution. At each checkpoint, the progress counter is used to evaluate the application's progress. Different approaches for the placement of calls to *update_progress* can be used, e.g., in [1], the authors use code analysis to identify optimal locations of such calls. Here, calls are placed a few milliseconds apart, details about this approach are beyond the topic of this paper. The cost of each call is a few extra instructions for decrementing an integer value.

Iterative Checkpoint Computation. Once the first checkpoint has been computed, the process is repeated in the following manner: we consider the remainder of a task's execution from the first checkpoint to the deadline. The previously obtained execution times for the best-, average-, and worst-case scenarios are adjusted to reflect the progress made and the new values are used to determine (a) if the clock frequency needs to be adjusted and (b) the location of the next checkpoint. Algorithm 3 summarizes these steps, which are repeated until either the value of the new checkpoint or the distance between the deadline and the new checkpoint are smaller than twice dt, the interval between two consecutive calls to the function decrementing the progress counter. In the first case, instead of computing new checkpoints, we simply evaluate the progress once per dt and in the latter case we are sufficiently close to the deadline to terminate the evaluation process.

```
index = maxindex;
while (index > 0) do
    if (ACET * factor[index] <= Td) then
        index − −;
    else
        if (index < maxindex) then
            index + +;
        end
        break;
    end
end
set_clock(frequency[index]);
return frequency[index];
```

Algorithm 3. Recursive frequency and checkpoint computation.

4   Evaluation

Application Profiling. The application under consideration is that of a scientific visualization tool for mobile devices. Here, data streams contain graphic objects in form of points and lines, which are then displayed and the pixels between end-points of a line are interpolated. The number of lines determines the overheads in displaying the images. Each data frame received contains a header indicating the number of lines in the frame. The relationship between the number of lines and the application run-times has been determined with off-line profiling and is shown in Figure 7(a). Using these results we are able to obtain functions (e.g., with linear regression) to describe the run-times for the best case (rt_{bc}), the average case (rt_{ac}), and the worst case (rt_{wc}), where the number of lines is indicated by $num(l)$: $rt_{bc} = 2.82*num(l)+650, rt_{ac} = 2.86*num(l)+665, rt_{wc} = 2.90 * num(l) + 680$.

These results show that $\Delta t = (WCET − BCET)/2$ is almost independent from the number of lines. We compare these results to the profiling results of another application, a video decoder, shown in Figure 7(b). Here, the deviations Δt increase with the size of the data. This increase can be explained with the larger variation in data content for video streams, i.e., the decompression depends not only on the data size but also on the image content. The resulting functions are as follows, where $size(d)$ is the size of the compressed data in kBytes: $rt_{bc} = 9.54 * size(d) + 4.6, rt_{ac} = 10.98 * size(d) + 8.1, rt_{wc} = 12.42 * size(d) + 8.4$.

The experiments are performed on the previously described Compaq iPAQ handheld and the power measurements are performed with a Picotech ADC-100 PC oscilloscope (100kSamples/s, 2 channels, and 12 bit resolution).

Iterative Checkpoint Computation. The goal of the iterative checkpoint computation approach introduced in this paper is to reduce the number of progress evaluations of a running task and the number of frequency changes.

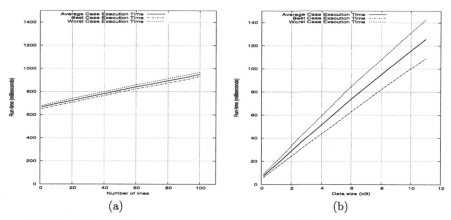

Fig. 7. (a) Scientific visualization application and (b) video decompression.

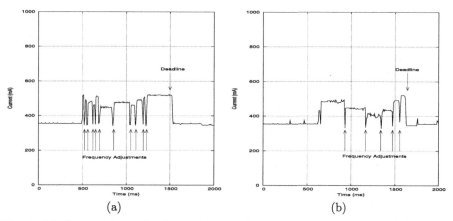

Fig. 8. (a) Current drawn by device for periodic progress evaluation and (b) current drawn by device for iterative progress evaluation.

Figure 8(a) shows a snapshot of an approach with periodic progress evaluation, with a period of $20ms$ between evaluations. This period has been carefully chosen, i.e., larger periods resulted in less frequency adjustments but more missed deadlines due to the reduced ability for the approach to react to variations, particularly close to the deadline. Smaller periods have resulted in larger overheads and more frequency adjustments and therefore also missed the deadlines more frequently. The arrows in Figure 8(a) indicate the times where the evaluation resulted in a clock frequency adjustment, e.g., 10 times in the example shown here. Further, due to the overheads caused by these frequent – and often unnecessary – adjustments, the deadline (as indicated in the graph) is ultimately missed by about $30ms$. In contrast, Figure 8(b) shows a snapshot of the same application, this time with the iterative checkpoint computation. The first checkpoint is after about 30% of task execution, the second one after 50%, etc., resulting in 5 checkpoints, each of which results in a frequency change. Compared to Figure 8(a), where 20% of all checkpoints result in frequency changes (50 checkpoints and 10 frequency adjustments), in our approach in Figure 8(b) 100% of all checkpoints result in frequency changes (5 checkpoints), while still ensuring that the application meets its deadline. That is, our approach is efficient in the sense that only 10% of the checkpoints – compared to the periodic approach – were needed, but *each* checkpoint resulted in a frequency adjustment.

Overhead Considerations. With our code, each checkpoint computation requires approximately $50\mu s$. In contrast, each frequency switch requires about $150\mu s$, however, the total measured delays can reach up to $20ms$. This is due to the way the used Linux version updates the SDRAM refresh rates for each frequency change. Figure 9(a) evaluates the achieved run-times of the scientific visualization application for the following three approaches: (a) no power management, (b) periodic checkpoints, and (c) iterative checkpoint computation. The number of lines is varied from 10 to 100, in all cases the application terminates before the deadline if no power management is deployed. If the iterative approach is used, the actual run-time is about 0–4% earlier than the deadline. However, if the periodic approach is used, the deadline is missed for most executions with number of lines of 40 and more. The reason is that the high number of evaluations and clock changes results in large overheads, which can ultimately push the execution time beyond the deadline. Figure 9(b) compares the average clock frequency for the two approaches: iterative checkpoints and periodic evaluations. Lower average clock frequency translates to lower energy consumption. For line numbers from 10 to 70, the iterative approach has lower average clock frequencies, thereby saving more energy than the periodic approach. After 70, the periodic approach has lower average clock frequencies, but note that this led to the missed deadlines in the previous graph. Similar results are shown by Figure 10(a) that show the energy consumptions as a function of the number of lines. Here, the periodic approach shows the worst results. The iterative

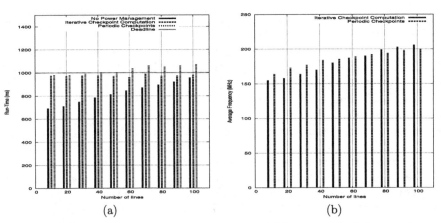

Fig. 9. (a) Measured application run-times and (b) average clock frequencies.

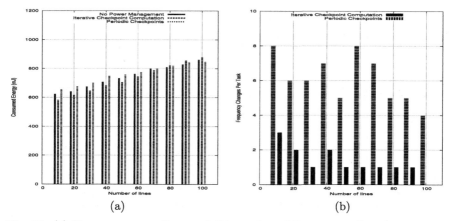

Fig. 10. (a) Energy consumptions and (b) number of frequency adjustments per application.

approach shows the best results up to about 70 lines. After that, the execution times are so large and the potential energy savings so little, that the overheads caused by our approach result in increased energy consumptions compared to the case without power management. This indicates the possibility of deploying a hybrid approach, where frequency scaling is only used *if* the potential energy savings outweigh the overheads introduced by the frequency scaling algorithms (this approach is left as future work). Finally, Figure 10(b) compares the number of frequency adjustments for the same application for both the periodic and the iterative approach at different numbers of lines, where the periodic approach requires on average 3.8 times as many clock adjustments.

5   Related Work

There has been substantial work on power management for mobile devices, including low-power modes for disks and networks [4, 6], power-aware scheduling policies [11], and energy management techniques for wireless communication [2, 12]. Frequency scaling [9] and voltage scaling [10] have been investigated in recent research. Both have been shown to be useful to reduce power consumption for a variety of application scenarios, including real-time systems [7, 10]. In [15], the authors exploit slack times to integrate fixed priority scheduling with power-awareness. The exploitation of idle times to preserve power in video decoding applications has been shown feasible in previous work [8, 13]. The focus of this work is on overhead reductions for dynamic frequency management for embedded real-time applications. Previous approaches have introduced methods to dynamically adjust the clock frequency to allow applications to meet their deadlines while minimizing the energy consumption [1, 3]. However, frequent execution of progress evaluations and frequent frequency changes reduce the utility of these approaches. This paper extends these approaches by introducing an iterative method of computing checkpoints, reducing the number of checkpoints and frequency changes required.

6   Conclusions and Future Work

The work presented in this paper builds on previous work on dynamic frequency and voltage scaling for real-time applications. Here, periodic comparison of actual task progress with predicted task progress is used to determine if and how to change the clock frequency. The problem with periodic evaluation of application progress is that frequencies may be changed too frequent, resulting in excessive overheads. The goal of this paper is to replace periodic checkpoints with iteratively computed checkpoints, resulting in less overheads for progress evaluation and frequency changes. The results show that in the case of a scientific visualization tool, the overheads can be reduced to 26% of the costs for the original periodic approach. Our future work will use techniques to evaluate task progress also to detect 'hot spots' of long running application code in terms of energy consumption. For example, the scientific visualization tool discussed in this paper is typically run for a long period of time and code optimizations of frequently executed segments of the application may help to reduce the overall energy consumption. Further, this paper considered a single real-time application for embedded systems, our future work will address situations with multiple real-time applications executing simultaneously. Finally, other architectures (e.g., Transmeta, XScale) offer different numbers of frequency levels and voltage levels; our work will explore the achievable overhead reductions on these architectures.

References

1. N. Aboughazaleh, B. Childers, D. Mosse, R. Melhem, and M. Craven. Energy Management for Real-Time Embedded Applications With Compiler Support. In *Proc. of Languages, Compilers, and Tools for Embedded Systems (LCTES) Conference*, June 2003.
2. S. Agrawal and S. Singh. An Experimental Study of TCP's Energy Consumption over a Wireless Link. In *Proc. of the 4th European Personal Mobile Communications Conference*, February 2001.
3. A. Azevedo, I. Issenin, R. Comea, R. Gupta, N. Dutt, A. Veidenbaum, and A. Nicolau. Profile-based Dynamic Voltage Scheduling using Program Checkpoints. In *Proc. of Design Automation and Test in Europe*, 2002.
4. S. Chandra and A. Vahdat. Application-specific Network Management for Energy-aware Streaming of Popular Multimedia Formats. In *Proc. of the USENIX Annual Technical Conference*, 2002.
5. G. Flavius. On Energy Reduction in Hard Real-Time Systems Containing Tasks with Stochastic Execution Times. In *Proc. of IEEE Workshop on Power Management for Real-Time and Embedded Systems*, 2001.
6. D. P. Helmbold, D. D. E. Long, and B. Sherrod. A Dynamic Disk Spin-down Technique for Mobile Computing. In *Proc. of the Intl. Conference on Mobile Computing and Networking*, 1996.
7. J. Liu, P. H. Chou, N. Bagherzadeh, and F. Kurdahi. Power-Aware Scheduling under Timing Constraints for Mission-Critical Embedded Systems. In *Proc. of Design Automation Conference*, 2001.

8. M. Mesarina and Y. Turner. Reduced Energy Decoding of MPEG Streams. In *Proc. of Multimedia Computing and Networking, San Jose, CA*, 2002.
9. A. Miyoshi, C. Lefurgy, E. V. Hensbergen, R. Rajamony, and R. Rajkumar. Critical Power Slope: Understanding the Runtime Effects of Frequency Scaling. In *Proc. of the 16th Annual Intl. Conference on Supercomputing*, 2002.
10. P. Pillai and K. G. Shin. Real-Time Dynamic Voltage Scaling for Low-Power Embedded Operating Systems. In *Proc. of the 18th SOSP, Chateau Lake Louise, Banff, Canada*, 2001.
11. C. Poellabauer and K. Schwan. Power-Aware Video Decoding using Real-Time Event Handlers. In *Proc. of the 5th International Workshop on Wireless Mobile Multimedia, Atlanta, GA*, September 2002.
12. C. Poellabauer and K. Schwan. Energy-Aware Media Transcoding in Wireless Systems. In *Proc. of the Second IEEE Intl. Conference on Pervasive Computing and Communications (PerCom 2004)*, March 2004.
13. J. Pouwelse, K. Langendoen, R. Lagendijk, and H. Sips. Power-Aware Video Decoding. In *Proc. of Picture Coding Symposium 2001, Seoul, Korea*, 2001.
14. S. Saewong and R. Rajkumar. Practical Voltage-Scaling for Fixed-Priority RT-Systems. In *Proc. of the 9th IEEE Real-Time and Embedded Technology and Applications Symposium (RTAS)*, May 2003.
15. Y. Shin and K. Choi. Power Conscious Fixed Priority Scheduling for Hard Real-Time Systems. In *Proc. of Design Automation Conference*, 1999.
16. E. Vivancos, C. Healy, F. Mueller, and D. Whalley. Parametric Timing Analysis. In *Proc. of the Workshop on Language, Compilers, and Tools for Embedded Systems*, 2001.
17. W. Yuan and K. Nahrstedt. A Middleware Framework Coordinating Processor/Power Resource Management for Multimedia Applications. In *Proc. of IEEE Globecom 2001, San Antonio, TX*, pages 1984–1988, 2001.

Towards Autonomic Networking
Using Overlay Routing Techniques

Kendy Kutzner, Kurt Cramer, and Thomas Fuhrmann

System Architecture Group, Universität Karlsruhe (TH), Karlsruhe, Germany
{kendy.kutzner,curt.cramer,thomas.fuhrmann}@ira.uka.de

Abstract. With an ever-growing number of computers being embedded into our surroundings, the era of ubiquitous computing is approaching fast. However, as the number of networked devices increases, so does system complexity. Contrary to the goal of achieving an "invisible computer", the required amount of management and human intervention increases more and more, both slowing down the growth rate and limiting the achievable size of ubiquitous systems.

In this paper we present a novel routing approach that is capable of handling complex networks without any administrative intervention. Based on a combination of standard overlay routing techniques and source routes, this approach is capable of efficiently bootstrapping a routable network. Unlike other approaches that try to combine peer-to-peer ideas with ad-hoc networks, sensor networks, or ubiquitous systems, our approach is *not* based on a routing scheme. This makes the resulting system flexible and powerful with respect at application support as well as efficient with regard to routing overhead and system complexity.

1 Motivation and Introduction

The Autonomic Computing vision outlines a future in which computing systems are self-managing. By this, the systems' administrative complexity is expected to be greatly reduced. Autonomic Computing techniques therefore lend themselves to the implementation of large-scale ubiquitous systems. There, networking plays a fundamental role as the systems' complex functionality only emerges from the *cooperation* of the otherwise less powerful embedded devices. When comparing the anticipated traits of Autonomic Computing with those achieved by peer-to-peer (P2P) networking, striking similarities can be discovered. We therefore see great opportunities in developing autonomic networking systems targeted at Ubiquitous Computing by employing P2P techniques.

In this paper, we present an important building block for the successful deployment of that idea, a novel routing scheme based on the combination of peer-to-peer overlay routing and source routing in the underlay. This combination is capable of pooling tens of thousands of small, network-enabled, autonomous devices – each with limited processing and memory capabilities – into a routable

M. Beigl and P. Lukowicz (Eds.): ARCS 2005, LNCS 3432, pp. 222–235, 2005.

network. The protocol is fully self-organizing and self-optimizing, has a low per-node control message overhead, and yields efficient path lengths as compared to globally optimized shortest-paths networks. Moreover, being based on distributed hash-table addressing, the resulting network also efficiently supports higher-layer functionality like look-up services, etc.

To our knowledge such an approach has not been studied well in the literature so far. Few authors already proposed to replace the Internet Protocol (IP) by a peer-to-peer overlay [4],[3]. But no definite results have been achieved by them yet. Hu et. al. proposed in [8] to combine Dynamic Source Routing with a DHT, however they were not able to eliminate the potential flooding of the whole network.

1.1   The Benefit of Overlays

One key aspect in the use of overlay networks is their capability of introducing an application specific addressing that abstracts from the physical necessities of the underlying network [2]. While in the Internet addresses should reflect the structure of the physical network, applications need to address logical entities. This is best seen with distributed hash tables (DHTs). There, logical addresses (identifiers, keys) are obtained by hashing the name of an object into a very large key space. The overlay network (e.g. CAN [12], Chord [16], Pastry [13], or Kademlia [9]) then maps these logical addresses to physical network nodes, thereby hiding the physical structure of the network. Applications can use this abstraction to, e.g., distributedly store files. Although this is probably the most popular use of overlay networks by now, other uses might be even more powerful. An example is the Internet Indirection Infrastructure [15], that employs the logical address space to create network services for mobility support, group communication, and the like.

This *separation of concern* is most useful in the area of pervasive and ubiquitous computing. For this reason many authors are combining peer-to-peer concepts with mobile ad-hoc networks, sensor networks, etc. ([7], [6], [14] and references therein) In general, these approaches employ a two-layered approach, where the basic connectivity is provided by some off-the-shelf routing protocol, like fish-eye routing [10], ad-hoc on-demand distance vector routing [11] or the ones compared in [1]. On top of this already fully routable underlay network, a separate overlay network of peer-to-peer mechanisms is established. While this provides the full benefit of the logical overlay addressing, this two-layered approach gives rise to inefficiencies. E.g., the nodes have to use their scarce resources for *two* different routing protocols, overlay *and* underlay. Moreover, the network is burdened with the control message overhead of *two* routing protocols. These inefficiencies are avoided by our approach, that inherently combines overlay and underlay routing. Before describing this combination, we briefly review those key aspects of overlay and underlay routing that form the ingredients for our novel protocol.

1.2   A Brief Review of Underlay and Overlay Routing

Routing can be viewed as being the task of applying general knowledge of a network's structure to a concrete packet (frame, message, datagram). Such a packet originates at one node of the network (source) and is destined to another node of that network (destination). Routing schemes can, among other properties, be classified according to *where* the knowledge of the network structure is stored:

With many dynamic routing approaches, especially with *distance vector routing*, but in essence also with *link state routing*, all the nodes in a network build up their specific part of the global knowledge that allows them to route a packet *towards* its destination. Each node stores its knowledge in a routing table. Thereby, these dynamic routing schemes benefit greatly from a well-organized address space that allows the nodes to aggregate large chunks of the address space into a single routing table entry. But with real networks, especially with organically growing ubiquitous networks, the aggregability of the address space deteriorates quickly. Especially the low-resource devices targeted in pervasive computing are not capable of storing and handling large routing tables.

Overlay routing with distributed hash tables, on the other hand, circumvents the aggregation problem by choosing peers that allow a perfect routing table. A simple algorithmic rule determines which peer is responsible for which address. Hence, the routing table has exactly p entries when a node has p peers. However, to work properly, a DHT overlay must be able to connect to all the peers prescribed by the algorithmic rule. This is no problem in overlays where an underlay routing mechanism provides full connectivity in the network. But it seems to be impossible to achieve in physical networks, where the neighbors of a node cannot be chosen at will.

Contrary to this seemingly obvious statement, we will show how a simple extension of the standard overlay approach can indeed create a DHT-like routing scheme in arbitrary networks. To this end, we combine a typical DHT routing (Chord) with two well-known underlay routing approaches: mutual state exchanges (as with distance vector routing protocols, DVRP) and source-routing. Both approaches are known to have severe drawbacks: DVRP scales badly to larger networks, while source-routing can only be employed in combination with some other routing means. But, as we will show, both obstacles are also overcome by the combination with the DHT-routing mechanism. (For the time being, we will not address other problems often associated with source routing, like e.g. security issues. These are severe problems in open networks with malicious users, but they are much less severe in our target scenario as described in the following section.)

1.3   Target Scenario Description

Before we describe our proposed routing approach in section 2 and report first results on efficiency with respect to traffic overhead and achievable path length in section 3, we briefly describe the scenario for which we designed this routing protocol. We also envisage our protocol being applied outside this specific scenario. Nevertheless, we also believe this particular application to be of growing importance in the near future.

Our novel routing approach targets networks of some tens or hundreds of thousand autonomous networked nodes that are connected by some physical communication links, be it wired or wireless. A typical example is a network of sensors and actuators in a large office building, a large factory plant, or a large municipal utility. The nodes have limited memory and processing capabilities. They are deployed redundantly, so that individual nodes may fail at any time, but we assume that they do so only at a moderate rate. We will, however, address the case that the entire system is shut down and re-started, as might happen with a power outage.

Individual nodes might be moved in the network (i.e. be detached and re-attached elsewhere), but we do not assume all the nodes to be truly mobile to a large extent. Moreover, we assume the nodes to be fully cooperative, i.e. we do not consider malicious nodes in this paper. This important issue is to be addressed in future work.

We assume the nodes to be redundantly linked to other nodes, typically in their vicinity. Communication requirements are assumed to be repetitive and of small data-rate. E.g. a light-switch will mostly signal to its associated lamps, the temperature sensor will mostly signal to the air-conditioning in the same room.

Additionally, many typical applications in the field of pervasive computing will benefit from the logical address space that the overlay aspects bring into our routing scheme. E.g. nodes can employ indirection mechanisms for service discovery, as well as for multicast, anycast, or concast. Moreover, addresses may be randomly assigned numbers, i.e. they can be hashes of device names, public cryptographic keys, etc. all of which greatly simplifies many applications in such a network (see [4] for a praise of these benefits).

We believe that the described network properties are typical for the described scenario of a large, but closed system. Although here centrally administered approaches would be applicable in principle, we do not believe that they are practically feasible in the in the light of a significant roll-out of such small autonomous embedded communication devices. To the contrary, we strongly believe, that only truly self-organizing systems will be able to pave the way to the large-scale deployment of distributed computing devices in all kinds of appliances. A technician installing such a device will well understand that it needs to be connected to the communication network, but he will probably not know the network topology, respect its original layout, register the device with a central facility, etc. Experience shows that in practice, people tend to apply quick hacks, i.e. they want to simply attach a device and expect it to work right away, and this is exactly what our approach accomplishes.

2   An Overlay-Underlay Routing Combination

We consider a network of randomly connected nodes with randomly assigned addresses. (The respectively employed definition of "randomness" is explained in section 3 where the simulation results are discussed.) Such a fully random network is the worst case assumption for a scenario like ours. In order to not complicate the description of our protocol, we begin with the assumption that the links are reliable point-to-point links. (Link and node failures as well as shared media will be addressed in section 2.3.) For simplicity, we also assume the network to be always connected and the addresses to be unique within this network. Provided sufficient redundancy, the former will hold for *almost every* network graph in the studied scenario. The latter is a typical assumption made with overlay networks where the address space is much larger than the number of nodes. Even if the address space was populated so densely that a collision became likely, conflict detection and resolution would be simple with standard overlay means (e.g. by having the neighbors of a newly attached node query for the node's address before accepting it as a neighbor).

Now the proposed protocol works as follows:

2.1   Bootstrapping Phase

Upon powering up a node, the node sends a $HELLO_1$ message to all its physical neighbors. They reply with a $HELLO_2$ message. If a new link is introduced between two existing nodes, both will send a $HELLO_2$ message. Both types of hello messages carry the respective node's address. Thus, after all hello messages have been exchanged, all nodes know the addresses of all their physical neighbors. This mechanism is known as *Neighbor Discovery*. There may be hardware technologies which support neighbor discovery and where therefore this mechanism is not necessary. We included it for completeness.

The neighbors' addresses are inserted into a constant size routing table. For an address space of 2^m unique addresses, each node's routing table contains m regular entries and one special purpose entry (see below). The organization of this routing table is such that the ith (regular) entry at a node with address a points to a node with address b whose distance $d(a, b) = (b-a) \bmod 2^m$ is at least 2^i and less than 2^{i+1}. In other words, the address space is circularly connected with a defined orientation so that distances are *asymmetric*. The larger i, the larger the chance that addresses fall into the respective interval. (Note that the 0'th entry can only be populated in the unlikely case that another node's address is the immediate successor of the node's address.) If more than one node is to be stored in the same entry of the routing table, one of them has to be chosen. An extension is to keep more than one up to k entries. The tradeoffs included are described in section 2.3. Upon start-up, when only physically neighboring nodes are known, this choice which nodes to keep has to be made at random. Later on, when the node has accumulated more "knowledge" about the network, the "better" node is chosen, where the term "better" is yet to be defined (see below).

Each entry in the routing table points to one node in the network. The entry itself is a string of node addresses, which describes a source route to the respective node. Upon start-up, all address strings trivially have length one. Later on, the strings will grow in size. The simulation results presented in section 3 show that for networks with 10 000 to 100 000 nodes, the length of these paths is on the order of the network diameter.

As soon as all physical neighbors have been entered into the routing table, the node sends all the nodes in the routing table an UPDATE message containing the full table. (It can do so, since by definition of the routing table it has either a source route to these nodes, or the destination is a direct neighbor.) Upon reception of an UPDATE message, the respective receiver takes that source route from the received table that leads to itself, inverts it and prepends the inverted source route to every other entry in the received table. If this address string concatenation leads to loops in the resulting path, these loops are cut so that the shortest possible path is formed. Finally, all the obtained paths are compared to the node's own routing table. Besides a new entry in the routing table there is one other reason to send an UPDATE message. Upon reception of an UPDATE message, the receiving node answers with such an message. It is important that these in turn don't lead to further messages. To avoid such an UPDATE-storm, every UPDATE message carries a flag whether the receiver should reply with another UPDATE message.

If a received path is better than the locally stored path for a given regular entry, the respective entry in the routing table is replaced. Here, a new entry is considered to be better, either if so far no path was available locally for the respective entry of the routing table, or if the new path is shorter. (Note that by replacing an entry in the routing table, that entry now points to a different node!)

The special purpose entry is used to store the path to the node's successor in the address space, i.e. the node with the smallest distance. This is necessary since otherwise the path to the successor might be replaced by a slightly more distant node (in the logical address space) which happens to have a shorter path (in physical network hops). Although this case is rare, it would lead to not being able to route to some of the nodes in the network (e.g. the successor).

After the routing table has been updated, the node sends a new UPDATE message to all the nodes currently stored in the routing table. (No update is sent if updating left the routing table unchanged.) In order to avoid an inflation of update messages, generation of the update is delayed by a timeout T_{update}. During this time potential further update messages can be processed. In a stable network without node churn, after a while, consistency will be achieved and no further updates will be sent. In real-world networks where nodes come and go, there will always be new update messages to be processed. Nevertheless, even there a sufficient level of consistency will permanently prevail in the network. Because newer and shorter routes are preferred by the selection algorithm, the network is constantly optimizing itself without the need for a central authority. Note that there are no flooded messages necessary to discover all routing table

entries, which is a clear improvement for the scalability of the system compared
to previous aproaches.

Very quickly after start-up of the entire network, the update mechanism fills
the routing table. (Clearly, due to the sparsely populated address space, the
low-index entries of the routing table typically remain empty.) In the further
course of operation the length of the stored paths shortens until an (almost)
stable state has been reached. But even before that time, the system is able to
route to arbitrary destinations.

2.2 Routing Phase

The routing table that results from the bootstrapping phase has all properties
required by the standard Chord routing algorithm. Accordingly, routing can
now be done in almost exactly the same manner as described with Chord. The
only difference is that we are using the source route paths that are stored in
the routing table instead of the transport addresses of a regular Chord. The
distinction between overlay and underlay present in Chord directly maps to the
use of two different packet types for routing in our proposed system: Type 1
packets contain a source route and can thus be directly forwarded towards the
respective destination. Type 2 packets only bear the destination address. In order
to be forwarded, a node must look up a source route. (In the Chord analogy,
type 1 packets are TCP/IP packets and type 2 packets are overlay packets.)

Consider the following example: A node with address a has to forward a
type 2 packet to a destination node with address b. To this end, it looks up that
source route path from the lower $\lfloor \log_2 d(a, b) \rfloor$ entries of the routing table that
has the shortest path length. This selection algorithm equals PRS with path
length as metric. It then encapsulates the type 2 packet into a type 1 packet
with that source route. (From a networking point of view this is in fact exactly
the same as what happens in normal overlay routing schemes. There, the overlay
messages are "encapsulated" into TCP segments and IP packets.)

As has been shown before [5], such an approach leads to a highly efficient
routing with path lengths that are only slightly larger than those of the optimal paths. Unlike the classical use as an overlay routing protocol *on top of
an already* existing network, our protocol does not require any underlying routing mechanism. This is a large benefit since it enables routing in scenarios like
those described in section 1.3. Nevertheless, we want to also investigate the performance of our protocol as compared to a hypothetical optimal shortest path
routing. (Note, that neither full-topology nor distance vector approaches are
feasible in our target scenario. Hence, this is only a benchmark indicating what
could be possibly achieved with much more resources in the individual nodes.)

2.3 Extensions for Practical Use

So far, we have presented the principles of our proposed new approach. Before we
present simulation results indicating that this approach indeed has the required
properties, we briefly sketch some extensions to the protocol that will be required

for practical use or allow tradeoffs between memory, number of messages and efficency. These extensions are subject of our current research efforts.

In real networks, packet loss is common due to node and link failures, queue overflows or problems on the link layer. Moreover, we expect in practice a moderate rate of node churn, i.e. nodes being attached and detached from the network. Given that the rate of such events is sufficiently low, our protocol is able to handle these situations. The argument is as follows: As will be demonstrated in the next section, our protocol converges rather quickly even for large networks. As long as the churn rate is below the convergence time, there will be no problem at all. If the churn rises, a growing number of inconsistencies will prevail in the network. At the same time, update messages do not cease any more, but perform constant maintenance of the network. I.e. routing table entries become soft-state. The actual thresholds which churn or packet loss rates lead to which rate of update messages and which level of correctness, are, however, to be determined by future simulation work.

The protocol described above maintains at most one source route per address space interval. An obvious extension is to keep more routes per interval, or to increase the number of intervals (provided the interval lengths are increasing logarithmically). This increased redundancy can be expected to reduce the achievable paths lengths and improve convergence. But it might also increase the amount of update traffic. The investigation of this trade-off, too, is subject of our ongoing work.

Another objection to the practical use of our protocol as described above might be that we described it only with point-to-point links. We believe this to be a minor technical detail. When the underlying hardware is based on a shared medium, as is typically the case in wireless scenarios, both the neighbor discovery and the exchange of update messages are accelerated since now several nodes can learn from each HELLO or UPDATE message. Since the protocol does not contain acknowledgments, etc., both message types can be considered as point-to-multipoint without further change. Moreover, the concept of source routes that always explicitly addresses the next hop during packet forwarding immediately carries over to shared media.

Finally, to reply to yet another potential objection with regard to the practical use of our proposed approach, we briefly mention the protocol overhead implied by using source routes. Consider a network with, e.g., a diameter of 20 hops and an address space size of 64bit. Then the source route can be expected to lead to a 160byte header for each packet. This is definitely not suitable for the low-resource devices of our target scenario. But, as stated in section 1.3, we expect communication to be repetitive and typically limited to a small set of destinations. Hence it is worth while to generate compressed headers, where the source route does not contain globally unique addresses but only labels that are locally unique to the respective nodes along the path. (We cannot elaborate the technical details here. See text books on ATM or MPLS for an explanation of this standard idea.) In a network with a node degree of $2^4 = 16$, this will lead to a packet header of only 4bit per source route hop.

3   Simulation Results

In order to be able to judge the achieved efficiency of our proposed routing protocol we implemented it as a simulation, focusing on the core aspects: the number of update messages and the length of the created source routes. The simulation program's source code is available from the authors on request.

The network's topology was modeled as random graph with constant node degrees of 3, 5, 10 and 20. (In detail: To ensure connectedness of the whole graph, first, a random permutation of all nodes was connected in form of a ring. Then additional links were entered between randomly drawn nodes until all nodes had acquired the respective degree.) Node addresses were drawn uniformly random from a 32bit address space, and duplicate address assignments were explicitly excluded. For each node degree various network sizes were simulated, ranging from 100 to 20 000 nodes.

At the beginning of each simulation run, all nodes were equipped with a routing table, each containing the node's physical neighbors (as it would result from exchanging the HELLO messages). Then the set of all nodes was traversed in consecutive rounds, according to the random permutation of the initial ring. For each node all the pending update messages were processed, and the resulting routing table sent to the nodes stored in the table.

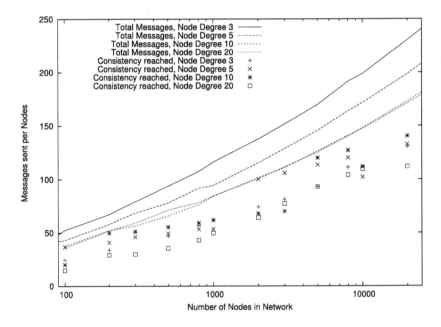

Fig. 1. Messages per node until consistency is reached

Figure 2 shows the average number of UPDATE messages per node that were exchanged during the various simulation runs as (normal, dotted, dashed) lines. Graphical approximations show that the number of UPDATE messages grows with $O(\log^2(n))$. A network of 10 000 nodes produces between 140 and 200 messages per node, depending on the degree of the nodes.

Long before all UPDATE messages have been exchanged, the system has already reached global consistency, where global consistency means that all nodes have stored their correct successor. The respective number of UPDATE messages needed for global consistency is shown as cross (star, box, plus) in figure 2. E.g., the 10 000 node networks reach global consistency after about 100 messages per node.

Once global consistency is achieved, the system is capable of correctly routing all packets. However, since global consistency can only be detected if global knowledge is available, the nodes have to keep sending UPDATE messages until these messages do not cause further changes in the regular routing table entries.

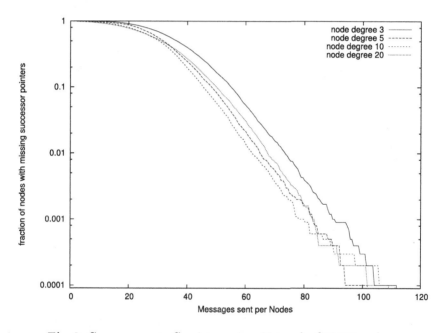

Fig. 2. Convergence to Consistency in a Network of 10 000 nodes

But even before reaching global consistency, the system is already able to correctly route most of the packets. Figure 2 shows how consistency proceeds during the simulation runs for the 10 000 node networks with node degrees of 3, 5, 10 and 20. At the beginning, nodes only know their physical neighborhood. Since for larger networks, it is highly unlikely that in this neighborhood there is a correct successor, almost 100% of the nodes lack their correct successor.

After a few rounds of update message exchange, the nodes learn more and more about nodes with similar addresses. (Note that the protocol is constructed to spread this knowledge in the address-neighborhood, not the physical neighborhood. Hence the quick exponential convergence.) The vast majority of the nodes (90%) have correct successor routes after about 40 – 50 exchanged messages. The rest of the time and update messages is spent to correct very few mistakes.

This entire bootstrapping process assumes the entire network to be powered up at once, as might be the case after a power outage. Such an extreme scenario is typically not studied in the field of overlay computing, since there one assumes a gradual extension of the network. However, we consider it a rare, but important "worst" case for our target scenario. Hence, the emphasis.

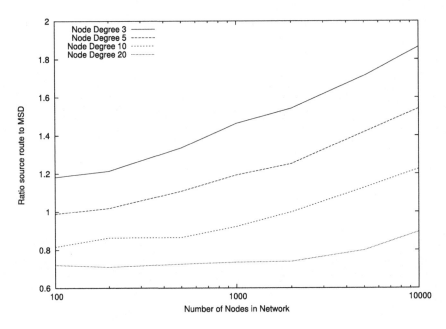

Fig. 3. Ratio of discovered source routes to the mean shortest distance

Our protocol does not aim at finding perfect shortest routes, however we strive to find good ones. Therefore, it is worthwhile to look at how good the selected routes are. Figure 3 shows the routing stretch for a single routing table entry, i.e. the ratio of the length of the source route and the mean shortest distance (MSD) of the graph. MSD is defined as the average of the shortest distance between two randomly selected nodes in the graph. Note the logarithmic scale. Since our algorithm is biased for smaller source routes (*proximity node selection*), it can select source routes shorter than the MSD. As can be seen from the graph, these source routes are typically in the order of magnitude of MSD, growing only logarithmically with the network size.

Note that, like with Chord, for routing to arbitrary nodes, $O(\log_2 n)$ of these source routes have to be traversed consecutively, where n is the number of nodes in the network. But, also like with Chord, there is a freedom of choice which source routes a packet should follow. [5] has shown that this *proximity route selection* (PRS) mechanism typically reduces the overall path length to about the length of the longest individual hop. (We are currently investigating the effects of PRS on our approach. First results are promising.)

4   Conclusion and Outlook

In this paper, we have presented a novel routing approach that is capable of efficiently routing messages in a random graph network where the nodes bear randomly assigned addresses. The latter is an important essence to the implementation of distributed hash tables (DHTs) on which many currently proposed middleware services are based. Like with DHTs, our approach distributes routing knowledge in the entire network so that a full route to an arbitrary destination can be found within $O(\log n)$ steps. It also limits the size of the routing table in each node to $O(\log n)$ entries, despite the random address assignment. Unlike other approaches, that promote the use of overlay techniques in mobile or pervasive network environments, we *do not require any underlying routing protocol at all*. Thereby, we are able to efficiently address much larger systems.

We motivated a target scenario for our propose protocol by considering a network of tens or hundreds of thousands of small embedded sensor actuator nodes that is extended with new nodes by and by. We pointed out that such a scenario highly benefits from a routing algorithm like ours, that is fully self-organizing even with the considered large random network topologies that could not be handled with conventional ad-hoc network or sensor network routing protocols. Moreover, since our protocol provides a DHT-like service to the application running on top of it, typical applications like look-up services, etc. are easy to be implemented efficiently.

We showed with the help of simulations that our approach leads to globally consistent routing tables after $O(\log^2 n)$ update messages where n is the network size. We also showed that partial correctness is achieved rather quickly, and that the number of routing inconsistencies decays exponentially. Furthermore, our simulations indicate that the resulting path lengths are on the order of the network diameter.

Nevertheless, our research towards the use of overlay networking techniques for autonomic networking is still at its beginning. Many interesting questions are to be resolved by future research. We see, e.g., considerable potential for further improving the efficiency of our approach, especially concerning overall path lengths. Additionally, we are currently studying the efficiency of our algorithm in a network with node churn, i.e. where nodes come and go or change their physical position in the network at a moderate rate. Besides these ongoing research activities, we still need to address many important questions like security and accounting, that would yield our approach applicable for open networks, too.

Altogether, we believe that the here proposed combination of overlay and underlay routing techniques is an important step towards the realization of truly autonomic computing systems.

References

1. Josh Broch, David A. Maltz, David B. Johnson, Yih-Chun Hu, and Jorjeta Jetcheva. A performance comparison of multi-hop wireless ad hoc network routing protocols. In *Proceedings of the Fourth Annual ACM/IEEE International Conference on Mobile Computing and Networking*, pages 85–97, October 1998.
2. Curt Cramer and Thomas Fuhrmann. On the Fundamental Communication Abstraction Supplied by P2P Overlay Networks. *European Transactions on Telecommunications*, 16:1–9, 2005.
3. Jakob Eriksson, Michalis Faloutsos, and Srikanth Krishnamurty. PeerNet: Pushing Peer-to-Peer Down the Stack. In *Proceedings of the 2nd International Workshop on Peer-to-Peer Systems (IPTPS '03)*, Claremont Hotel, Berkeley, CA, USA, February 2001. Springer Verlag.
4. Bryan Ford. Unmanaged Internet Protocol. *ACM SIGCOMM Computer Communications Review*, 34(1):93–98, January 2004.
5. P. Krishna Gummadi, Ramakrishna Gummadi, Steven D. Gribble, Sylvia Ratnasamy, Scott Shenker, and Ion Stoica. The impact of DHT routing geometry on resilience and proximity. In *Proceedings of the ACM SIGCOMM Conference*, pages 381–394, Karlsruhe, Germany, August 2003.
6. Tobias Heer, Heiko Niedermayer, Leo Petrak, Simon Rieche, and Klaus Wehrle. On the Use of Structured P2P Indexing Mechanisms in Mobile Ad-Hoc Scenarios. In *Proceedings of the 34. Jahrestagung der Gesellschaft für Informatik*, volume 2, pages 239–244, Ulm, Germany, September 2004.
7. Hans-Joachim Hof, Erik-Oliver Blaß, Thomas Fuhrmann, and Martina Zitterbart. Design of a Secure Distributed Service Directory for Wireless Sensornetworks. In *Proceedings of the 1st European Workshop on Wireless Sensor Networks*, Berlin, Germany, January 2004.
8. Y Charlie Hu, Himabindu Pucha, and Saumitra M Das. Exploiting the synergy between peer-to-peer and mobile ad hoc networks. In *Proceedings of HotOS-IX: Ninth Workshop on Hot Topics in Operating Systems*, May 2003.
9. Petar Maymounkov and David Mazières. Kademlia: A Peer-to-Peer Information System Based on the XOR Metric. In *Revised Papers from the First International Workshop on Peer-to-Peer Systems*, pages 53–65. Springer-Verlag, 2002.
10. Guangyu Pei, Mario Gerla, and Tsu-Wei Chen. Fisheye state routing in mobile ad hoc networks. In *ICDCS Workshop on Wireless Networks and Mobile Computing*, pages D71–D78, 2000.
11. Charles E. Perkins and Elizabeth M. Royer. Ad hoc on-demand distance vector routing. In *Proceedings of the 2nd IEEE Workshop on Mobile Computing Systems and Applications*, pages 90–100, February 1999.
12. Sylvia Ratnasamy, Paul Francis, Mark Handley, Richard Karp, and Scott Shenker. A Scalable Content-Addressable Network. In *Proceedings of the SIGCOMM 2001 conference*, pages 161–172. ACM Press, 2001.
13. Antony Rowstron and Peter Druschel. Pastry: Scalable, distributed object location and routing for large-scale peer-to-peer systems. In *Proceedings of the IFIP/ACM International Conference on Distributed Systems Platforms (Middleware) 2001*, Heidelberg, Germany, November 2001.

14. Rüdiger Schollmeier, Ingo Gruber, and Florian Niethammer. Protocol for Peer-to-Peer Networking in Mobile Environments. In *Proceedings of the 12th International Conference on Computer Communications and Networks*, Dallas, Texas, USA, October 2003.
15. Ion Stoica, Daniel Adkins, Shelley Zhuang, Scott Shenker, and Sonesh Surana. Internet Indirection Infrastructure. In *Proceedings of the 2002 ACM SIGCOMM conference*, pages 73–86, Pittsburgh, PA, USA, 2002. ACM Press.
16. Ion Stoica, Robert Morris, David Karger, M. Frans Kaashoek, and Hari Balakrishnan. Chord: A Scalable Peer-to-peer Lookup Service for Internet Applications. In *Proceedings of the SIGCOMM 2001 conference*, pages 149–160. ACM Press, 2001.

Context-Based Storage Management
for Wearable and Portable Devices

Alexandros Karypidis and Spyros Lalis

Computer and Communication Engineering Department, University of Thessaly
{lalis,karypid}@inf.uth.gr

Abstract. In our information-rich world, managing the data we collect is becoming a significant bottleneck for users. This issue has triggered considerable research in so-called semantic file systems, relying on the attachment of metadata to files. Such data is useful for dynamically arranging files in virtual directories, according to the user's request or task at hand. However, current research typically concerns the desktop and little work has been done taking into account mobile devices, which in addition to being generators of data themselves are now also capable of carrying significant amounts of information. In this paper we discuss how context information can be exploited to attach semantics to files residing on portable devices, and we show how such information can be used by the storage system itself to enhance data management while on the move. We also describe a storage framework which integrates smoothly with semantic file systems by facilitating automatic annotation of files generated by portables, as well as by exploiting this information to better integrate with infrastructure data stores.

1 Conglomeration of Computing Devices: A New Personal System

Portable, handheld and wearable computing devices are becoming increasingly popular. Mobile phones, PDAs, digital photograph cameras and GPS receivers are just a few examples of consumer electronics which can be readily bought at the local electronics store. The vision of ubiquitous and pervasive computing has also led to the embedding of processors in objects such as coffee cups [1], clothes [18], jewellery [5] and other items that could be worn or carried by people. As a result, computing is moving beyond the physical – and mental – boundaries of the desktop, posing yet another challenge to system designers, namely that of flexibly combining the available devices to support personal computing.

Cooperation amongst wearables and between wearables and the infrastructure can be useful in several cases, be it to overcome usability and capacity limitations, comply with social norms, or adhere to privacy requirements. For example, one may prefer to read his personal e-mail on his PDA rather than a public wall-sized display. Conversely, it could be more convenient to redirect the display from a PDA to the same wall-sized display when reviewing a map and use the PDA just for navigation control. Given the variety of circumstances it is unlikely for one specific device to fit all purposes. In fact, different devices may be candidates for the same task, and the best option may often be the combination of many different devices rather than a single device. In [17] the term symbiosis is used to refer to the need for cooperation among handhelds and

M. Beigl and P. Lukowicz (Eds.): ARCS 2005, LNCS 3432, pp. 236–248, 2005.

displays, in order to overcome device limitations. A framework which extends inter-device cooperation to several aspects of application development has been implemented in [11], exploring the concept of a personal system that can be built in an ad-hoc fashion by combining various computing elements together.

In this paper we focus on the issue of storage management for the case where the user employs several portable and wearable devices which can also interact with fixed infrastructure. We outline opportunities for cooperation on the storage front, taking into consideration the forthcoming generation of semantic file systems and context-aware applications. We highlight the problems which must be addressed to achieve this and then go on to present our storage framework, which was designed with these requirements in mind.

2 A Scenario Involving Storage and Wearables

We begin by presenting a scenario that provides a starting point for our discussion on the possibilities but also the issues of storage management in a multi-device and multi-user setting.

Jim is a photographer for a major newspaper network. He is visiting Eve, the network's correspondent in an area suffering from a long-standing regional conflict. On their first day in the field, Jim prepares to go out. His only concern is to have several spare batteries for the camera and mobile phone. Eve carries a PDA, and is wearing her voice-memo recorder necklace and a wristwatch with an embedded GPS receiver.

Inside the conflict zone Jim is constantly alert, both due to sporadic gunfire but also to spot scenes worth a photograph. Eve leads the way, pointing out important settings while taking memos for her reportage on her recorder. As Jim takes various photos, thumbnails of them are opportunistically uploaded to the newspaper office whenever GPRS coverage is available. The thumbnails are tagged with location information regarding the place where they were taken, obtained from Eve's wristwatch GPS.

At some point, street fighting intensifies and they are forced to take cover in a deserted house. Eve takes some time to write a quick report on her PDA, and Jim is reviewing the pictures on his camera to select the best ones for publication. At the same time, the chief editor at the newspaper headquarters is browsing the thumbnails received, looking for candidates for tomorrow's issue. Selections by both will be uploaded in full quality to the office, once an Internet connection can be established.

As the fighting settles down, they head back to the streets. On their way to the hotel the phone catches a strong signal and the selected photographs are uploaded to the newspaper servers, just in time to meet the press deadline. As soon as they enter the hotel, all photographs are quickly uploaded via the fast local area wireless network. Inside his room, Jim is using the HDTV set to review his work.

A sudden nearby explosion causes both colleagues to grab their stuff and run down to the street. Jim is taking many photographs in a frenzy. As the camera starts running out of space, old photographs that have been uploaded to the main servers are being deleted automatically. When things calm down, they head back to the hotel where they meet Emanuel, another colleague who was also at the explosion scene. As they discuss the events of the day, Jim shows him the photograph selected for tomorrow's publication, which is still on the camera together with the most favourite selections of the day.

3   Context, Storage and Wearable Devices

A large variety of popular portable devices such as digital cameras, music players and mobile phones, already provide significant amounts of storage space. As wireless ad-hoc communication is rapidly becoming the norm, many devices also come with built-in wireless communication capability, e.g. Bluetooth is already available on most mobile phones and PDAs. It is thus possible to let devices make their resources – including storage – available to other devices within communication range. This increases the potential for using the devices and the data they contain, creating new prospects for exploitation. In the following we analyse the scenario of Section 2, which introduces several such possibilities, partly in an implicit way. We then outline the technical requirements of a storage management framework designed to exploit this potential.

3.1   Wearable Storage Management and Context Exploitation

The explosion of the data being created and handled, even by casual users, has magnified the importance of semantic information. Attaching meta-data to files is therefore expected to play a central role in the management of storage [6, 7, 20, 22]. On desktops, this information is typically used to provide flexible views of the contents of huge collections [20].

Such information can be harvested to a large extent from sensors, worn by people or part of the infrastructure, in order to relieve the user from the tedious operation of manually annotating files. One such example is the case with the location-stamp of files, which can be obtained from a GPS receiver, just as time-stamps are a standard part of conventional file systems. It is important to note that wearable devices are especially suited for automatically producing meta-information as they are in close *contextual proximity* to the user who generates or captures data.

Semantic information can also be harvested from user input that is being provided while working towards a *high-level* goal rather than explicitly just for the sake of entering meta-data. This is the case in our scenario when Jim and the newspaper's editor mark the best photographs, asynchronously and without any explicit communication. Nevertheless, through this selection they implicitly introduce various levels of significance: photos chosen by both, photos chosen by one of the two and photos chosen by neither.

The storage framework can exploit the generated meta-data to adjust it behaviour. Specifically, photographs of no significance are uploaded as thumbnails, whereas significant ones are uploaded to the backend server in full quality and with higher precedence. Photographs that have been backed up can be deleted, with the less significant ones being eagerly deleted from the local store and the most significant photographs being preserved the longest possible.

As wearables can be constantly carried by the people, opportunity for their use may arise at any moment. With conventional file management tools for uploading, moving, copying and deleting files, the user may be required to deal with such issues unexpectedly and continuously. Such interaction may also be extremely awkward if not impossible to perform using simple wearable interfaces. As a result, user attention is forcibly shifted from one's real work to the resolution of technical issues. In the last scene of our scenario, if Jim were required to manually delete photographs, in a hurry, this may well have translated to missed opportunities and perhaps incorrect decisions on his part. This is in contrast with the vision of ubiquitous computing where systems provide a distraction-free environment and the user is not bothered with technical and/or untimely decision-making. We believe that our approach of combining context with storage management support is a good step towards eliminating such problems and achieve a *collective device behaviour* that is in accordance to the ubiquitous computing advocacy.

3.2 Overview of Technical Issues

The first requirement from a technical standpoint is the management of meta-information. A light-weight semantic information store must be present on the portable device. To exploit this semantic store, the system needs to provide facilities for associating meta-information with the files generated on the portable. The mechanism employed must allow any meta-data generating device or application to transparently 'hook into' the file generation process and add its piece of meta-information to the file's annotations.

While our focus is on wearables one can not ignore the possibility of exploiting infrastructure on the move. For instance, we assume that an always-on backend storage server is available. This could be a common personal computer, or a special household appliance in the user's home. Alternatively, it could be provided as a network backbone service from a service provider or organisation. Mobile phones or hot-spots may also be exploited in order to reach the server while on the move.

The system must be flexible enough so as to allow collaboration among wearables which belong to the same as well as different users, in order to extract meta-information. Specifically, the storage on wearables sensing prolonged co-presence among users should cooperate to produce additional meta-information for files produced by their owners. An example of such cooperation is the tagging of photographs with location information throughout the day.

Naturally all the technical challenges present in ad-hoc distributed systems apply. Service discovery must be performed for the detection of other devices and interoperable communication protocols must be employed to support the multitude of computing platforms. Last but not least, all this functionality must be implemented with the limited resources of wearable and portable devices in mind.

4 Implementation

4.1 Model

Our system is built around a global hierarchical namespace used to identify users, devices and files. Each user has a node representing him in the namespace. For example: *com.newsagency.employees.jim*. When users add devices to the system, each device is identified by a subordinate name: *com.newsagency.employees.jim.devices.DeviceID*. As a result, files on the storage embedded in a device go by fully-qualified names of the form: *com.newsagency.employees.jim.devices.DevID..store.filename*. In addition to the

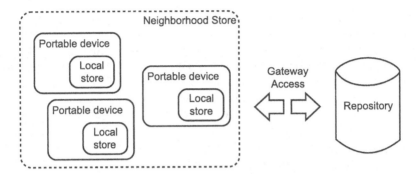

Fig. 1. Our storage model.

local store of each device, the system requires that users have a central data repository where all their data is collected. This is identified by the name *com.newsagency.-employees.jim.infrastrure.MainStore*.

We have also defined three scopes of the storage universe (Figure 1): the *Repository*, the *Neighbourhood Store* and the *Local Store*. These scopes have clean and strong associations among them and have been conceived to simplify the user's mental model for the behaviour of the storage system:

- The *Repository* is the backbone storage server which contains all data ever created by the user. It is the place where all data eventually end up, regardless of the location and the device of creation. The Repository is expected to be permanently available and accessible via the Internet.
- The term *Neighbourhood Store* refers to the collective local storage of a group of devices within range of each other. The user (and application developer) perceives this as a single entity where files can be stored and retrieved from[1].
- The term *Local Store* refers to the storage of a single device.

As a last note regarding the design of our storage model, we decided to employ the approach of immutable files. This simplifies implementation and eliminates various sycnhronisation issues that are hard to solve in loosely coupled distributed systems. It is also in accordance with recent trends towards deep archival systems[13, 16, 19].

4.2   Core Services

Before focusing on the storage system, we briefly mention some base services provided by our middleware, whose layout is depicted in Figure 2. Particularly, we note that the issues of nearby device discovery, capability introspection and point-to-point communication among devices, are taken care of by the core system services. The corresponding APIs hide the actual type of wireless communication technology in use. We further point out that the active modules in our design are only the discovery and storage services, shown with dotted frames in Figure 2. Thus, apart from the application(s) running on the device, there are only two threads of control.

---

[1] This aspect of the storage system is outside the scope of this paper and is orthogonal to the ideas and system architecture described here. We simply mention it for completeness.

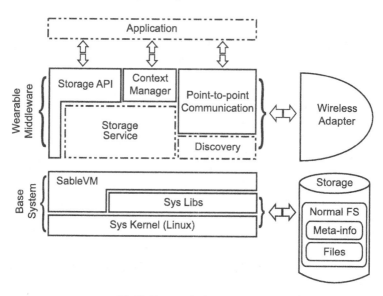

Fig. 2. System design overview.

4.3   Context Manager and Discovery

A core system module is the context manager, a data space whose contents at any given instant constitute the active context as observed by the device. The data is maintained in the form of a tuple space where each entry has four fields: key, value, scope and time-to-live (TTL). This data is generated by applications hosted on the device as well as from any of the core system modules.

An indicative sample of possible context manager contents is shown in Table 1. The key and value are open unrestricted sets. Applications are free to introduce keys under any name and interpret their values as they see fit. Examples of how the system itself uses its own keys are given later in this section and in Section 4.4. We first discuss the meaning of the scope and TTL fields.

A time-to-live (TTL) value must be defined for each entry by its submiter. This value specifies how long the entry should persist in the local context manager. When the TTL expires, the entry is automatically removed. We point out that since keys – as will be shortly discussed – may propagate to other devices, they are passed on with updated TTL values. This does not require devices to share absolute time and performs well even with relatively significant clock drifts. In practice, clock synchronization has proven to be a non-issue.

The scope field controls whether key propagation occurs in the first place. The submitter of the entry must choose one of the following values:

- *Local*: No propagation at all.
- *Owner*: Propagation to 'persistently nearby' devices of the same owner.
- *Neighbours*: Propagation to 'persistently nearby' devices, disregarding owner.

The term 'persistently nearby' implies that devices are near each other for a while, as opposed to a short encounter. For example, when a person enters his office briefly a device he carries may detect other devices he owns in the office. Context exchange among these would not occur at all, as no entries may be exchanged. But if that person takes with her an extra device from the office, then *owner* entries would eventually be exchanged among this device and the one already carried by the user. The *neighbours* scope restricts context exchange in the case where two people meet in a corridor as opposed to the case where these two people are walking to the building's cafeteria. It should be noted that context exchange always requires some long-lasting co-presence among the participating devices. This prevents a device's perception of context from being influenced by the 'noise' of opportunistic encounters.

The context manager provides a mechanism for system components, including applications, to capture and share context information across different layers (and even systems when exchange occurs). For example the discovery subsystem tries to maintain co-location information with other wearables. When the discovery service detects that another wearable has been in close proximity for a while[2], it will locally advertise this fact by posting a *neighbour* entry with *private* scope to the context manager. This context information is used in various ways by the system itself and is further available to applications for their own purposes. For example, as would be expected, context managers use this key to decide whether to exchange information with each other, as only devices which have been declared 'neighbours' are considered for exchanging entries.

The context exchange is tightly coupled with the device discovery and introspection cycle. At the end of each cycle the discovery service calls into a method of the context manager which implements the exchange. This approach eliminates the need for an extra control thread for this task, plus allows for a more efficient implementation of the communication, e.g. reusing an already open connection between devices. The only side-effect is that there is no context manager thread to update the TTL values and remove expired entries. For this reason TTL fields are updated (and stale entries removed) on-the-fly, during context retrieval calls. In addition, to avoid uncontrolled context dissemination, the scope of imported entries, received from remote devices, is converted to *private* and is thus not forwarded to other devices.

4.4 Storage Functionality

Using the storage system, applications may create immutable files on the wearable. Each file may also be associated with a so-called *summary*. For photographs this could be a thumbnail, for voice memos an excerpt or a speech-to-text conversion, for songs the chorus, etc. Applications may optionally do this during initial file creation, or a later time. Moreover, files may be annotated with semantic information by attaching key-value pairs to them. This is the traditional approach used in semantic file systems [6, 7], though RDF-based annotations have recently been suggested [22]. Our system attempts to automatically annotate files by attaching the active context[3] as observed by the context manager.

---

[2] The definition of *long-lasting co-presence* is given through a user-configurable time threshold, which can be set separately for different devices depending on type and ownership.

[3] Only the key and value fields are stored in the semantics database file – the scope and TTL fields of the context manager are ignored.

Table 1. Sample context manager contents.

Key	Value	Scope	TTL
neighbour	$Device_x ID$	private	12min
neighbour	$Device_y ID$	private	15min
gpsstamp	$X^d Y^m (N/S), K^d L^m (E/W)$	neighbors	2min

The meta-information attached to a file is not necessarily a snapshot of the current context-manager contents. An application may intervene and flexibly control the annotation, introducing additional keys, altering the values of existing ones, or even removing some of the keys being attached to the files. In terms of programming, this is achieved by letting applications install handlers via the storage API. For example, a handler which prevents files from being annotated with the devices which were neighbours at the time is shown in Listing 1. As would be expected, applications can also inspect and alter file annotations at any time after the files have been created, using appropriate storage API methods.

In an analogous fashion, the storage system attaches and exploits annotations to files for its own purposes, by the keys shown in Table 2. The *dirty* key indicates the status of each file regarding its backup progress in the Repository. The storage service automatically transfers files to the Repository when connectivity is available and updates this key accordingly. The order of upload is determined by using the *rating* key, which is also added to files created by the storage system with an initial value of zero. Files with higher rating have precedence over other files when the storage system uploads contents to backend storage. For files of equal rating the order of creation is used. In accordance to our open storage management scheme, applications may alter the rating as they see fit, for example the camera device application does so when the user marks a photograph as significant. An indicative file annotation life-cycle using context information is depicted in Figure 3.

The storage system keys are further used to automatically create free space when a device runs out of space, by automatically deleting the oldest files with the lowest significance that have already been uploaded to the Repository. This can be done based on the *dirty*, *rating* and *timestamp* metadata entries. This procedure is executed, in a blocking mode, within API calls that request storage space. A call fails only when all files on the device are dirty and there is not enough free space. In order to avoid blocking

```
public void annotationHandler (ContextSnapshot toAttach) {
    Iterator it = toAttach.iterator();
    while (it.hasNext()) {
        // iterate through the "to be attached" annotations
        ContextPair cp = (ContextPair) it.next();
        if (it.getKey().equals(Discovery.NEIGHBOUR_KEY))
            it.remove(); // remove "neighbour" keys
    }
}
```

Listing 1.1. A sample file annotation handler.

Table 2. Storage-system annotations.

Key	Value Range	Interpretation
dirty	Yes/Summary/No.	Indicates whether a file has been fully backed up, or has only had its summary uploaded, or has never been uploaded to the backend storage server.
rating	Integer value.	Indicate the significance of a file.

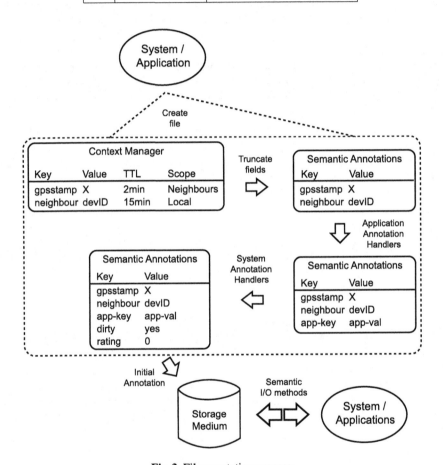

Fig. 3. File annotation process.

of applications, it is possible to set values for (a) the minimum free space (MFS) and (b) desired free space (DFS). In this case the storage system asynchronously initiates a corresponding garbage collection/backup algorithm each time the MFS threshold is passed. The asynchronous garbage collection stops when the DFS value is reached (or no more space can be recovered). Applications may further request a call-back from the storage service when the cleanup algorithm cannot free space, for example in order to warn the user to manually delete files.

4.5   Base System and Middleware Runtime

Our storage framework is implemented as part of a middleware system for cooperating wearable devices. This implementation is the evolution of our previous work on co-operating wearable devices [11]. The new version is implemented in the Java language and comprises of the elements marked as 'wearable middleware' in Figure 2. The entire runtime components and application API make for a self-contained system which is not dependent on the standard Java classes. Such an approach would add significantly to the footprint of the system, also providing functionality that is not needed[4]. The footprint of the wearable middleware layer is less than 1MB, to which a base runtime of a VM and a native interfacing layer to devices must be added.

A flexible configuration for a base system (Figure 2) is the use of the Sable [4] vir-tual machine and the Linux kernel. Although not a particularly lightweight approach[5], it is sufficiently small for the purposes of experimentation, provides a comfortable de-velopment/testing environment and can be installed on several PDAs and ARM-based devices (e.g. our 'data-wallet' described in [11]), while also leaving ample room for applications.

5   Related Work

An accumulating body of research advocates the transition towards file systems based on semantic information [6, 7, 15, 22], with [7] giving a most comprehensive compari-son. However, to our knowledge all previous research focuses on the desktop and does not consider wearables; they are disregarded both as a significant storage medium or as a source for meta-information. In fact, the process of generating meta-information is often overlooked or relies upon explicit user input. As content-based access becomes popular, the importance of automatically extracting meta-information will increase to the point of becoming a prevalent issue. This issue was immediately identified as even in early research [6] on semantic file systems, an approach to tackle the probelm was suggested: the use of transducers[6]. Other methods for extracting such information were recently described in [20], with a focus on desktop-oriented activities. In some ways, our work extends this approach to consider wearables.

The issue of storage in ubiquitous computing environments is discussed in [8], but in a complementary manner since focus is mainly on the surrounding infrastructure and backend servers. Personal data is made available through data-references carried by the user, which allows backend-servers holding the files to supply their content as users enter and leave the smart space. Applications may attach context information to files using the typical key-value pair approach in semantic file systems [6] and to browse virtual directory hierarchies using queries on the attached meta-data [7, 22]. The novelty is that the smart space has a special virtual 'current' directory which contains the files whose semantics match the smart space's context. In this manner the system filters and channels the data to pertinent to the current context to applications in the room. Interestingly, by moving a file into the special 'current' directory, the user may attach the current context as observed by the smart space to the file.

---

[4] For resource-rich portables (e.g. PDAs) one may include a standard Java installation.

[5] Kernel (600kb), POSIX libraries (1900kb) and VM (400kb) on ARM architecture.

[6] Specialised drivers for extracting semantic information by interpreting contents.

Wearable devices can assist in collaboration among people. The potential of 'wearable communities' – social networks of collaboration built around mobile devices – is described in [10]. The Proem framework [9] facilitates the development of such applications through a development kit for implementing 'peerlets', collaborative peer-to-peer applications for ad-hoc networks. We append to this work the possibility of collaboration revolving around a central mechanism that integrates context and data management. Furthermore, our implementation is based on a framework which aggregates several wearable devices owned by one user into a single platform, rather than taking the approach of each device being an application platform.

The use of a wearable device as a first-class citizen concerning storage is taken to the extreme in the case of the Personal Server [21]. The author suggests that it will be feasible to hold all of a user's data on a handheld device, which will be constantly carried around and accessed via the infrastructure. While this approach seems to be in contrast to our view of multiple cooperating personal devices, the distinction is artificial since a Personal Server fits nicely into our framework taking the role of a general-purpose storage device for all wearables present. In fact, we have developed a wearable data-wallet [11] along this exact concept, viewed through our prism of a multi-device wearable system, also supporting the integrated management of multiple such storage devices.

Our implementation is in part inspired by recent work in vertically shared information across adaptive network protocol layers. This principle is introduced in [2], termed as *situation-aware* communication, giving birth to a trend of designs with controlled cross-cutting of network layers [3]. The idea is to store the communication context of a node in a central module that is accessible by all protocol layers and applications for adaptive decision making. We follow a similar principle, by using the context manager as a shared context space across all system layers to keep context generation and consumption open and flexible. In addition, context managers of different devices communicate with each other by exchanging (certain) information. This has similarities with work on mobile tuple space based communication [14], in fact the collective context of neighbour devices can be thought of as a distributed tuple space that is gradually assembled by each participant as a function of co-presence.

6   Discussion

Our framework's ultimate goal is to explore functionality emerging as a side-effect of people's high-level activities rather than as a consequence of conscious and rigid programming. Contrary to the usual *hard* properties of a computer, this often concerns *soft* properties that are likely, but not guaranteed, to be achieved. We believe that investigating such functions will become increasingly important as we strive towards a new mental model for the ubiquitous computing era.

Our storage framework uses context information to semantically annotate files transparently using the context manager. As a result, the meta-data which may be added to files is inherently extensible. Annotations of any type may originate from any other device with no requirements on the part of application developers to anticipate, pre-program or negotiate meta-data collection. For example, the minimal 'application part' of a digital camera or a voice recorder need only consist of code that performs data capture and storage.

The possible annotations to the data being generated are limitless and depend on previous but also future ideas for other wearable devices and applications which may provide context. While the developer may foresee some meta-data and possible usage in conjunction with specific applications, it is likely that many other options cannot be a priori conceived in order to be built into the system at design time. An open and flexible approach is therefore mandatory, which is one of the key properties of our system.

The exploitation of meta-information has practically no limits, and is open to imagination. However, as with the case of the semantic web, standardisation of annotations through ontologies [12] is required to achieve portability and wide usage of annotation-aware subsystems and applications. The approach must be simple, general and extensible. Even though in our implementation we have introduced only a very small set of predefined entries, this has created the potential to support several different aspects of functionality, some of which were actually identified after the core system had been implemented.

References

1. Michael Beigl, Hans-W. Gellersen, and Albrecht Schmidt. Mediacups: experience with design and use of computer-augmented everyday artefacts. *Comput. Networks*, 35(4):401–409, 2001.
2. Michael Beigl, Albert Krohn, Tobias Zimmer, Christian Decker, and Philip Robinson. AwareCon: Situation Aware Context Communication. In *Proceedings of Ubicomp 2003*, Seattle, USA, October 2003.
3. Marco Conti, Gaia Maselli, Giovanni Turi, and Silvia Giordano. Cross-layering in mobile ad hoc network design. *Computer*, 37(2):48–51, 2004.
4. Etienne M. Gagnon and Laurie J. Hendren. SableVM: A Research Framework for the Efficient Execution of Java Bytecode. In *Proceedings of the Java Virtual Machine Research and Technology Symposium*. USENIX Association, April 2001.
5. Maribeth Gandy, Thad Starner, Jake Auxier, and Daniel Ashbrook. The gesture pendant: A self-illuminating, wearable, infrared computer vision system for home automation control and medical monitoring. In *Proceedings of the 4th IEEE Internation Symposium on Wearable Computing*, pages 87–94, October 2000.
6. David K. Gifford, Pierre Jouvelot, Mark A. Sheldon, and James W. O'Toole, Jr. Semantic file systems. In *Proceedings of the thirteenth ACM symposium on Operating systems principles*, pages 16–25. ACM Press, 1991.
7. Burra Gopal and Udi Manber. Integrating content-based access mechanisms with hierarchical file systems. In *Proceedings of the third symposium on Operating systems design and implementation*, pages 265–278. USENIX Association, 1999.
8. Christopher K. Hess and Roy H. Campbell. An application of a context-aware file system. *Personal Ubiquitous Computing*, 7(6):339–352, 2003.
9. Gerd Kortuem, Jay Schneider, Dustin Preuitt, Thaddeus G. C. Thompson, Stephen Fickas, and Zary Segall. When peer-to-peer comes face-to-face: Collaborative peer-to-peer computing in mobile ad hoc networks. In IEEE, editor, *1st International Conference on Peer-to-Peer Computing (P2P 2001)*, pages 75–92. IEEE Computer Society, 2001.
10. Gerd Kortuem and Zary Segall. Wearable communities: Augmenting social networks with wearable computers. *IEEE Pervasive Computing*, 2(1):71–78, 2003.
11. Spyros Lalis, Alexandros Karypidis, Anthony Savidis, and Constantine Stephanidis. Run-time support for a dynamically composable and adaptive wearable system. In *Proceedings of the 7th IEEE Internation Symposium on Wearable Computing*, pages 18–21, October 2003.

12. A. Maedche, B. Motik, and L. Stojanovic. Managing multiple and distributed ontologies on the semantic web. *The VLDB Journal*, 12(4):286–302, 2003.

13. Mallik Mahalingam, Chunqiang Tang, and Zhichen Xu. Towards a semantic, deep archival file system. In *Proceedings of the 9th IEEE Workshop on Future Trends of Distributed Computing Systems (FTDCS'03)*, pages 115–121. IEEE Computer Society, May 2003.

14. Marco Mamei and Franco Zambonelli. Programming pervasive and mobile computing applications with the tota middleware. In *Proceedings of the Second IEEE International Conference on Pervasive Computing and Communications (PerCom'04)*, pages 263–276. IEEE, March 2004.

15. B. Clifford Neuman. The Prospero File System: A Global File System Based on the Virtual System Model. *Computing Systems*, 5(4):407–432, 1992.

16. Sean Quinlan and Sean Dorward. Venti: A new approach to archival storage. In *Proceedings of the Conference on File and Storage Technologies*, pages 89–101. USENIX Association, 2002.

17. Mandayam Raghunath, Chandra Narayanaswami, and Claudio Pinhanez. Fostering a symbiotic handheld environment. *Computer*, 36(9):56–65, 2003.

18. J. Rantanen, J. Impi?, T. Karinsalo, M. Malmivaara, A. Reho, M. Tasanen, and J. Vanhala. Smart clothing prototype for the arctic environment. *Personal and Ubiquitous Computing*, 6(1):3–16, 2002.

19. Douglas S. Santry, Michael J. Feeley, Norman C. Hutchinson, Alistair C. Veitch, Ross W. Carton, and Jacob Ofir. Deciding when to forget in the elephant file system. In *Proceedings of the seventeenth ACM symposium on Operating systems principles*, pages 110–123. ACM Press, 1999.

20. Craig A. N. Soules and Gregory R. Ganger. Why can't I find my files? New methods for automating attribute assignment. In *Proceedings of HotOS IX: The 9th Workshop on Hot Topics in Operating Systems*. USENIX Association, May 2003.

21. Roy Want, Trevor Pering, Gunner Danneels, Muthu Kumar, Murali Sundar, and John Light. The Personal Server: Changing the Way We Think About Ubiquitous Computing. In *Proceedings of the 4th International Conference on Ubiquitous Computing*, 2002.

22. Zhichen Xu, Magnus Karlsson, Chunqiang Tang, and Christos Karamanolis. Towards a semantic-aware file store. In *Proceedings of HotOS IX: The 9th Workshop on Hot Topics in Operating Systems*. USENIX Association, May 2003.

A File System for System Programming
in Ubiquitous Computing

Christian Decker, Michael Beigl, and Albert Krohn

Telecooperation Office (TecO), University of Karlsruhe,
Vincenz-Priessnitz-Str. 1, 76131 Karlsruhe, Germany
{cdecker,beigl,krohn}@teco.edu
http://www.teco.edu

Abstract. In Ubiquitous computing small embedded sensor and computing nodes are one of the main enabling technologies. System programming for such small embedded systems is a challenging task involving various hardware components with different characteristics. This paper presents a file system for sensor nodes platforms providing a common organization structure and a light-weight and uniform access model for sensors and all other resources on sensor nodes. This mechanism forms an abstraction from different hardware, makes functions re-useable and simplifies the development on such systems. With ParticleFS an file system implementation on a sensor node platform is shown. As an example a telnet application running on sensor nodes was implemented demonstrating the usage of the approach for system programming on such platforms.

1 Introduction

In Ubiquitous computing (Ubicomp) and Pervasive Computing environments people are surrounded by a multitude of different computing devices. Typical representatives are PDAs, PCs and - more and more - embedded sensor nodes. Platforms are able to communicate, preferably wireless, and exchange information with each other. By collecting and interpreting information from sensors and network such devices can improve the functionality of existing applications or even provide new functionality to the user. For example, by interpreting incoming information as a hint to the current situation, applications are able to adapt to the user requirements and to support him in various tasks. Prominent examples where such technology is developed and tested are AwareHome[10] and Home Media Space[13].

An important area within Ubicomp is the embedding of sensor nodes in mundane everyday objects and environments. Such applications were explored for instance in a restaurant context at PLAY Research[12]. Within the scenario sensor enhanced objects supported dynamic workflows, information displays, and new interactions. Implemented applications checked for freshness of food or automatic negotiation of prices between menus depending on their history. The central enabling technologies for this application are small sensor nodes that are embedded into various objects in the restaurant. Devices used in this restaurant setting were Smart-Its[1], but similar devices exist including Berkeley Motes[9], Ember[6] and MITes[15]. In general,

M. Beigl and P. Lukowicz (Eds.): ARCS 2005, LNCS 3432, pp. 249–264, 2005.

these devices integrate computing capabilities – primarily an 8bit microcontroller – a wireless communication protocol – often customized – and various sensors. Most of the device platforms follow a modular concept where additional sensors can be added according to the needs of the application. The devices are battery powered and use energy saving mechanisms to last for months or even years. In particular for integration aspects they are very small. Figure 1 shows a 1 cubic centimeter (cm³) device with a microcontroller, communication interface, sensors and battery.

Fig. 1. TecO's Particle[16] (1 cm³ integrating microcontroller, sensors, communication, battery).

System programmers of such embedded and integrated devices have to be aware of many constraints. The microcontroller is often a resource restricted 8-bit type, providing typically between a few kilobytes (KB) up to 512KB of Flash memory for storing programs and also small amount of RAM. Application programs are primarily written in assembly language or C. As a consequence of the embedding in everyday objects, applications heavily access the sensors as primary information source. Most systems provide developer support in one of two ways: An operating system protects access to resources by shielding lower level functions from direct access through the application. Communication between applications and system is made through events, such as in the TinyOS[9] used by the Motes. The other possibility is a library shielding the access to (sensor) hardware by providing abstract function interfaces. This concept avoids the overhead of event dispatching. Common to both methods is that they are not able to completely shield and protect the application due to restrictions of the used microprocessor platforms.

The approach we chose to follow in this paper, when designing the system software, places the developer at the center of interest. Our goal is to maximize the support for the system programmer, who is implementing applications for Ubicomp settings. We believe that a compact, simple-to-understand and simple-to-remember programming interface contributes most to the support for such a programmer. This assumption is supported by experiences that we gathered in various Ubicomp development projects presented in the next section. These experiences are motivated by examples in the next section. Based on these findings we present our system approach in section 3. In the center of this architecture stands the concept of a file system. All resources of the system are accessible only through the file system via a uniform access method, formed by six primary operations of the file system. We believe that this method of access is most appropriate for the programmers of small, embedded, wireless devices, as it provides a lightweight and compact interface to system functionality. We will show that such a compact file system architecture is also appropriate in terms of low resource consumption.

2 Analysis: Ubicomp Development

We implemented various applications on the wireless networked embedded sensor platform Smart-Its Particles[16]. Many of these applications are clustered in larger settings. An example is the Aware Office[2] – an office environment running different applications distributed over several dozen of wireless embedded sensor and computing nodes. Most of these nodes are embedded into everyday objects such as chairs, tables, windows, pens and whiteboards. The available applications support different activities in office settings including meeting support, activity and occupation detection. When implementing such applications programmers can choose from a variety of different sensors on the Smart-Its Particle hardware. It is known that the use of multiple sensor sources tend to improve the quality of the output. Nevertheless we experienced that in practice programmers use mostly one sensor as input to the system. They also tend to use the sensor they have used in a project before if applicable or a sensor where they can re-use example programs. Being asked for the reason they answered that from their experience their unfamiliarity with (the access functions of) other sensors would delay the development process.

Other experiences with a library based access interfaces to resources come from the eSeal[5] project. In this project sensor devices are embedded in physical goods measuring environmental and logical conditions in which the goods are situated. The nodes acquired, interpreted and shared sensor data among each other in order to detect violations pre-defined limits. This compelled the programmer to use several different sensors. Sensors are accompanied by various options to enable and disable them in order to save energy. In the analysis we found that the system programmers always used the simplest but most energy consuming way to power sensors on and off. Although this results in higher energy consumption programmers explained that the complexity of various interfaces but also of the overall distributed application is too high, so they decided to lower complexity on other parts of the program as much as possible. Another finding in this context was interface breach. Each sensor is accessible through its own interface taking the sensor's features into account. This interface is often only slightly different from another sensor's own. Nevertheless, even though the difference is only small, development got often stuck in debugging because of not noting the differences in the interface when accessing the sensor.

From the findings in the conducted experimental analysis we conclude that supporting the programmer to follow the simplest and uniform way to access sensors should be major principles for system programming. These principles also apply to other resources like communication and memory of the sensor nodes. Such an approach allows programmers freedom to concentrate more on other important aspects like distributed programming logic.

We propose a file system as an appropriate abstraction for implementing these principles. The coherent, hierarchical name space is able present resources in general.

Therewith, it creates a clear and simple-to-recognize structure of all resources. The file system operations are applicable to all files and form an uniform access model on the structure. This enables the system programmer to follow the simplest way in the development process. Finally, we believe, that the familiarity and long-term experience of system programmers with established file systems will help to standardize programming on the various present and upcoming sensor node platforms.

The paper continues with the system architecture of a sensor node incorporating a file system. The understanding is deepened in an analysis of the resources of a sensor node. As a result a suitable name space and operations of a file system are derived. In section 4 we present our implementation of ParticleFS and discuss its performance. With the telnet application utilizing the ParticleFS in section 5, it is demonstrated how a file system supports the system programmer. Section 6 discusses related work on file systems before the paper is concluded in section 7.

3   System Architecture

The file system provides a uniform access layer for an application on top of all resources available on sensor nodes (figure 2). An application has access to direct and mediated resources via the file system. Direct resources are the representation of available hardware on the sensor node. Mediated resources aggregate and interpret information from direct resources, but can also represent other functionality provided by an application. If mediated resources access direct resources, this is also carried out via the file system.

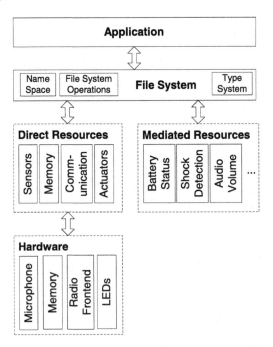

Fig. 2. System Architecture of a Sensor Node integrating a File System.

The file system is composed of a name space presenting all resources in a hierarchical structure, file operations responsible for the uniform access to the resources and a type system supporting compatible operations on multiple resources. It is important to note, that the application has no direct access to the hardware. All calls are made through the file system. In the next subsections the components of the architecture will be explained in detail.

3.1 Resources

The above-mentioned sensor nodes (Motes, Ember, MITes and Particles) have a microprocessor unit (MPU) at their core and incorporate various sensor, wireless communication, memory and actuation hardware. They are typically powered by regular batteries. We will analyze available resources and their methods of access on these sensor nodes and thereby distinguish between direct and mediated resources.

Direct Resources

Direct resources are represented by hardware components available on the sensor node device. The sensor nodes have access on

- various sensor hardware, e.g. light, audio, acceleration, temperature sensors,
- wireless communication interface
- memory in form of internal, i.e. contained in the MPU, and external memory
- power supply, typically regular batteries
- actuators, e.g. LEDs, buzzer or small display

Sensors. Sensor hardware is accessed with a multitude of possibilities. Analog sensors are sampled via the MPU's analog-digital converter. Digital sensors provide for instance a duty cycle, which needs to be sampled and interpreted, or they provide a bus interface. Typical interfaces used on sensor nodes are I2C and 1-Wire bus.

Communication. A widely used access method to the wireless communication interface is a serial line communication connected to communication component. The communication component with the transceiver is then responsible for the channel access, data modulation and the communication protocol. On other platforms like Smart-Its Particles the transceiver is completely controlled by the MPU, including methods for channel access, data modulation and an own communication protocol.

Memory. The MPU's internal memory consists of Flash-ROM for programs and RAM for program variables. The Harvard architecture common for MPUs on the considered platforms imposes the separation of both types. A system programmer has only limited control over the internal memory because the compiler determines the usage. This makes the internal memory inappropriate to be accessed via a file system. External memory is included in form of flash memory or EEPROM devices. Storage for arbitrary data is provided ranging from a few kilobytes up to half a megabyte. External memory components provide typically a serial interface like I2C or SPI interface.

Power Supply. Energy is one of the key resources for sensor node platforms. Batteries are a crucial component and often limit the usage of the platform. Having access to this resource enables the application to optimize its runtime behavior. Motes and Smart-Its Particles are both able to measure the voltage of the supplying battery.

Actuators. Embedded sensor nodes have capabilities to present states and events. Commonly used on all mentioned sensor node platforms are LEDs. Current Motes and Smart-Its Particles integrate a buzzer for acoustic notifications. Complex actuators are displays, controlled via serial line, I2C or by a proprietary protocol. However, displays are seldom used, because they require a lot of energy and often the embedding in everyday objects prohibits their usage.

Mediated Resources

These resources apply operations like combination, aggregation an interpretation on data from direct resources. An example for a mediated resource is the average volume level of a sound source. It requires the aggregation of an array of audio samples from the direct resource microphone, which are then used to compute the average volume level. Mediated resources may access a multitude of other direct and also mediated resources. The concept of mediated resources can even be applied to functions within an application. A system programmer can separate functions from the application and present them in the file system. In this way even pure computational functions can be presented as mediated resources. In order to serve as a uniform access layer to direct and mediated resources a file system has to organize them in an appropriate name space. In order to retrieve information from these resources a file system needs a suitable and applicable set of operations for accessing these resources.

3.2 Name Space

In the file system resources are organized in a hierarchical name space. Files are the smallest entities and directly identify resources. Files are further organized in directories which are special files identifying a collection of files. By recursion a file tree can be built up with a single top directory representing the root. A resource in this tree is then clearly identified by the complete path starting from the root down to the single file along the tree structure. In order to separate the directories from each other along this path the delimiter "/" is used. A single "/" indicates the root directory. There are 3 predefined directories in the root directory. The directory /dev/ holds all direct resources. In /context/ the system organizes mediated resources based directly or indirectly on sensors. Finally, resources for storing application data are located in /usr/. Within these directories the resources may further hierarchically ordered using subdirectories. Arbitrary data is physically stored in the external memory which is represented as the direct resource /dev/eMem. In order to include those data in a structured manner, the /usr/ directory contains a file system view of the /dev/eMem resource. This is considered as a mediated resource and therefore files in /usr/ are also mediated resources.

Table 1. Example of a Name Space of Resources presented as File System.

Resource	Explanation
/	This identifies the root directory.
/dev/	Directory containing files providing access to direct resources.
/dev/SLI0	File representing a light sensor. SLI1 is the second one, if available.
/dev/SAU	This is the file for retrieving for sampled the microphone.
/dev/SVC	This is the file for retrieving the battery voltage.
/dev/eMem	The external memory is accessed for reading and writing via this file.
/dev/comm.	This file provides access to the communication interface.
/context/	This directory contains files for accessing mediated resources
/context/audiovolume	This file is for computing the audio volume
/context/batterystatus	Mediated resource describing battery in 3 states (full, good, weak)
/usr/	Application stores arbitrary data as regular files in this directory.
/usr/myfile	File containing arbitrary application data; created by an application

In table 1 we present an example of a name space. For sensor hardware in the /dev/ directory we used a three-letter-abbreviation indicating a sensor. We found it more expressive than the technical name of the sensor and reusable on different platforms. For instance, SLI indicates a Sensor for LIght. If there is more than one sensor of a type available, the sensors may be enumerated by an additional number behind the identifier.

3.3 File-Based Operations

After the analysis of available resources and organizing them in a name space, a suitable set of operations is needed in order to access them. A communication interface is accessed by the widely-used operations send() and receive(). Similar to that, widely-used access methods for memory are read() and write(). Both approaches abstract from detailed processes going on below, e.g. a specific organization of the memory, or channel access of the communication interface. This enables a shielding of hardware differences on different platforms. Taking those considerations into account we analyzed the usage of read() and write() for other resources. Both are generically understood for transferring data in both directions which makes them suitable for accessing various resources. We identified them as fundamental for the access model. However, their implementation is different depending on the platform and the resources. As a consequence we demand that each resource is coupled to its specific read() and write() operations. Hereby, the file system only references these specific operations. Their implementation remains in a specific access library for a resource. In that way an abstraction is achieved, since the generic read() and write() are called, but the specific access behavior on a resource is kept by transparently calling the specific read() and write() through the file system. Additionally, every resource presented as a file is coupled with a type as a file attribute. Types can be used to check for compatibility when accessing different resources in combination. This is important for mediated resources since they may be derived from other resources. The type system will be explained in more detail in the next section. The access model supports types in the process of mounting and by providing type queries. The set of operations is summarized in table 2. It bases on our long-term practical experience with the Smart-Its Particle platform and insights of similar platforms. We use the C syntax for the operation set. Note, size_t is an abstract data type which can be replaced with an appropriate platform specific one.

Table 2. Generic Access Functions of the File System.

Operation	Explanation
size_t read (int fd, void* buf, size_t n)	Reads n data bytes from the resource identified by fd to buf; returns number of bytes or -1 if error occurred
size_t write (int fd, void* buf, size_t n)	writes n data bytes from buf to the resource fd; returns number of bytes or -1 if an error occurred
int open(char* resource_path)	Returns a descriptor for the resource; -1 if it is not valid.
int getType(int fd)	Returns the type of a resource fd; -1 if fd is not valid.
int mount (char* resource_path, int type, (*pFunc) read, (*pFunc) write)	Creates a resource in the name space. Type and function pointers to their specific read and write operations are given. -1 is returned if the resource_path already exists.
int umount(char* resource_path)	Removes a resource; -1 is returned if it is not valid.

Our access model is now based on read() and write() operations which are coupled to specific resources and a type system supporting compatible operations across different resources. Both read() and write() operations are also fundamental in POSIX[17]. POSIX, the portable operating interface, defines data types, return codes, functions for file operations, process handling, security issues and error reporting. The definitions describe an interface which is designed in a way making them easily portable to other systems. Both operations apply to all functions (e.g. processes, file operations etc.) within the standard. Indeed, it was intended to use the POSIX syntax for read() and write() operations. From the POSIX point of view, we achieved a very lightweight file access model by leaving out access permissions, security issues and process handling. Return codes where simplified and there is no detailed error reporting mechanism like errno() in POSIX.

3.4 Type System

The type of a resource allows to check for compatible resources, when using them together. For example: The communication interface may not accept raw sensor values from the /dev/ resources. They should be extended by meta information. This is done by reading them not directly from /dev/, but from a mediated resource in /context/. By checking the type of the resource the communication interface /dev/comm can decide whether to accept or not accept the resource. Furthermore, higher-level functions aggregating data from low-level resources can adapt their behavior according to the types. The designed file system knows the following types:

Table 3. Types used within the File System.

Type	Explanation
directory	indicating directories, such as /dev/ or /usr/.
regular file	each file containing arbitrary data in /usr/ is considered to be a regular file.
custom types	these types are defined by a system programmer for all other resources, e.g. each file identifying a direct resource in /dev/ has its own type.

While the directory type and the regular file type are integrated in the system, custom types can be defined freely. It enables the system programmer to define the compatibilities between resources. However, the system programmer has to take care of declaring resources with consistent types. For instance, using resources together which work on different data formats, but are accidentally declared with the same type may result in unexpected behavior of an involved resource. The system does not provide checks for such inconsistencies.

4 Implementation

We implemented the previously suggested design in a file system called ParticleFS for our Smart-Its Particle platform. The devices comprise a communication board with a PIC18f6720 microcontroller. The communication uses a TR1001 transceiver with the customized protocol AwareCon[3] especially designed for ad-hoc networking in Ubicomp environments. Furthermore the board carries a 512KB flash memory component. Various forms of sensor and other add-on boards can be attached to the communication board. The following sensors are currently implemented on the sensor board: two 2D-accelerometers enabling the measurement in three dimensions, a light sensor, a microphone, a force sensor and a temperature sensor. The boards are powered by a single AAA battery. The implementation was carried out with the goal to limit the resource consumption of the file system. Internal memory usage regarding RAM and ROM on the microcontroller was aimed to be kept minimal. Furthermore, the file system's effects on the overall runtime behavior were analyzed in order to estimate consequences for calls on hardware operations, e.g. sensor sampling via the file system.

4.1 ParticleFS

ParticleFS implements a main table, a subdirectory table and a file storage table (figure 3). The main table holds all resources including directories, the type of the resource and the function pointers to the resource specific read() and write() operations. Each entry is preceded with a number – the resource descriptor. Additionally, the main table is linked to the subdirectory table. Latter table orders all resources or directories from the main table by referencing back all subdirectories and resources for each directory.

Regular files in the main table are also referenced by the subdirectory pointer. However, since the type of regular files differs from the directory type, the pointer is interpreted as a reference to the storage table. Each entry of that table represents the content of a regular file and is preceded by its file size attribute. The storage table is stored on the external flash. Therefore only the first two tables are kept in RAM, minimizing the overall consumption. Directed and mediated resources are only referenced in the main table along with their function pointers. As a positive effect, the system programmer can benefit from this organization since it enables an easy way to re-use common functions.

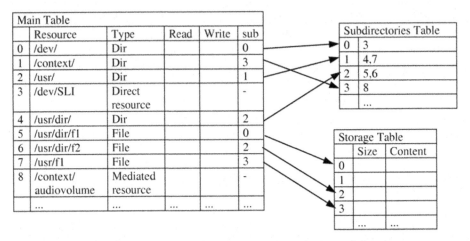

Fig. 3. File Tables of the ParticleFS (function pointers are left out).

4.2 Functionality of ParticleFS

During the boot up of the hardware when the ParticleFS starts it mounts several resources. It creates the /context/ directory for mediated resources, the /usr/ directory for file storage and the /dev/ directory for direct resources. The file system also mounts the known sensors in the /dev/ directory. Resources mounted at startup, in particular sensors in /dev/, are not expected to be umounted during the runtime of the file system. Each sensor driver has to provide a specific read() and write() function referenced in the file system. Additionally, there is a file library providing read() and write() functions for regular files and directories. Now, consider the following two representative scenarios:

Access a direct resource (e.g. /dev/SAU – the audio sensor). Figure 4 illustrates the access of the audio sensor through the file system. In the first step a call of the open() operation is needed to retrieve the resource descriptor from the main table. The system's read() operation uses the descriptor to retrieve the function pointer for the resource's specific read() function, here readMic(). The specific read() function is called and starts sampling the microphone using the MPU's analog-digital-converter. The sampled values are then returned in the given buffer from the read operation.

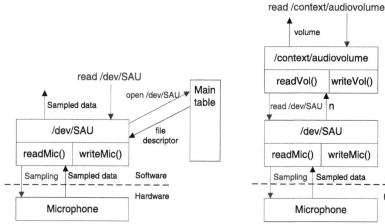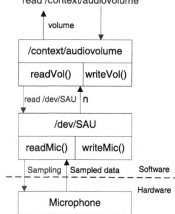

Fig. 4. Reading a Sensor (Direct Resource).   **Fig. 5.** Reading the Audio Volume (Mediated Resource).

Access a mediated resource (e.g. /context/audiovolume). In figure 5 the file system's read() operation will call the specific read() function of /context/audiovolume, here readVol() in order to compute the average volume for n samples from the microphone. That read() function will invoke the system's read() operation for /dev/SAU like in the previous scenario, but n times. The resource descriptor of /dev/SAU can be re-used minimizing the effort to find the entry in the main table when the audio sensor is accessed again. Finally, the average volume for the period of samples will then be computed and returned to the file system's call on /context/audiovolume.

Accessing sensors does not necessarily mean only read accesses. All sensors have to provide a specific write() operation. Usually, it refers to an empty function. However, some sensors implement a non-empty one for configuration purposes. For instance, write() functions of analog sensors may configure the bit resolution of the analog-digital converter when sampling.

4.3   Discussion of ParticleFS

In our current implementation the main table can hold up to 50 resource entries where each one is 30 characters long at maximum. Additional for each resource is a type of one byte, function pointers for the specific read/write functions – each 2 bytes long – and the subdirectory pointer consisting of one byte identifying the position of the entry holding all subdirectories or resources in the parent directory. The subdirectory table can reference 15 subdirectories or other resources for each parent directory. However, there are only 10 parent directories possible. It is important to note that the focus of the implementation was not to create deep and complex file trees. We do not believe that this will be convenient on the systems we are targeting. We expect that the structure is rather flat with many resources distributed over a few directories. The storage table uses the external flash of 512KB to store files. The structure of this table imposes a 50 byte segment alignment of all data. Files smaller than this size do not use the remainder. Larger files will allocate a multiple of 50 bytes segments. The design decision was made according to our expectation, that our system will handle large file for sensor logging, and small files for intermediate results or configuration data. Altogether, the file system consumes 1850 bytes of RAM for holding the tables and has access to the complete external memory. However, in future implementations parts of the main and subdirectory table will be swap out to the external memory. The implementation of the minimal set of operations from section 3.3 required 2106 byte program Flash memory.

Currently, the ParticleFS implementation does not support an event mechanism and has no notion of interrupts. All file system operations run synchronously, i.e. the call returns after the completion of the operation. When accessing a resource through the file system the resolution process to determine the specific read() or write() function slows down the execution process. However, once the file descriptor is obtained, it can be reused for further uses. So, each access to a resource is then only preceded by a table lookup for the specific read() or write() function and call of this function. On the Particles' 18F6720 MPU the delay for the lookup and the additional call is below 5 microseconds. The delay of the analog-digital-converter to sample a new sensor value is about 30 microseconds. I2C sensors are even slower. So, the resolution of the access through the file system had no noticeable effect on sensor sampling.

Both read() and write() operations are character oriented. We found, that exchanging arrays of byte is the most generic way to deal with the diversity of resources. Mediated resources can transform those raw data to structured ones and can further work with them. In order to ensure the semantic meaning the types were introduced to check for compatibility. Nevertheless, the view on the resources is local. Up to now, we have not implemented a mechanism which can combine file systems of multiple device.

The current implementation for regular file storage does not focus on frequent updates of files. Such updates will trash the storage table. As a consequence, a continuous writing of a large file for sensor logging might fail, if there is an insufficient number of consecutive 50 bytes segments left. Compacting files regularly may be a solution. However, read() and write() calls on regular files are resolved to specific functions in the file library which is not part of the file system. This flexibility makes it easy to transparently implement a new concept for storing data files. This shows how the file system fulfills the principles from the motivation by providing a uniform access to resources and supports the system programmer to follow a simple way.

5 Application: Telnet for Smart-Its Particles

Telnet is a console to remotely access all functionality of the file system ParticleFS and let users inspect all resources of an embedded sensor node interactively. It enables a user to actually login on the Particle and browse the file system, read sensors and activate actuators.

5.1 Components

The telnet application is divided into a proxy and a telnet server. The proxy as shown in figure 6 runs on a personal computer connected to a UDP network. It is responsible for sending commands to the server running a specific. A bridge in the UDP network transports messages from the proxy to the RF network of the Smart-Its Particles and vice versa. The proxy awaits a connection from a regular telnet client. If connected, each string encapsulated in the telnet protocol from the client is extracted by the proxy's command parser and given to the Particle communication module. The latter is sending this string to the telnet server encapsulated in the Particle protocol.

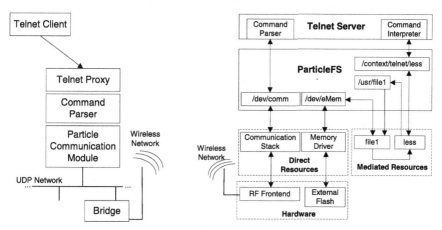

Fig. 6. Telnet Proxy on Personal Computer.

Fig. 7. Telnet Server on Particle demonstrating "less /usr/file1".

The telnet server is implemented on a Particle (figure 7). It places a command interpreter on top of the file system. The interpreter enables more complex operations for inspecting, copying, moving or deleting of regular files. A command parser reads strings from the communication interface using the file system's /dev/comm resource. The strings are parsed and forwarded to the interpreter for invocation. All interpreter operations are mounted in the file system as mediated resources under /context/telnet/ and can be called as commands in the telnet console.

5.2 Functionality of Particle Telnet

Once a telnet client is connected to the proxy and finally to the telnet server on the Particle, commands can be remotely invoked on the Particle's file system. We representatively describe the invocation of the command "less /usr/file1" as it is shown in figure 7. The command displays the content of a file /usr/file1. We present further commands where the file system supports the telnet application.

The command parser parses "less /usr/file1" and identifies the command, here "less" and the parameter, here "/usr/file1". These information are given to the interpreter which invokes "/context/telnet/less" by calling the file system's read() operation on it. The file system resolves this call into the mediated resource "less" and invokes the specific implementation for read() on it. In the same way the "less" resource resolves the parameter "/usr/file1" into the "file1" resource. By invoking "file1" it accesses /dev/eMem and therefore resolves this direct resource into the read() function in the memory driver. Finally, this function accesses the file on the external flash memory. The file content is returned to next previous caller until it is written to /dev/comm by the command parser and then presented in the telnet console of the client.

Browsing and File Operations. The interpreter provides commands like "dir", "copy", "delete", "write" for listing directories, copy, deletion and writing of files. The commands allow to interactively inspect the file system and all available resources on the embedded sensor node. Further, these commands support modifications of the file system, since one can create and delete own directories and files and store arbitrary data.

Accessing Sensors. The "less /context/dev/SLI" command prints the current light sensor value on the console. However, the "less" command denies the access on the direct resource /dev/SLI, because those resources return raw data which may contain non-printable characters. The file system supports this behavior by providing resource type information. The "less" command decides accordingly, whether the access to a resources is granted or not. Access to resources under /context/dev/ is granted since they return sensor values in a printable format.

Combining Resources. The file system supports combination of resources. Commands utilize resource type information in order to adapt their behavior accordingly. The command "write /dev/comm /dev/SLI" reads a light sensor value and sends it via the communication interface. The "write" command can also be applied for strings in combination with regular files, e.g. "write /usr/file 'hello world!' ". Hereby, the type information causes the write command to store the given string in /usr/file.

New Commands. The set of commands which the interpreter can invoke may not be sufficient for an embedded sensor node. The file system contributes to the integration of new commands of the interpreter by mounting them as mediated resources in the file system. As a consequence, all telnet functionality is disclosed by adequate mediated resources in the file system. This enables a system programmer to easily add and interactively test new functions.

6 Related Work

UNIX operating systems and various derivates like Linux incorporate peripheral devices such as keyboard, mouse, sound card as special files in their file system. Plan9[14] implements this idea consequently. All resources are accessed in a file-based manner with file-based operations. Our work was mainly inspired from this idea, but differs in the way the application sees the resources. In contrast to Plan9, there are no client specific local name spaces imposed on the file system. As a result file servers managing theses views are not needed. This forms a very lightweight access model especially appropriate for resource limited sensor nodes.

In Ubicomp the idea of file systems is also already established for system-wide data access and sharing method as well as for data storage on sensor nodes. Dynamo[11], a file system for smart room applications residing in Stanford's iRoom, is targeted on office collaboration scenarios. Hereby, file-oriented data is consistently replicated across various devices from personal computer infrastructure down to personal devices, such as PDAs. Further, users can choose situations like meetings, coffee breaks and others, in which they want to share certain portions of their file system. The context-aware file system (CFS) [8] integrates this principle consequently. The user's personal data are organized in directories using his name while context driven data is organized based on contextual information. Contexts may be physical presence, location or data format requirements of the user's personal device. According to the current context, the file system's awareness limits the visibility of data stored in this file system. These examples show, that file systems are thought of middleware solutions for data management in mobile scenarios. The Dynamo and CFS rely on strong infrastructure support provided by personal computers. The smallest entity using those middleware services is a PDA-like device. In contrast, our approach with ParticleFS is self-contained and implements the file system on individual sensor nodes, small enough to be integrated in everyday objects. Berkeley Motes and the BTNodes[4] from the ETH implement sensor node file systems. Motes follow with MatchBox[7] a very straight approach for storing data on an external Flash memory component. The file system supports only sequential reads and appending writes. This distributes write accesses over the entire Flash memory space and contributes to the memory's life time especially under high write access loads. The Micro-ROM implementation of the BTNodes provides a simple program space file system. Hereby, data files are linked together as part of the application program. This results in a read-only data structure only suitable for the application it was linked with. In contrast to those examples we extend the file system concept by integrating other resources like sensors, memory and communication into the file system. Apart from data storage, the file systems forms a uniform access model and supports system developers for embedded sensor nodes.

7 Conclusion and Future Work

By bringing the file system approach down to the sensor node we continue existing system support concepts in Ubicomp. System programmers are provided with a compact, easy-to-understand interface, with which they are very familiar. The uniform interface and the consistent integration of all resources in one name space support system programmers to follow the simplest way during development. The capability of extension by just adding another file/resource let them easily add new functions on the sensor node while maintaining the uniform interface. Having the file abstraction directly on the sensor node enables also a homogeneous integration of small sensor systems into previous work in system support for Ubicomp in particular for middleware solutions.

In future work we will integrate an event mechanism, which is able to present and handle hardware interrupts and self defined events in the file system. The research on the minimal set of file system operation will proceed, as more experience will be gained. Future file systems for sensor nodes will also incorporate remote resources in the local file system. Finally, with the telnet application we have implemented an evaluation environment for rapidly testing these new file system capabilities.

References

1. Beigl, M., Zimmer, T., Krohn A., Decker, C., Robinson, P.: Smart-Its - Communication and Sensing Technology for UbiComp Environments. Technical Report ISSN 1432-7864 (2003)
2. Beigl, M., Zimmer, T., Krohn, A., Decker, C. Robinson, P.: Creating Ad-Hoc Pervasive Computing Environments. In the Adjunct Video Proceedings of the Pervasive 2004, Vienna, Austria (2004)
3. Beigl, M., Krohn, A., Zimmer, T., Decker, C., Robinson, P.: AwareCon: Situation Aware Context Communication. Proceedings of UBICOMP 2003, Oct. 12-15, Seattle, USA
4. BTnodes - A Distributed Environment for Prototyping Ad Hoc Networks. Available online: http://www.btnode.ethz.ch [Accessed: 01/2005]
5. Decker, C., Beigl, M, Krohn, A., Kubach, U., Robinson, P.: eSeal - A System for Enhanced Electronic Assertion of Authenticity and Integrity of Sealed Items. Pervasive 2004, Austria
6. Ember – Wireless Semiconductor Solutions. Available from: http://www.ember.com/
7. Gay, D. The Matchbox File System. Available online: http://webs.cs.berkeley.edu/tos/tinyos-1.x/doc/matchbox-design.pdf [Accessed: 01/2005]
8. Hess, C., Campbell, R. An application of a context-aware file system. In Personal and Ubiquitous Computing Volume 7, Issue 6, pp. 339–352, December 2003, ISSN:1617-4909
9. Hill, J., Szewczyk, R., Woo, A., Hollar, S., Culler, D., and Pister, K.: System Architecture Directions for Networked Sensors. ASPLOS-IX, 2000.
10. Kidd, C.D., Orr, R.J., Abowd, G., Atkeson, C.A., Essa, I., MacIntyre, B., Mynatt, E., Starner, T. and Newstetter, W.: The Aware Home: A Living Laboratory for Ubiquitous Computing Research. In the Proceedings of CoBuild'99. October 1999.
11. Lamarca, A., Rodrig, M.. Oasis: An Architecture for Simplified Data Management and Disconnected Operation. ARCS 2004, Augsburg, Germany
12. Maze, R. Holmquist, L.E.: Smart-Its Workshop on Interactive Scenarios. Available online: http://play.tii.se/projects/smart-its/restaurant.html [Accessed: 09/2004]
13. Neustaedter, C. and Greenberg, S. The Design of a Context-Aware Home Media Space: The Video. Video Proceedings of UBICOMP 2003, Seattle, USA (2003)
14. Pike, R. Presotto, D., Dorwards, S., Flandrena, B., Thompson, K., Trickey, H., Winterbottom, P.: Plan 9 from Bell Labs. Computing Systems, vol.8, no.3, pp.221-254, 1995.
15. Tapia, E.M., Intille, S., Larson, K.: MITes: Wireless Portable Sensors for Studying Behavior. In Adjunct Demo Proceedings of UBICOMP 2004, Nottingham, UK (2004)
16. TecO Smart-Its Particle: http://particle.teco.edu [Accessed: 09/2004]
17. The OpenGroup. IEEE Std 1003.1, 2004 Edition. Available online: http://www.unix.org/single_unix_specification/ [Accessed: 09/2004]

Author Index

Lecture Notes in Computer Science

For information about Vols. 1–3322

please contact your bookseller or Springer

Vol. 3370: A. Konagaya, K. Satou (Eds.), Grid Computing in Life Science. X, 187 pages. 2005. (Subseries LNBI).

Vol. 3369: V.R. Benjamins, P. Casanovas, J. Breuker, A. Gangemi (Eds.), Law and the Semantic Web. XII, 249 pages. 2005. (Subseries LNAI).

Vol. 3368: L. Paletta, J.K. Tsotsos, E. Rome, G.W. Humphreys (Eds.), Attention and Performance in Computational Vision. VIII, 231 pages. 2005.

Vol. 3366: I. Rahwan, P. Moraitis, C. Reed (Eds.), Argumentation in Multi-Agent Systems. XII, 263 pages. 2005. (Subseries LNAI).

Vol. 3365: G. Mauri, G. Păun, M.J. Pérez-Jiménez, G. Rozenberg, A. Salomaa (Eds.), Membrane Computing. IX, 415 pages. 2005.

Vol. 3363: T. Eiter, L. Libkin (Eds.), Database Theory - ICDT 2005. XI, 413 pages. 2004.

Vol. 3362: G. Barthe, L. Burdy, M. Huisman, J.-L. Lanet, T. Muntean (Eds.), Construction and Analysis of Safe, Secure, and Interoperable Smart Devices. IX, 257 pages. 2005.

Vol. 3361: S. Bengio, H. Bourlard (Eds.), Machine Learning for Multimodal Interaction. XII, 362 pages. 2005.

Vol. 3360: S. Spaccapietra, E. Bertino, S. Jajodia, R. King, D. McLeod, M.E. Orlowska, L. Strous (Eds.), Journal on Data Semantics II. XI, 223 pages. 2005.

Vol. 3359: G. Grieser, Y. Tanaka (Eds.), Intuitive Human Interfaces for Organizing and Accessing Intellectual Assets. XIV, 257 pages. 2005. (Subseries LNAI).

Vol. 3358: J. Cao, L.T. Yang, M. Guo, F. Lau (Eds.), Parallel and Distributed Processing and Applications. XXIV, 1058 pages. 2004.

Vol. 3357: H. Handschuh, M.A. Hasan (Eds.), Selected Areas in Cryptography. XI, 354 pages. 2004.

Vol. 3356: G. Das, V.P. Gulati (Eds.), Intelligent Information Technology. XII, 428 pages. 2004.

Vol. 3355: R. Murray-Smith, R. Shorten (Eds.), Switching and Learning in Feedback Systems. X, 343 pages. 2005.

Vol. 3353: J. Hromkovič, M. Nagl, B. Westfechtel (Eds.), Graph-Theoretic Concepts in Computer Science. XI, 404 pages. 2004.

Vol. 3352: C. Blundo, S. Cimato (Eds.), Security in Communication Networks. XI, 381 pages. 2005.

Vol. 3351: G. Persiano, R. Solis-Oba (Eds.), Approximation and Online Algorithms. VIII, 295 pages. 2005.

Vol. 3350: M. Hermenegildo, D. Cabeza (Eds.), Practical Aspects of Declarative Languages. VIII, 269 pages. 2005.

Vol. 3349: B.M. Chapman (Ed.), Shared Memory Parallel Programming with Open MP. X, 149 pages. 2005.

Vol. 3348: A. Canteaut, K. Viswanathan (Eds.), Progress in Cryptology - INDOCRYPT 2004. XIV, 431 pages. 2004.

Vol. 3347: R.K. Ghosh, H. Mohanty (Eds.), Distributed Computing and Internet Technology. XX, 472 pages. 2004.

Vol. 3346: R.H. Bordini, M. Dastani, J. Dix, A.E.F. Seghrouchni (Eds.), Programming Multi-Agent Systems. XIV, 249 pages. 2005. (Subseries LNAI).

Vol. 3345: Y. Cai (Ed.), Ambient Intelligence for Scientific Discovery. XII, 311 pages. 2005. (Subseries LNAI).

Vol. 3344: J. Malenfant, B.M. Østvold (Eds.), Object-Oriented Technology. ECOOP 2004 Workshop Reader. VIII, 215 pages. 2005.

Vol. 3343: C. Freksa, M. Knauff, B. Krieg-Brückner, B. Nebel, T. Barkowsky (Eds.), Spatial Cognition IV. Reasoning, Action, and Interaction. XIII, 519 pages. 2005. (Subseries LNAI).

Vol. 3342: E. Şahin, W.M. Spears (Eds.), Swarm Robotics. IX, 175 pages. 2005.

Vol. 3341: R. Fleischer, G. Trippen (Eds.), Algorithms and Computation. XVII, 935 pages. 2004.

Vol. 3340: C.S. Calude, E. Calude, M.J. Dinneen (Eds.), Developments in Language Theory. XI, 431 pages. 2004.

Vol. 3339: G.I. Webb, X. Yu (Eds.), AI 2004: Advances in Artificial Intelligence. XXII, 1272 pages. 2004. (Subseries LNAI).

Vol. 3338: S.Z. Li, J. Lai, T. Tan, G. Feng, Y. Wang (Eds.), Advances in Biometric Person Authentication. XVIII, 699 pages. 2004.

Vol. 3337: J.M. Barreiro, F. Martin-Sanchez, V. Maojo, F. Sanz (Eds.), Biological and Medical Data Analysis. XI, 508 pages. 2004.

Vol. 3336: D. Karagiannis, U. Reimer (Eds.), Practical Aspects of Knowledge Management. X, 523 pages. 2004. (Subseries LNAI).

Vol. 3335: M. Malek, M. Reitenspieß, J. Kaiser (Eds.), Service Availability. X, 213 pages. 2005.

Vol. 3334: Z. Chen, H. Chen, Q. Miao, Y. Fu, E. Fox, E.-p. Lim (Eds.), Digital Libraries: International Collaboration and Cross-Fertilization. XX, 690 pages. 2004.

Vol. 3333: K. Aizawa, Y. Nakamura, S. Satoh (Eds.), Advances in Multimedia Information Processing - PCM 2004, Part III. XXXV, 785 pages. 2004.

Vol. 3332: K. Aizawa, Y. Nakamura, S. Satoh (Eds.), Advances in Multimedia Information Processing - PCM 2004, Part II. XXXVI, 1051 pages. 2004.

Vol. 3331: K. Aizawa, Y. Nakamura, S. Satoh (Eds.), Advances in Multimedia Information Processing - PCM 2004, Part I. XXXVI, 667 pages. 2004.

Vol. 3330: J. Akiyama, E.T. Baskoro, M. Kano (Eds.), Combinatorial Geometry and Graph Theory. VIII, 227 pages. 2005.

Vol. 3329: P.J. Lee (Ed.), Advances in Cryptology - ASIACRYPT 2004. XVI, 546 pages. 2004.

Vol. 3328: K. Lodaya, M. Mahajan (Eds.), FSTTCS 2004: Foundations of Software Technology and Theoretical Computer Science. XVI, 532 pages. 2004.

Vol. 3327: Y. Shi, W. Xu, Z. Chen (Eds.), Data Mining and Knowledge Management. XIII, 263 pages. 2005. (Subseries LNAI).

Vol. 3326: A. Sen, N. Das, S.K. Das, B.P. Sinha (Eds.), Distributed Computing - IWDC 2004. XIX, 546 pages. 2004.

Vol. 3325: C.H. Lim, M. Yung (Eds.), Information Security Applications. XI, 472 pages. 2005.

Vol. 3323: G. Antoniou, H. Boley (Eds.), Rules and Rule Markup Languages for the Semantic Web. X, 215 pages. 2004.